Pinaki Roy (ed.)

Words from India in the West
A Critical Approach to Select Writings by the Diasporic Indian Litterateurs

Pinaki Roy (ed.)

WORDS FROM INDIA IN THE WEST
A Critical Approach to Select Writings by the Diasporic Indian Litterateurs

Bibliografische Information der Deutschen Nationalbibliothek
Die Deutsche Nationalbibliothek verzeichnet diese Publikation in der Deutschen Nationalbibliografie; detaillierte bibliografische Daten sind im Internet über http://dnb.d-nb.de abrufbar.

Bibliographic information published by the Deutsche Nationalbibliothek
Die Deutsche Nationalbibliothek lists this publication in the Deutsche Nationalbibliografie; detailed bibliographic data are available in the Internet at http://dnb.d-nb.de.

Cover illustration: © Sreeparna Chattopadhyay, 2022

ISBN-13: 978-3-8382-1718-5
© *ibidem*-Verlag, Stuttgart 2023
Alle Rechte vorbehalten

Das Werk einschließlich aller seiner Teile ist urheberrechtlich geschützt. Jede Verwertung außerhalb der engen Grenzen des Urheberrechtsgesetzes ist ohne Zustimmung des Verlages unzulässig und strafbar. Dies gilt insbesondere für Vervielfältigungen, Übersetzungen, Mikroverfilmungen und elektronische Speicherformen sowie die Einspeicherung und Verarbeitung in elektronischen Systemen.

All rights reserved. No part of this publication may be reproduced, stored in or introduced into a retrieval system, or transmitted, in any form, or by any means (electronical, mechanical, photocopying, recording or otherwise) without the prior written permission of the publisher. Any person who does any unauthorized act in relation to this publication may be liable to criminal prosecution and civil claims for damages.

Printed in the EU

Dedicated To:

Prof. (Dr.) Deb Narayan Bandyopadhyay,
Vice-Chancellor, Bankura University

(The Teacher, The Administrator, The Critic...)

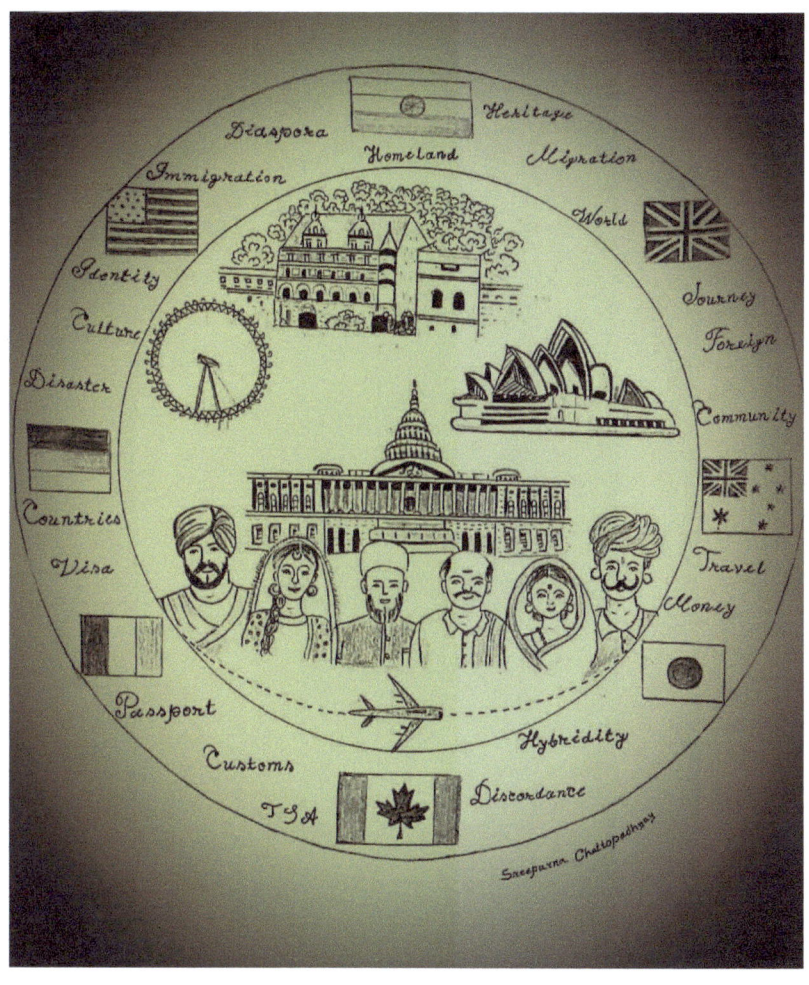

Illustration: *Vasudhaiva Kutumbakam: The Indian Diaspora and the World* by Sreeparna Chattopadhyay, 2022

Foreword

I grew up as a boy in a North Bengal village during the 1960s, hearing people of my grand/parents' generation lament the loss of a life of abundance in their *desh* (homeland) that they had to leave behind following the partition of India in 1947. Intrigued by the discriminatory aspects of India's Citizenship Amendment Act of 2019, which continues to encounter protests against its impending country-wide implementation, I fished out of an old family trunk a 1948 document issued by the Government of West Bengal that registers the name of my (paternal) grandfather as head of a family of refugees that sought *ashroy* (refuge) in a new land. The paradox apart — those who lived in an undivided India ('East Bengal' pre-partition) were now treated as refugees in a partitioned India — I saw in their eyes pangs of loss and separation, nostalgia for and swelled pride in the soil they were uprooted from and yet an unflinching resolve to make a new home here in the face of overwhelming odds. Despite all conceptual distinctions made today between refugees and diasporas, and the hostland being the West in the title of Pinaki Roy's present volume, I could not open the foreword disregarding the location from which I am writing and the convoluted history of dislocation/relocation that those people had suffered. Loss, backward-looking, mourning and labored homemaking define both refugees and the 'old' diaspora. But when I look at their third or fourth generation, on the other hand, I find many of them settled in the West (Britain and North America) and that if they remember their home at all, it is the present-day Bengal and not the land (Bangladesh now) their ancestors came from because they were never there. They form the 'new' diaspora in other lands through re-migrations in my brief narrative.

As we enter into the broader frame of Indian diaspora in Roy's book, of Indian diasporic literature in the West, an engagement with the fast-changing trajectory of diaspora is in order, a trajectory also borne out by the editor's arrangement of chapters. In fact, diaspora as concept and praxis is ever in a diasporic state because its nature is to keep crossing borders and frontiers 'of language, history, race, time and culture' (Zhang 2004: 69). The essays collected in Roy's volume are about Indian diasporic writing from two spatiotemporal zones popularly known as, or broadly divided into, old and new diaspora. It is common knowledge that while the 'old' stemmed from 'colonial capital' (Rai and Reeves), the new is an outgrowth of globalization—although world theories or globalization approaches often differ from diaspora studies in that the latter is limited to a set of particular geographic and sociocultural spaces (Faist 2010: 15). The 'old' tells of 'a forced dispersion' (Chaliand and Rageau), of slavery and indentured labour; the 'new' of 'individual choice', 'hypermobility' and '(post)modern ascendancy' (Mishra 2007: 3). Notwithstanding this old-new binary in studies of migration and dislocation, assimilation and adaptation, homelessness and homemaking, the concept of diaspora today evokes a plethora of new movements, developments and their interconnections. The Jewish diaspora may still be considered 'the fundamental ethnic model for diaspora theory', as Vijay Mishra maintains, but it must also be 'reread through alternative models much more attuned to spatio-temporal issues' (6).

Words from India in the West makes it plain that diaspora is a challenge to the narrow precepts of nation and nationalism, territoriality and its interior hegemony. Yet it is always defined by its relationship to nation—in one way or another. The old diaspora happened when the (home)lands that 'supplied' labour, or from which people were exiled, were not independent nations. Decolonization and the birth of nation-states in quick succession during the middle of the twentieth century not only changed the very patterns of migration from former colonies but boosted the migrants' morale in their fight for rights in the land of settlement (Shukla 2018: 169) and included them as subject in the host nation's political and cultural discourses. Noteworthy in this context is the US Immigration and Naturalization Act of 1965 that awarded greater visibility to South Asians, especially Indians, in broader national debates on race, ethnicity and difference (166). Diaspora also functions as the nation's Other. The suspicion about the immigrant as an alien, especially since 9/11 and also following unplanned migrations caused by war, poverty and natural calamities, interferes with what Žižek (online) calls the 'National Thing', the majoritarian imaginary of home/nationhood that is supposedly violated by the racial/ethnic Other coming from outside. The 'Nation qua Thing', however, was always already 'contaminated' by the alien within. The alien within is the enemy within in terms of their skin colour or faith, caste or gender and sexuality, as the case may be. They spoil all 'pure enjoyment' of 'the real Thing' (Nation), as Mishra correctly argues after Žižek (2007: 14).

The concept of home(making) remains a recurring motif in the essays collected in Roy's volume. Insofar as home to a diaspora is an absence that is sought to be overcome through 'domophilia' (Raychaudhuri), home as a fictive construct, Avtar Brah's 'homing desire' aptly explains contemporary diasporic imaginary and diaspora's altered relationship with nation. This homemaking is not a yearning for a return to the home left behind; home (or the homeland) as the point of origin is at once changed by history and mediated by unreal expectations from an(other) adopted location. Nor does it turn the hostland into a substitute for the abandoned home; it can at best produce a 'liberatory nostalgia' (Raychaudhuri 2018: 12) that helps the diasporic subject fight the double jeopardy of total assimilation and discrimination in the hostland. On the other hand, the new diaspora, the rich/affluent rather than the working class, lives in both worlds simultaneously — physically as well as virtually, problematizing further the ideas of home and nation. Under neoliberal globalization aided by free market, the Internet, transterritorial hiring of labour, fast and cheap travel and dual citizenship, diaspora is now considered not only a 'precursor to transnationalism' (Rai and Reeves 2009: 5) but synonymous with it in spite of their different sociopolitical histories and 'intellectual genealogies' (Faist). Transnationalism has become, especially since the 1990s, the experience of international migrants, changing notions of home (belonging), nationality and citizenship. Arjun Appadurai's concept of 'deterritorialization' acquires renewed relevance in appreciating this 'spatial turn' (Collyer and King), a flexible/liquid notion of space, though the everyday of transnational activities including the movement of people and the creating of sociocultural fields also retains a sense of embeddedness in real place. This may not return us to methodological nationalism even as national ideologies and interests are peddled through 'transnational diasporic circuits' (Hegde and Sahoo 2018: 2). Diaspora as a concept may still appear somewhat inseparable from a community's ethno-cultural distinctiveness, or its sense of home. Yet contemporary diasporas, as Tölölyan observed as early as 1996, are 'the exemplary communities of the transnational moment' (online). Overcoming the debate on the 'ideal type' of cosmopolitanism by shifting the focus from communities to practice (Faist 2010: 20), transnational diaspora has come to mean for us a constant negotiation between multiple spaces indicating the 'shifting terrains of habitus' (Bandopadhyay).

Roy's volume also suggests that diaspora studies, for India or for any other former colony, is connected to postcolonial studies. Whether or not displacement, global movement and transnational network—conditions for defining contemporary diaspora—can be part of postcolonial studies that initially built on home, nation and belonging remains a debatable issue. Yet it is evident that the South Asian diaspora expanded steadily after the decolonization of the subcontinent and postcolonial migration. Postcolonial discourse, for us, connects to this phenomenon especially by providing 'a cultural turn in globalization studies' (Ashcroft 2014: online). As Bill Ashcroft would say, globalization is not singularly economic—it has many forms, cultural globalization being the most important in our context. The figure of the postcolonial migrant that increasingly turned transnational in patterns of movement that go past the human (see Thomas Nail 2015), soon became the carrier of local practices that affected the nature of the global diaspora by undermining the Eurocentric narrative of nation (and of modernity in general) with questions of difference and alterity, diversity and hybridity (Ashcroft 2014: online). And postcolonial literature, a good part of which is also diasporic, is 'the ultimate border crosser' (the border within is included) and therefore 'inherently postnational' (Ashcroft 2020: online). Even on the economic front, postcolonialism is closely related to 'the new global capitalism' (Dirlik 2000: 309) that transnationalizes for the contemporary diaspora the process of production. The 'contemporary figuration' of capitalism that camouflages the totalizing structure within the transnational system of 'apparent disintegration and fluidity' and subverts 'possibilities of resistance' is very much part of the postcolonial critique today. It is not a question of returning to 'national loyalties' for the transnational diaspora, although Prime Minister Narendra Modi recently described the Indian diaspora as 'brand ambassadors of India', but one of recognizing its own position in global capitalism (316).

The Indian diaspora is the world's largest overseas diaspora today. The present volume aptly recognizes the global Indian diaspora's burgeoning contribution to the literature and culture of our times and is, therefore, an important addition to diaspora studies. Many of the literary works and cultural texts under scrutiny here, have received international recognition. Divided into seven distinct sections, based on the diversity of genres the works belong to, the book contains theoretical forays into (Indian) diaspora as well as essays on diasporic fiction, non-fiction, and even theatre and filmmaking. 'Words' in the volume's title acquires special import in two different senses: theatre and film are viewed in the interstices of text (word) and performance; secondly, the essays/chapters represent a plethora of voices from South Asia vying for greater recognition in the global register of literary-cultural studies. Building on the perspectives of 'India-based critics', as Bashabi Fraser points out, on literature produced in the Anglophone world of Britain and North America, the volume makes a political choice that reinforces the contemporary nature of encounters between the home and the world.

Apart from his introduction as volume editor, Pinaki Roy has another essay here that provides an 'overview' of the novelists of the Indian diaspora since Kamala Markandaya and thus helps in quick mapping of the terrain. The volume, on the whole, discusses Indian diasporic literature across the spectrum of exile and migration, displacement and alienation, assimilation and adaptation, transnationalism and transculturalism. Within these broader spatiotemporal tropes of diaspora, the essays collected in this volume probe trans-oceanic border-crossing and its travails (Munshi), the 'performatives and [...] counter-performatives of belonging'

(Mukherjee and Sarkar), the dilemma of diasporic experience and the duality of identity (Singh), the interweaving of myth, reality and magical realism (Dubey), poetic ruminations on home and the magical power of memory (Arora), gender identity amidst cultural encounters (Swarnakar), and the interaction of self and nation within a colonized space (Mallick). There are also essays in the volume on other cultural forms — on Indian diasporic theatre which is still a marginalized genre because of its very composite nature (Dutta); on visual culture including India-made films that explore 'heterogenous identities' in 'transnational communities' (Samajdar); and on the steady overseas journey of Indian cuisines (Chattopadhyay).

Words from India in the West should cater well to the needs of anyone pursuing higher studies in South Asian/Indian diaspora anywhere in the world.

Works Cited:

Ashcroft, Bill. 2014. 'Rethinking Post-Colonialism: An Interview with Bill Ashcroft.' https://www.academia.edu/10376946/Rethinking_post_colonialism_An_interview_with_Bill_Ashcroft

Ashcroft, Bill. 2020. Don Bosco Distinguished Lecture Series. https://www.youtube.com/watch?v=JgNeoWFNYGY

Dirlik, Arif. 2000. 'The Postcolonial Aura: Third World Criticism in the Age of Global Capitalism.' In *Contemporary Postcolonial Theory*. Edited by Padmini Mongia. Delhi: Oxford University Press. 294-321.

Faist, Thomas. 2010. 'Diaspora and Transnationalism: What kind of Dance Partners?'. In *Diaspora and Transnationalism: Concepts, Theories and Methods*. Edited by Rainer Bauböck and Thomas Faist. Amsterdam: Amsterdam University Press. 9-34.

Hegde, Radha Sarma, and Ajaya Kumar Sahoo, eds. 2018. Introduction. *Routledge Handbook of the Indian Diaspora*. Abingdon: Routledge. 1-14.

Mishra, Vijay. 2007. *The Literature of the Indian Diaspora: Theorizing the Diasporic Imaginary*. Abingdon: Routledge.

Nail, Thomas. 2015. *The Figure of the Migrant*. Stanford: Stanford University Press.

Rai, Rajesh, and Peter Reeves, eds. 2009. Introduction. *The South Asian Diaspora: Translational Networks and Changing Identities*. Abingdon: Routledge. 1-12.

Raychaudhuri, Anindya. 2018. *Homemaking: Radical Nostalgia and the Construction of a South Asian Diaspora*. London: Rowman and Littlefield.

Shukla, Sandhya. 2018. 'South Asian Migration to the United States: Diasporic and National Formation'. In *Routledge Handbook of the South Asian Diaspora*. Edited by Joya Chatterji and David Washbrook. Abingdon: Routledge. 166-80.

Tölölyan, Khachig. 1996. "Rethinking *Diaspora*(s): Stateless Power in the Transnational Moment." *Diaspora: A Journal of Transnational Studies* 5, no. 1 (1996): 3-36. doi:10.1353/dsp.1996.0000.

Zhang, Benzi. 2004. 'Beyond Border Politics: The Problematics of Identity in Asian Diaspora Literature'. *Studies in the Humanities* 31.1: 69-91.

Žižek, Slavoj. Online. 'Eastern Europe's Republics of Gilead'. https://newleftreview.org/issues/i183/articles/slavoj-zizek-eastern-europe-s-republics-of-gilead

Ashis Sengupta
Professor of English, University of North Bengal
January 27, 2023

Contents

Ashis Sengupta
Foreword 9

Bashabi Fraser
Introduction 19

Pinaki Roy
Editor's Introduction 31

Deb Narayan Bandyopadhyay
Re-Structuring the Diaspora Imaginary: A Critique 37

Jaydip Sarkar
Theorising Indian Diasporic Writings: A Brief Reflection 49

Pinaki Roy
Carving out Niches for Themselves: An Overview of Select
Indian Novelists of the Diaspora 57

Auritra Munshi
Coolie Diaspora: A Trans-Oceanic Border Crossing 87

Lata Dubey
Portrait of India in Chitra Banerjee Divakaruni's Fictional
World 105

Amrit Sen
'The Forgotten Voices': Indian Indentured Women in Select
Diasporic Novels 117

Indrajit Chattopadhyay
Curry Nation/Carry Nation: Indian Diasporic Cuisine 129

Saptarshi Mallick
A Historical Understanding of the National Mores: The
Autobiography of an Unknown Indian... 145

Neha Arora
Home and Memory in the Cross-Border-Musings of Indian
Diaspora: A Poetic Survey 161

Rupayan Mukherjee & Jaydip Sarkar
Poetics of Denial: Negotiating the Performative in
Contemporary English Poetry by Diasporic Indian Women
Poets 181

Tanima Dutta
Raising The Curtain of Indian Diasporic Theatre: An Insightful
Overview 195

Lalan Kishore Singh
The Indian Diaspora and the Short Story: Critical Reflections
on Jhumpa Lahiri 231

Neha Swarnakar
Cultural Encounters and Feminine Identities: A Re-Reading
of Short-Stories by Select Indian Diasporic Writers 255

Subhrajit Samanta & Soumyajit Samanta
From Text to Screen: Searching for the Roots of the Indian
Diaspora in Select Films 273

Saunak Samajdar
Mathematics, Motherhood and Migrations: Gyno-Film and
Diaspora in Shakuntala Devi 301

About the Contributors 311

Introduction

Words from India in the West: A Critical Approach to Select Writings by the Diasporic Indian Litterateurs

In this anthology of critical essays, Deb Narayan Bandyopadhyay, in his chapter entitled, 'Re-structuring the Diaspora Imaginary: A Critique', speaks of the 2009 protocols issued by the Scottish Government on transnational mobility which encouraged not just emigrant Scottish communities from across the globe to re-engage with their ancestral homeland, but also recognised those temporarily displaced from Scotland as part of her diaspora. It was an astute economic and political move to encourage tourism with Destination Scotland as the centripetal force for diasporic communities with links to the Scottish nation. 2009 was significant as it was the 'Year of the Homecoming', which called on Scots across the world to reclaim their ancestral antecedents in a reimagined celebration of their Scottish roots, organised by Event Scotland to mark the 250th birth anniversary of Scotland's national bard, Robert Burns.

It was also the year when Scotland was the Theme Country at the Kolkata Boi Mela/Book Fair in January 2009, where the Scottish Pavilion took centre stage and representatives of the Scottish literary establishment conglomerated in India's cultural centre to speak about and emphasise a long-shared history commemorated in literature and preserved in Scottish libraries, museums and galleries. My epic poem, *From the Ganga to the Tay* (2009) was launched by the British Council during the Boi Mela in the country of my birth. This is a concrete poem which is in the form of a conversation between two iconic rivers in their respective countries, talking about their shared Indo-Scottish historic heritage, while reflecting on the contemporary reality of migration and diaspora. The same book was launched at the Edinburgh International Book Festival later that year in August in my adopted nation. The endeavour of the Scottish Government and India's cultural literary milieu to bring the hiatus of diaspora into focus, confirms the undeniable reality of the history of migration and the emergent patterns of diasporic communities impacting on governmental positions, socio-economic concerns and the literary expressive modes that give voice to resettled communities abroad, across a spatio-temporal axis that bridges centuries and continents. The narrative of diaspora is thus epic in dimension, marked by a diversity that defies a unilateral definition.

Diasporic individuals have been diversely referred to as expatriates, exiles, itinerants (Fry 2001), which are positive appellations, often self-adopted/selected or used to describe voluntary migrants from the more affluent, developed world, resettled or as temporary migrants elsewhere. The term sojourner (Siu 1952) has been used for those who migrate with the idea of returning to their home country, like the first generation of Chinese in America, while the broader term, economic migrant, denotes individuals looking for better opportunities of employment and livelihoods abroad, which includes Europeans choosing their careers paths in the East during colonial times and the migrants to the richer west from the rest of world today. Yet terms like immigrants, aliens, refugees and asylum seekers, have negative connotations, perpetually casting such groups as the 'Other'. We may wish to distance ourselves from Edward Said's (1978, 1993) thesis of the need for societies to create/seek out/designate the 'Other' as irrelevant in a postcolonial, postmodern, globalised world, but the politics of a nation's need to create the enemy within or identify the 'alien' from without, continues to drive the rhetoric of many electoral candidates today. This argument is often resorted to as a vote winning strategy to legitimise those perceived as truly belonging to a nation in order to reaffirm and retain the primacy and rights of a national 'majority' (e.g., White British in Britain, Black Africans in Uganda), against those who are labelled as outsiders or the enemy within who are usually minorities and easy targets for exclusion from citizen's rights, who are thus perpetually pushed to the margins.

However, terms like cosmopolitan (Appiah 2015) and transnational have been used to describe diasporic communities and their descendants, many from the Global South to the Global North. Said's reference to how and where people are positioned will always determine how groups are perceived as those who 'belong' to a nation and those who are considered peripheral to it. There have been writers like Paul Gilroy (1987, 1992) and in more recent times like Afua Hirsch (2018), David Olusoga (2016), Charlotte Williams (2002) and Sathnam Sangheera (2021) who have reviewed their dual heritage and identity, affirmed their sense of belonging, and reviewed the process of assimilation of their diasporic communities which has not been as smooth and easy as mixing sugar in a bowl of milk. Through their racial and/or mixed heritage positioning, they have considered how they see themselves and how others see them. They have, through their research, their review of personal histories and experiences and their very act of writing, claimed their place amongst their compatriots with a shared history of migration in an estimation of diasporic corollaries. They record what their parents have brought to their nation, which has not just made the nation what it is, but built and enriched it. Their books have fuelled the debate round the Black Lives Matter Movement and Sanghera's book in coinciding with it, makes it both timely and significant, underscoring the fact that 'Black Writers Matter' and the brown population, in political terms is subsumed by the positive connotation of 'Black' as inclusive of Black and Asian, which suggests, non-White.

In this particular volume, *Words from India in the West*, edited by Pinaki Roy, we encounter literature written by writers of the Indian diaspora, writing from the Anglophone world of Britain and North America, which is analysed by India-based critics. This is an act of transnational positive academic assertion, which recognises an affinity that brings the homeland academic and the hostland writer in a continuum of interchange and literary dialogue in what is, a two-way process—of the diasporic writer writing about life experiences in the hostland, and the India-based critic engaging with and interpreting the literary texts with a deep understanding and sensitivity that is inevitable when the homeland critic unpacks with confidence the migrant writer whose links with the ancestral land might have been disrupted and interrupted, but has not quite been ruptured with any finality, that promotes this transnational interchange/communication.

The term diaspora has been defined and revisited extensively by critics like Sheffer (1986), Safran (1991), Clifford (1992) and Cohen (1997). There are two interpretations of the Greek root words pertaining to agricultural practices: *speiro*, meaning to sow, and the preposition, *dia*, meaning over, which fits the settler colonies of Caucasians in the New World. And there is the other interpretation of the Greek *diaspeirein* which means to scatter, signifying the dispersal from a homeland, used extensively of the Jewish and Armenian populations. It is the latter meaning of scattering, of dispersal, that also describes the migrants from the sub-continent.

This reality is reflected in the Indian diaspora in the United States, the United Kingdom and Canada, whose ethnically Indian writers and filmmakers and their work, form the subject matter of this volume. As Musarrat Shameem (2016) points out, the journeys undertaken by the Indian diaspora has not occurred at any one particular point in time, caused by momentous events. Their movements have been sporadic, spread over time. Hence, we have a scattering rather than a sowing of a population, with people dispersed, rather than a mass movement from a dangerous/unliveable place, towards a safe haven where they can down set their roots and find peace. For the Indian population, their transnational fluidity of movement has been across sub-continental borders, intra-national borders before and after Partition and continents, effecting multiple departures and arrivals. So even if the homeland remained a place of longing, holding many memories and arousing a sense of nostalgia for a life left behind, the desire for return was not of paramount interest or a burning desire amongst the displaced.

Diasporic communities are affected by the 'myth to return'. One such example is that of the Chinese immigrant to the USA, the itinerant, who migrated with the plan to earn enough economic stability which would then enable them to return to homeland China. The myth to return originates in the Old Testament, which narrates the punishment God meted out to the followers of Moses for their unfaithfulness to God, for which they were exiled from their land. What sustained them was the wish to return to the promised land, the 'myth to return', when God was once again happy with the Israelites.

What is pertinent here in relation to Indian communities of the first and second (and even third) generations, living and writing in and from the Anglophone world, is that they are not necessarily afflicted by the desire to return to the homeland. They do not suffer from the sense of despair that comes from their ancestral land being the place of no return. The Indian diaspora in the United Kingdom, the USA and Canada, whose writing is the subject of this book, continues to have links with their country of origin. This remains one of the fundamental definitions of modern diasporic communities, the recognition of a common place of origin and the continuing links with the homeland. While many first generation Indian migrants in the 1960s and 1970s harboured a desire to return, the second generation's links to the parents/grandparents' homeland has been more tenuous, unaffected by the 'myth to return'. The first generation of diasporic Indians migrating from the 1980s till today, retain links with the homeland through visits, periodic or intermittent, to see their parents and have their parents visiting them in their adopted country, which confirm the diasporic description of scattered populations maintaining links with the homeland. Cheaper and faster modes of air travel, easier connectivity made possible through the internet (Sahoo 2019), have helped to sustain a diaspora's communication with family and friends in their country of origin. The desire to return thus assumes mythical proportions as various realities intervene, such as the receding of job opportunities in the homeland or business prospects in a competitive market for returnees, or the consideration of their children being settled in the hostland and any uprooting of their education and prospects subsequently seen as a disruption. Moreover, the loss of family members and close friends in the homeland often creates a void in the once attractive socio-familial circle in the homeland, which can be a factor which dissipates the myth of return in a diaspora. And sometimes, the social and political changes in the country of origin make it an unfamiliar and even dangerous place for would-be returnees (Cakmak 2021).

In many cases, the sacrifices made by parents to raise the funds to send their children abroad for what they deem an education that will bring better prospects for their progeny, lead to a sense of loneliness and isolation that the older, left-behind generation feels, which is explored in much of the literature by Indian diasporic writers. The remittances sent by migrants to their families in the homeland and the investments they may make in the homeland, are ways of maintaining links with the family and community at home. Other links that are retained by diasporic communities with the homeland who have settled in the hostland, are through the diaspora following traditional social customs, observing rituals carried over from the homeland, the celebration of festivals, modes of worship, cuisine and dress and assembling, celebrating and meeting in community spaces. There is the recognition of the need to retain the mother tongue in the home, through community-led language classes, watching films from the sub-continent, learning Indian vocal and instrumental music and dance and participating in artistic performances.

Though people of Indian origin do come into contact with the host population in educational institutions, their workplace and businesses, Indian diasporic communities in general in Britain, the USA and Canada continue to identify with their compatriots in their hostland in their social sphere, as their broad circle of friends remain those who have come from the sub-continent (via Africa in some cases), as is seen in many of the texts discussed in the book. Another feature that marks diasporic communities from the sub-continent is the affinity they feel and sustain across postcolonial borders, e.g., between Punjabi speaking migrants from India and Pakistan and Bengali speakers from India and Bangladesh—the continuum arising from a regional contiguity and a shared language, literature and culture, especially significant for first generation migrants and passed on to their offspring.

The relevance of the diasporic experience can be dismissed when the assimilation process in the hostland is effectively complete. If one goes back to the Saidian idea of positioning which affects the perception by the host population of the incomer, it is noticeable that the process of assimilation is not something that can be effected by propensity or the will of the immigrant to fit in and a desire to integrate. Assimilation and integration can happen when acceptance by the host community allows such seamless enfolding and embracing of diasporas to become a reality. The racial visibility of the Indian diaspora makes them distinguishable and identifiable, rendering their blending-in problematic. However, as they study alongside the mainstream population in educational institutions, especially in the United Kingdom which has not been afflicted by segregation, and as they are absorbed more and more into the work force at different levels and in various professions, the acceptance of their employability and contribution makes their 'here to stay' (Latif 36) a reality which the hostland has to ultimately acknowledge, reluctantly or graciously as the case may be. Policies of multiculturalism, positive discrimination, diversity and inclusion, which entail a recognition of diversity and an acknowledgement of what diverse populations from elsewhere have brought to the UK, USA or Canada, have gone a certain way to stress the value of more than the addition of colour to the socio-economic fabric in these nations. This is the diversity that Indian writing in English exemplifies as Indian writers in the diaspora are the 'voice' of their communities. Departures thus become a thing of the past. The arrival has happened and from this entry point, the struggle to make a home away from what they knew as the 'home' — the place from which they had migrated, the wish to 'fit in' in a foreign society, the sacrifices and choices made to give the second generation the education and opportunities the parents desire for them, make the diasporic experience in Hall's (1996) terms a fluid one, shaped and influenced by the transforming experience of the migrant, where 'becoming' rather than 'being' becomes the defining identity of the diaspora. Deleuze and Guattari (1987) too have considered identity as always being transformed, coming into being or becoming, which Nic Craith (2020) sees as 'the simple fact of becoming that is behind the creation of the rhizome' which 'exploits and enjoys continual change and connection' (163) with the homeland and with the diaspora abroad.

It is this process of becoming that creates the hybridity — the botanical metaphor that defines the transformation that occurs in the Third Space (Bhabha 1994) of a cultural encounter, which occurs here between the immigrant community and the host community in the adopted nation. In this context, another botanical term become pertinent, the rhizomatic nature of the migrant process where the ability of rhizomes to send out shoots laterally, as well us upwards, marks a quality of creative adventurous adjustment which allows transformations that become the survival tactics that mark hybrid communities as roots and shoots are modified by adaptational decisions determined by circumstantial realities.

This ability to become through transformation is what links a diaspora's past to the future, an assured future in the hostland for the transnational citizen. As Shuval notes 'Diaspora theory is also linked to the theoretical discourse on transnationalism and globalisation.' She quotes from Tololian (1991) who states, 'Diasporas are the exemplary communities of the transnational moment' (Shuval 44). Thus the conversation between the homeland and hostland continues as historic connections are recognised, renewed and transformed in the skein first woven by the English language imposed by Macaulay's Minute on Education in 1835. The linguistic link has come a long way as today Booker Prize winners like Salman Rushdie and Arvind Roy give Indian diasporic writing global recognition, with Salman Rushdie winning the Booker of Bookers, while Jhumpa Lahiri has been awarded the Pulitzer Prize for her first publication. These writers have claimed language of the former coloniser as their own, just as English remains one of India's multilingual tool for communication in a vast publication market.

We began this Introduction with a reference to Scotland where I live and write and from where I maintain links with my country of birth. Returning to the Scottish context, I would like to draw the reader's attention to Chitra Ramaswamy's memoir, *Expecting: The Inner Life of Pregnancy* (2016) which was awarded the National Book of the Year Prize by the Saltire Society in Scotland, endorsing the British Indian writer's acceptance as one of the foremost writers of Scotland. Ramaswamy's *Homelands: The History of a Friendship* is a strong contender for the Saltire Non-Fiction Award of 2022. It weaves the story of two unlikely friends, a second generation woman of Indian heritage in her late thirties to early forties and an elderly Jewish man from Germany, who is now ninety six, being one of the last survivors of children who came by the Kindertransport, escaping Hitler's ethnic cleansing of the Jewish population. In one book, we have commemorated the story of individuals and families of a scattered diaspora—of Indian and Jews, who migrated to Britain for very different reasons. Chitra's family came to avail of better opportunities while the Kindertransported boy, Henry Wuga, came to escape a cataclysmic event that annihilated most of his extended family members.

This narrative is like the conversation of rivers which flow with confidence through time, like that of the Ganga and the Tay, the Mississippi and the Nile, conscious of shared histories that have engendered the flow of populations from their banks to other shores. Pinaki Roy's edition of *Words from India in the West: A Critical Approach to Select Writings by the Diasporic Indian Litterateurs* brings together critiques of different genres: the novel, short fiction, poetry, drama, memoir and film as well as reflections on the forgotten or silenced stories of indentured labour and of the journeys made by culinary flavours also captured in literature, which have seeped into and transformed the taste of the hostland population. The experiences that have been voiced and explored by diasporic Indian writers in this critical anthology, embody the transnational narratives of diasporic individuals and communities, contributing to their hostland's literature through their representation of different cultural signifying systems, that widen the social fabric, adding fresh and distinctive strands to an expanding literature of their adopted nation. As Friedman (2006) implies, there is a narrative shift as nation-based paradigms are disturbed and one can add, dismantled, to incorporate 'transnational models emphasizing the global space of ongoing travel and transnational connection' (Friedman 906). This is what literature of migration and diaspora has brought to the literary canon that is being shaped now, as it assists and influences the decolonisation movement in educational institutions, augmenting the existing canon with the cosmopolitan experience of the transnational writer who has crossed and recrossed nation-state boundaries while maintaining a meaningful communication and association with the homeland. For them, as we have seen, their ancestral land is no longer a mythical place of origin, but one they have carried over in their lifestyle and memory, and with which they stay in touch with viable means that technology and travel enable. This is certainly a paradigm shift from the time when our generation studied English Literature at Indian universities where Indian Writing in English was not considered as worthy of inclusion in the syllabus. It has taken some time to rectify this lacunae, but it is a welcome development and this volume joins a rich raft of critical literature by Indian scholars who value and assess Indian Writing in English today, and in this case, of diasporic Indian writing.

Their texts wield their language tool with a confidence that comes from mastering the craft of writing, making films and creating flavours, in a language that they have helped to shape, enrich and claimed as their own, writing from the metropolitan centre as it were, from Edinburgh, London, Chicago or Toronto, in what is, a dialogue with their compatriots in their ancestral homeland, their host country audience and the global Anglophone readership. Their sub-continental critics have, in this book, assessed their idea of 'home' and 'memory', of belonging and becoming, of the diasporic struggle and achievements in chapters that unpack and unfold the significant contribution of Indian diasporic writers who continue to write and create in the Anglophone world, speaking meaningfully to sub-continental readers and critics in a language that remains a significant interweaving thread in India's richly diverse linguistic fabric that recognises the transnational Indian writer's dual heritage and identity.

Works cited:

Appiah, Kwame Anthony. *Cosmopolitanism: Ethics in a World of Strangers.* London: Penguin Books, 2015.

Bhabha, Homi K. *The Location of Culture.* London and New York: Routledge, 1994.

Cakmak, Mustafa. "'Take Me Back to My Homeland Dead or Alive!': The Myth of Return Among London's Turkish-Speaking Community." *Frontiers of Sociology* 6 (2021): 1–11.

Clifford, James. "Diasporas." *Cultural Anthropology*, 9.3 (1994): 302–338.

Cohen, Robin. *Global Diaporas: An Introduction*. London: UCL Press, 1997.

Friedman, Susan Stanford. "Migrations, Diasporas, and Borders." *Introduction to Scholarship in Modern Languages and Literatures*. Ed. David Nicholls. New York: MLA, 2006. 899-941.

Fry, Michael. *The Scottish Empire*. East Lothian: Tuckewll Press and Edinburgh: Birlinn, 2001.

Gilroy, Paul. *There Ain't No Black in the Union Jack: The Cultural Politics of Race and Nation*. London: Hutchinson, 1987.

Hall, Stuart. "Culture Identity and Diaspora." Ed. Jonathan Rutherford. Identity: Community, Culture, Difference. London: Lawrence & Wishart, 1990. 222–237.

Hirsch, Afua. BRIT(ish): *On Race, Identity and Belonging*. London: Vintage, 2018.

Latif, Tariq. *The Minister's Garden*. Tordmirden, Lancashire: Arc Publishers, 1996.

Nic Craith, Máiréad. "From Bengal to Scotland: Hybridity, Borders and National Narratives." Eds. Cicilie Fagerlid and Michelle A. Tisdel. *A Literary Anthropology of Migration and Belonging: Roots, Routes, and Rhizomes*. Switzerland: Palgrave Studies in Literary Anthropology, 2020. 157–180.

Olusoga, David. *Black and British: A Forgotten History*. London: Pan Books, 2016.

Safran, William. "Diasporas in Modern Societies: Myths of Homeland and Return." *Diaspora* 1.1 (1991): 83–93.

Sahoo, Ajaya K. "Migration, diaspora and development: a study of familial bonds of Indians in the diaspora." *Migration and Development* 9.3 (2020): 467–477. https://www.tandfonline.com/doi/full/10.1080/21632324.2019.1701840?scroll=top&needAccess=true_28 November 2022.

Said, Edward. *Orientalism*. Harmondsworth: Penguin Books, 1995.

---. *Culture and Imperialism*. London: Vintage, 1994.

Sanghera, Sathnam. *Empireland: How Imperialism Has Shaped Modern Britain*. U.K.: Viking, An Imprint of Penguin Books, 2021.

Shameem, Musarrat. "Narrative of Indian Diasporic Writing: A New Perspective on the Women Writers of the Diaspora." *Rupkatha Journal on Interdisciplinary Studies in Humanities* VIII. 1 (2016): 186–196.

Sheffer, G., ed. *Modern Diasporas in International Politics*. Sydney: Croom Hill, 1986.

Shuval, Judith T. "Diaspora Migration: Definitional Ambiguities and a Theoretical Paradigm." *International Migration* 38.5 (2000): 41–55.

Siu, Paul C. P. 1952. "The Sojourner." *American Journal of Sociology* 58.1 (1952): 34–44.

Tölölyan, Khachig. "The Nation-State and Its Others: In Lieu of a Preface." *Diaspora: A Journal of Transnational Studies* 1.1 (1991): 3–7.

Walkowitz, Rebecca L. "The Location of Literature: The Transnational Book and the Migrant Writer." Ed. Richard J Lane. *Global Literary Theory*. London: Routledge, 2013. 918–929.

Williams, Charlotte. *Sugar & Slate*. Wales: Planet Books, 2002.

Dr Bashabi Fraser, CBE
Professor Emerita of English and Creative Writing
Edinburgh Napier University

The Editor's Introduction

It is an incontrovertible fact that the late-20th and the early-21st century-literary-world is dominated by the writers of the diaspora—a sizeable number of whom are of Indian origin. In the recent years, a mentionable number of the reputed and popular literary awards and recognitions have been achieved by authors who are parts of the so-called 'diaspora', and the number of Indians/NRIs/People of Indian Origin (PIO) on this ever-expanding 'list' is worth noticeable—Anita Desai, Amitav Ghosh, Bashabi Fraser, Jhumpa Lahiri, Kiran Desai, and so on. What transpires out of this is the conclusion that the Indian voices in the postmodern world of literature are no longer being 'ignored'. Rather, contrary to the oft-quoted *Spivak-ian* dictum that the 'subaltern cannot speak', the Indian authors (whose ancestors, with their fellow-countrymen, suffered from umpteen numbers of vices of imperialism from the mid-18th to the early-20th century) are—right now—among the more well-recognised writers of the literary world! The 'Literature of the Indian Diaspora' (LID), 'Writings by People of Indian Origin' (WPIO), or 'Indian Diasporic Writers' (IDW) are some of the terms that are being progressively included in international lexicons of readers and intellectuals. With the number of Indian immigrants steadily increasing in (especially) the Western countries, the growing political and social influences of one of South Asia's larger nations, and the overwhelming military strength that India has acquired in the early-21st century, the IDWs are litterateurs who can no longer be relegated to the 'margins'. They are constantly shifting their 'positions' from the so-called 'literary peripheries' to the 'centres'. If a survey *were* to be made on the countries whose cultures have mentionably impacted the postmodern scenario, India would certainly top the 'list'.

But—are the Indians who are settled in the Western countries and writing their literary masterpieces—'happy' and 'satisfied' with their so-called 'diasporic conditions of existence'? This is a question which is both relevant and thought-provoking because, unlike most of the diasporic authors of (for example) African origin, the Indian diasporic writers migrated to the West—especially, to the U.S.A., the U.K., Canada, and Germany—by their own choice (though, 'migration-after-marriage' is an issue that needs to be taken into account). They have settled down in different important American, British, Canadian, and German cities, have tenured employment (mostly as professors), and are usually considered to be 'important' inhabitants of the places where they live. So, the themes that are recurrent in their writings (mostly in the novels and poetry)—including senses of loss, alienation, anxiety, consciousness regarding 'hyphenated identity', *in-between*-ness, hybridity, nostalgia, ideas about the perceived 'hostilities' of the 'host-nations', and 'burning desires' for returning to home—seem to be outrightly 'paradoxical' because these writers are *immigrants-by-choice*, and, as numerous surveys published in newspapers and periodicals have lately revealed, they have no 'real' or 'lasting' desire or intention to permanently return to their country-of-origin. However, one could wonder whether these writers employ or explore these themes right out of their *subconscious* minds—they are, probably, dissatisfied, in different aspects, from the core of their heart, and might have suffered from 'guilt-consciousness' for, or 'problematised perceptions' regarding the whole issue of 'leaving' or 'abandoning' their country-of-origin altogether. These 'issues of perception', in turn, might have percolated into their exploration of the above-mentioned themes in their publications, which have received rave-reviews globally. With the increasing relevance of India—to reiterate—in the 21st-century socio-economic-cultural-political milieu, these writers—it needs no special mentioning—are here to stay, and to be heard! It is not for nothing that their publications are attracting thousands of doctoral researchers every year. However, even in the third decade of the 21st century, there is a distinct dearth of quality reference-materials on the writings of the Indian diasporic authors. This is what makes *Words from India in the West: A Critical Approach to Select Writings by the Diasporic Indian Litterateurs* so much relevant!

The anthology of critical approaches to different aspects of Indian diasporic writings has been divided into seven distinct sections: (a) theoretical approaches to Indian diasporic writings; (b) novels by the diasporic writers of Indian origin; (c) non-fictional prose by the Indian diasporic writers; (d) Indian diasporic poetry; (e) drama by the diasporic playwrights of Indian origin; (f) short-stories by Indian diasporic authors; and (g) films on/by the Indian diaspora. These seven 'sections' have been chosen and arranged so that all the genres—or, arguably, the 'sub-genres'—of Indian diasporic writings/culture are 'covered'.

In the first section, Deb Narayan Bandyopadhyay (to whom the anthology is 'dedicated'), an eminent theorist, administrator, and academician from the field of diasporic-literary-criticism, and Jaydip Sarkar (a well-known teacher, editor, and activist) have contributed essays on their individual thoughts on different aspects of Indian diasporic-literary-criticism.

The second part consists of four essays on the Indian diasporic novels. While Lata Dubey (a widely-published academician from Banaras Hindu University) writes specifically about the portrayal of 'India' in different novels by Chitra Banerjee Divakaruni, Auritra Munshi—an assistant professor of Raiganj University, academician, editor, and a doctorate in diasporic writings—writes about the 'coolie-diaspora': an area which, in the recent years, has attracted intense critical attention. In the third essay of this section, the editor of this present volume, who is addicted to reading Indian diasporic novels and has supervised different theses on diasporic writings, presents an overview of select publications by the West-settled-novelists of Indian origin. The fourth essay—by the widely-recognised academician, professor, traveller, and the present Director of the Publishing Department of Visva-Bharati, Prof. Amrit Sen—rereads different dimensions of the female diasporic experiences. This has immensely contributed to the overall coverage and quality of the anthology.

Indrajit Chattopadhyay and Saptarshi Mallick—two recognised academicians and writers—have enriched the section on the non-fictional writings by the Indian diasporic authors through their two essays—respectively—on the 'presentation' and 're-presentation' of the Indian cuisines in Western culture, and Nirad C. Chaudhuri's (oft-criticised) non-fictional prose.

While Neha Arora—professor, traveller, and editor from the Central University of Rajasthan—in the section on critical approaches to the Indian diasporic poetry, provides an overall-assessment of the Indian diasporic poets, Rupayan Mukherjee and Jaydip Sarkar—colleagues, writers, and professors from the University B.T. and Evening College, Cooch Behar—chose to focus on select works by select poets of the Indian diaspora. Their jointly-written-essay would provide important information to the researchers who seek to work on Indian diasporic poetry.

Tanima Dutta, editor of a reputed literary-journal and an assistant professor of Buniadpur Mahavidyalaya, Dakshin Dinajpur—in her voluminous essay on the Indian diasporic theatre—has exhaustively analysed different aspects of the genre. The forthcoming second-volume of this anthology is likely to include another essay on this area by two recognised academicians, thespians, and writers who have carved niches for themselves in the field of drama-criticism.

Lalon Kishore Singh (a reputed professor of English of Gauhati University, and a widely-published editor) and Neha Swarnakar (researcher, writer, and lecturer) have focussed, in their respective essays, on different short-stories by writers of Indian origin.

The final section of the anthology contains two essays—one by the brilliant professor Saunak Samajdar, a J.N.U.-alumnus and teacher of Cooch Behar Panchanan Barma University, and the other (written jointly) by Mr. Subhrajit Samanta (a journalist and film-maker) and Prof. Soumyajit Samanta, formerly of the University of North Bengal—on films on/by the Indian diaspora. This section forms the conclusion to the anthology. The editor of this anthology takes his liberty to humbly acknowledge Prof. Soumyajit Samanta as his doctoral research supervisor, and registers his sincere gratitude to him.

The editor of the edited-volume takes upon himself the responsibility for the delays related to this project. It was begun in the background of the *Covid-19* pandemic, and the length of its 'continuation'—understandably—caused different inconveniences to some of the writers who were problematised by 'unkind maladies' and several other problems and complicacies. The ever-helpful and noted academician, Prof. Ashis Sengupta, has been kind enough to contribute a very important 'Foreword' to this anthology. With relevant theoretical aspects in the background, it also summarises the different essays collected in the book. The editor registers his sincere thanks and deep reverence and gratitude to Prof. Bashabi Fraser, C.B.E., of the Department of English, Edinburgh Napier University—a very popular, widely-read, and critically-acclaimed Indian diasporic writer—for finding time out of her busiest schedule to write an 'Introduction' for the volume. Dr. Sreeparna Chattopadhyay, an I.C.S.S.R. Post-doctoral Fellow of the Department of Political Science, Raiganj University, has kindly prepared the cover-page-illustration for this volume, and has contributed one of her paintings on the theme of this edited volume. I owe my thanks to her too!

I am grateful to the owner(s) and officers of *Ibidem Verlag/Columbia University Press* for their patience and benevolent guidance while I struggled frantically to meet the deadlines, and, above all, for their all-out efforts to make my dream project a success.

On the occasion of the 'materialising' and publication of this project, I register my sincere thanks and gratitude to my teachers of/from Visva-Bharati and University of North Bengal, to the authorities of and my colleagues at Raiganj University (and former colleagues of Cooch Behar Panchanan Barma University and Malda College), and to my closest relatives, friends, and acquaintances from Balurghat (my dearest home-town) and Raiganj.

(Pinaki Roy),
Professor of English,
Raiganj University

Re-Structuring the Diaspora Imaginary
A Critique

—Deb Narayan Bandyopadhyay

Diaspora 1990-2010: Development and Dissemination:
Critiquing diaspora in 2022, after a long evolutionary process since (the Armenian-American academician) Khachig Tölölyan's publication of the journal *Diaspora: A Journal of Transnational Studies* in 1991, is essentially complex. This diaspora evolution in terms of its pre-settlement phase leading to shifting responses to new geo-cultural forms raises multiple issues. With the gradual dwindling of the pre-settlement or semi-settlement phase of diaspora community, it is time now we had perceived new connotations and new cultural forms.

Edward Said's configuration of intellectual movements showing 'decentred and exilic energies' (332) seems extremely irrelevant after a long passage of time—after a gap of roughly twenty-nine years. The new epistemic turn in terms of dual territoriality or cultural and political laterality, as evident in Paul Gilroy's *The Black Atlantic: Modernity and Double Consciousness* (1993) or Stuart Hall's *Cultural Identity and Diaspora* (1990) is also by now an over-debated issue seeking no new connivance and critical vindication.

In the long phase of diaspora-criticism—spanning, approximately, from the 1990s to 2010s—there is, of course, an emphasis on a connotative episteme that re-defines and re-shapes the view of the American politician, Zebulon Baird Vance, posited more than hundred years back in his lecture delivered in 1874. Vance, in his lecture *The Scattered Nation*, begins with a potential imagery of the Gulf Stream and then he relates it to the evolving designs of the Jewish diaspora community: "There is a lonely river in the midst of the ocean of mankind". The lonely river is a powerful referential frame for the diasporic history of the Jews. Vance, therefore, celebrates the scattered identity of the Jews and comments: "[...] for eighteen hundred years, [they] they have been scattered far and near over the wide earth; their strange customs, their distinct features [...] and their scattered unity, make them still a wonder and an astonishment" (Vance 64).

The 19th century-American senator's impassioned speech delivered in 1874 seems to foreshadow the initial incipient pattern of thinking through the *problematics* of the diaspora. Despite being so popular and intense in the nineteenth and early twentieth-century U.S.A., Vance's ideal is now completely extraneous in view of the Jewish community now settled within the framework of nationhood. The imaging of a 'scattered nation' seems to develop a contradictory resonance insofar as it interrogates the concept of unitary, homogeneous, territorial bonding.

The decentring of nationhood is also significantly evident in the American-Iranian writer Azar Nafisi's *Reading Lolita in Tehran* (2003) or the Iraqi-litterateur Nuha al-Radi's *Baghdad Diaries* (1998). Both writers reify their memories of a nation being splintered in different ways. Such memoirs and re-descriptions challenge and critique the monolithic and uniform homogeneity of nation state, so rhetorically aggrandised, over-stated and etherealised by Benedict Anderson's 1983-thesis of 'imagined community'. The Anglo-Irish political scientist seems to posit and articulate the neo-capitalist agenda of resisting the developing tendencies of multiformity and pluralism. This sense of non-compliance to the structuration of nation is also evident in Nafisi's self-pity caused by helplessness:

"Life in the Islamic Republic was as capricious as the month of April, when short periods of sunshine would suddenly give way to showers and storms. It was unpredictable: the regime would go through cycles of some tolerance, followed by a crackdown. Now, after a period of relative calm and so-called liberalisation, we had again entered a time of hardships. Universities had once more become the targets of attack by the cultural purists who were busy imposing stricter sets of laws, going so far as to segregate men and women in classes and punishing disobedient professors" (Nafisi 6).

Nuha al-Radi (1941-2004) may be regarded as an iconic representation of a transnational woman. Born in Iraq, she moves—in her writings—beyond boundaries through India, Egypt, Lebanon, Jordon, the U.K. and the U.S.A. In her *Baghdad Diaries*, she represents the daily tortures inflicted on the Iraqis, the geopolitical unrest and the consequent political disjunctions. While commenting on Nuha al-Radi's narrative, Dalia M.A. Gomaa prefers to call it 'unhomely diaries', thereby contesting the traditional diaspora perception of 'homeland' and 'hostland':

> "In that sense, not only does *Baghdad Diaries* blur the boundaries between the private/domestic and the public/political, but also, more importantly, between the personal and the global. I examine *Baghdad Diaries* as an 'unhomely diary'" (Gomaa 55).

This naturally raises the issue of 'de-housement' and 're-housement'. In other words, it is a continuous search for negotiating the contestation of 'homeland' and 'hostland'. Bharati Mukherjee in her 1989-novel *Jasmine* celebrates her exiled identity:

> "We are the outcasts and deportees, strange pilgrims visiting outlandish shrines, landing at the end of tarmacs. [....] We ask only one thing: to be allowed to land, to pass through, to continue" (101).

But there is a transformative mode in shaping the metonymic ideology of 'home'. In an interview with Geoff Hancock, she says:

> "New York is my home now, and you know, in many ways, it isn't too different from Calcutta. Like Calcutta, New York has a delightfully arrogant sense of itself as the history and intellectual centre of the universe. And of course, both cities have sizeable communities of homeless people living on sidewalks. May be it's the gradual Calcuttisation of New York that makes me feel so at home here" (qtd. in Hancock 10-11).

This inter-linearity of urban space in terms of New York and Kolkata seems to resolve, erase and terminate the "outcasts and deportees" psychosis. The contentions of border-crossing now come to be replaced by theneo-nomadic cogito of shifting terrains of habitus. What Bharati Mukherjee intends to assert is the inflective nature of trans-spatiality in multiple geo-cultural situations. Mukherjee therefore finds no tangible difference in the global urban centres and the concept of 'home', as a result, becomes ubiquitous.

The diaspora phase from 1990s to 2010s has operated in alliance with the postcolonial narratives of nation, cultural citizenship, and hybridity; and it has therefore been largely built around cross-theory assumptions, each contributing to the other. The American Chicana theorist Gloria Anzaldua's negotiations of the 'Mestiza' thesis of interpermeation and mixed identities inflecting on the issues of borderlands may also be a contributing factor to the first phase of diaspora theory. Despite the rich potential of the borderland thesis that even moved beyond the problematic of Chicana existence, it finally could be considered compatible with questions of mixed identities and hybridities so intensely debated in diaspora theory.

The *S.O.A.S.*-affiliated author Gurharpal Singh—in *Culture and Economy in the Indian Diaspora*—has tried to develop three critical issues: (a) conceptualising Indian diaspora and configuring the correlated issues; (b) inter-relation of globalisation and Indian diaspora; and (c) multiple formations of labour mobility and emigration. Singh, further, asserts that "[…] the significance of the Indian diaspora will increase within the host countries and in its relationship with India" (Singh 12).

But these key issues so articulately discussed and developed seem to have been profusely debated and finally these debates exhaust themselves in order to make way for new theoretical ramifications.

In the earlier diaspora experiences, memory and exile used to play a significant role. In such cultural forms, elegiac yearning was an important constitutive element in the context of the 'homeland' trope. In ancient tradition of literary trope called *paraklausitheron*, there is an emphasis on the note of elegiac love song sung by a lover addressed to the door that separates him from the object of love. These songs are loaded with sentiments of separation, loss and yearning for re-union. The diaspora memory seems to show a metonymic compatibility with the design of this trope. We note this *paraklausitheron* sentiment even in the medieval Jewish poet Yehudah Halevi's longing for the Holy City Jerusalem:

> "O City of the world, with sacred splendour blest,
> My spirit yearns to thee from out the far-off west,
> A stream of love wells forth when I recall thy day,
> Now is the temple waste, thy glory passed away.
> Had I an eagle's wings, straight would I fly to thee,
> Moisten thy dust with wet cheeks streaming free.
> Oh! How I long for thee" (Halevi 238).

In most of the diaspora writers, there is a definitive emphasis on elegiac resonances contextualised in terms of memories of separation and a desire for return and re-union. This specific trope of *paraklausitheron* is therefore built on an epistemic question of associationist cognition of the moment of departure, disjunction and separation. *Paraklausitheron* or the elegiac moment and the correlated associationism can be best understood only when perceived in terms of a teleologic future. In other words, diaspora critique presupposes the theme of evolving 'settlement' across different geopolitical and geocultural boundaries. Hence it primarily critiques 'evolving settlements' under the general rubric of displacement memories of homeland.

As a result, the future of diaspora is essentially associationist because it reifies the homeland memories and the phases of new settlements. In this context, it is worthwhile to note the Freudian concept of *nachtraglichekeit* or 'afterwardness' which Sigmund Freud uses to interpret the modes of belated understanding of events. Diaspora memory may be considered in Freudian terms. As diaspora is constitutive of multiple event chains, such as geopolitical contentions, departures, dissociative factors, loss and trauma, re-contextualisation and re-definition of national cultures and identity, there is always an attempt to re-configure and re-articulate the diaspora experience. This mode of 'afterwardness', therefore, becomes explicit in narratives, fiction, poetry and history. Such modes of writing are procedures for taking into account the event patterns of the diaspora past caught and enshrined in a post-settlement phase. This method of 'afterwardness', therefore, objectifies the scattered moments of the experiences of disjuncture. 'Afterwardness' acts as a principle of objective reconstruction through associationist modes of memory. This helps to move beyond singular, subjective levels of experiential perception; it objectifies and distances the recollective process of the pre-settlement diasporic past.

Diaspora 2010: Transnational and the Neo-nomadic:
Diaspora theory disseminated though varying degrees of socio-cultural temporalities has been particularly possible because of changes in international dynamics. Despite the presence of discrepant economies and multiple figurations of the socio-cultural formations in the world order, the ideal of linkages across nations and cultures came to be an acceptable theoretical trope. India's decision to stride across boundaries in the wake of globalisation and the proliferation of the policy of F.D.I. (Foreign Direct Investment), themes of national culture and citizenship gradually began to acquire new meanings.

Since the cataclysmic *9/11 Destruction of the W.T.C.-Twin Towers in Manhattan*, diaspora space has become more complex with the emergence of the growing distrust of unipolarism and pre-emptive western centrism. Gradually the rise of global political economy, the new strength acquired by the Chinese Yuan or the Korean Won in the context of the developing G.D.P. began to re-shape the world order. It, therefore, challenges the dominance and celebration of the Euro-American currency. Moreover the Indian declaration of *Act East and Act West Policy* brought about new challenges in the global economic order.

The post-9/11 terror-ridden world brought restrictions in immigration policies and visa-rules, thereby bringing impediments to free mobility. To put it more polemically, the new world order began to envisage mobility and citizenship as fomenting contestations and debates. Since 2005, terrorism, apprehensions in international mobility, aggression across borders complicated the earlier significations of diaspora mobility.

There are now cases of 'situational' diaspora caused by war, poverty and disease. In 2015, hundreds of thousands of Syrian migrants entered Germany because of war and poverty. (The-then

German Chancellor) Angela Markel's Government granted citizenship to a large number of Syrian migrants. U.N.H.C.R. reports that a huge number of migrants and refugees sought asylum in different European countries, though it was not always favourably looked upon; the migrants had to experience push-backs or detention[1]. O.E.C.D. (*Organisation for Economic Co-operation and Development*) also reports that since the beginning of the internecine war between Ukraine and Russia in early 2022, more than 5.3 million refugees fled to Europe; it has been further estimated that that approximately one child has turned into a refugee per second. The government of Ukraine calls these refugees temporarily displaced hoping for return of the refugees in future[2].

In 2009, the Scottish Government initiated a controversy on questions of determining the diaspora identity. It underlines the following decisive protocols:

a) Trans-territorial mobility
b) Descendants of earlier emigrants re-engaging with ancestral home
c) Sporadic, nomadic movements

The Scottish government even recognised temporarily displaced persons as part of diaspora population. It even includes a special category called 'affinity diaspora' who, having temporally located in a different country, may return to the home country and yet cherish proximity to trans-locality.

The Scottish project of profiling diaspora may be looked as a form of acceptance of a community's negotiated subjectivity. It is a state-sponsored political and cultural diplomacy in terms of its approval of worldwide mobility, engagements with the point of origin (P.O.I.), and neo-nomadic movements across the world[3].

But the transformative factor is identified in the category constituted of temporarily displaced persons. This may involve certain economic and political questions. As a result, there is an interface of origin-ary territory and transnational territories. It posits an interweaving of the relationship of P.O.I. and N.R.I., appearing to be strengthened by possibilities of F.D.I. or even transnational 'sweatshop' regimes spread across the world or even T.N.C.-s and M.N.C.-s working hard for hiring cheap labour beyond all borders. Such temporalities no longer raise questions of citizenship, cultural nationalism, and identity. In other words, diaspora specificities undergo new academic or disciplinary transformations. Thus a *Centre for the Study of the Indian Diaspora* (C.S.I.D.) so enthusiastically inaugurated in 1996 in an Indian university as promoting a distinctive form of interdisciplinary *Area Study Programme* under *University Grants Commission* seems to have gradually exhausted its strength and energy in 2022 with much of its earlier energy and innovations being curtailed. Even an extensive reading list of books on diaspora shows that most of its critical literature seems to have been almost completed by 2010.

This is not meant to be a critique on the end of diaspora, its inadequacy or incompleteness. Rather it is an attempt to see how national governments and international economic or political policies bring multiple changes in the world order, thereby shaping new subjectivities and connotations.

With the rise of *Global Political Economy* (G.P.E.) as an attempt to form a new global consortium determined by international relationships, labour mobilities, strategic clustering of world powers, there seems to have occurred complex replacements and changes in the prevailing ontological mechanism[4].

Multilateral geopolitics comes to be significantly dominated by Foreign Direct Investment, Free Trade Agreement involving the participating countries. India began to look forward to the Indian N.R.I.-s for restructuring the new economic destiny of India. It was being done in a moment of international anxiety in trade and economic sectors, especially in view of India's perception of a definitive threat from China's 'Yuan trap' and unfair currency competitiveness. Moreover China's O.B.O.R. (*One Belt One Road*) initiative, though aiming at worldwide Chinese economic ascendancy, was an innovative mechanism at 'borderless' perception of trade regimes. This may be interpreted as a borderless journey into multiple nation states. Again the international organisations like A.S.E.A.N., E.U., B.R.I.C.S., and

Q.S.D., and so on, show further emphasis on transnational redefinition of international relationship.

The earlier projections of diaspora theory involving the trajectories of memory, exile, border, hybridity and nationhood begin to move towards a phase of definitive transformation. The diaspora journey of a community and its search for settlement has almost exhausted itself to be consequently metamorphosed into multiple variations of cultural forms.

In an international poetry festival called *Anantha Poetry Festival* on Indian diaspora poets based in the U.K. held on 5 May 2022, a debate was initiated on the nature of their poetic identity. It was unanimously agreed that the label 'diaspora poet' may no longer be assigned to them, especially when most of them are substantially settled in the U.K. and prefer to describe themselves as British poets. In a new twist in the critical argument, it was decided that 'transnational poet' would be an appropriate description for such poets. This new theme was further continued as the same group of poets clustered themselves in another web-poetry-festival organised on 7 June 2022 by Bankura University (West Bengal, India) on the theme '*Thresholds*: Transnational Poets Speak'.

These two events show the pattern of change. Despite their strong alliance with the postcolonial and the diasporic, all of these poets suffer from a sense of anxiety in relation to their creative identity. In a changed neo-liberalist world order, it is no longer preferable to accept a predicated identity or an identity celebrated in colonial and diasporic jargon. This group of poets that included the first generation as well as second or even third generation immigrants no longer found it relevant to describe themselves U.K.-based diaspora poets after long years of settlement and saturation in the U.K. Even the second or third generation poets with a blurred, faded historical memory find it difficult to coalesce with the homeland and their forefathers they left long ago. This generates a new transnational psychosis which inflects on a re-definition of their poetic identity.

Conclusion:

With wider mobility and transactions at multiple levels, there is a growing tendency to stride across national boundaries. This naturally conduces to relational multiplicity of the diaspora community traversing through shifting patterns of language, culture, cartography and history. In other words, people moving across a transnational world have become part of neo-nomadic communities.

Notes:

1. "*U.N.H.C.R. – Desperate Journeys*: Refugees and Migrants arriving in Europe and at Europe's Borders". *U.N.H.C.R.* Accessed on 23 October 2022 <*https://www.unhcr.org/desperatejourneys/*>
2. "*War in Ukraine*: Tackling the Policy Challenges". *O.E.C.D.* Accessed on 20 October 2022 <*https://www.oecd.org/ukraine-hub/en/*>
3. "The Scottish Diaspora and Diaspora Strategy: Insights and Lessons from Ireland". *Scottish Government – Online* 29 May 2009. Accessed on 20 October 2022 <*https://www.gov.scot/publications/scottish-diaspora-diaspora-strategy-insights-lessons-ireland/pages/4/*>
4. See Robert Gilpin's *Global Political Economy: Understanding the International Economic Order* (Princeton: Princeton University Press, 2001), 3-24.

Works cited:

Gomaa, Dalia M.A. "Remembering Iraqis in Nuha al-Radi's *Baghdad Diaries: A Woman's Chronicle of War and Exile*". *Feminist Formations* 29. 1 (2017): 53-70.

Halevi, Yehudah. "Oh! City of the World". *The Standard Book of Jewish Verse*. Ed. George Alexander Kohut. New York: Dodd Mead and Co., 1917.

Hancock, Geoff. "An Interview with Bharati Mukherjee". *Conversations with Bharati Mukherjee*. Ed. Bradley C. Edwards. Jackson: University Press of Mississippi, 2009.

Nafisi, Azar. *Reading Lolita in Tehran: A Memoir in Books*. New York: Random House. 2003

Mukherjee, Bharati. *Jasmine*. New York: Grove Press, 1989.

Said, Edward W. *Culture and Imperialism*. London: Vintage Books, 1994.

Singh, Gurharpal. "Introduction" *Culture and Economy in the Indian Diaspora*. Eds. Bikhu Parekh, Gurharpal Singh, and Steven Vertovec. New York and London: Routledge, 2003.

Weinstein, Maurice (ed.). *Zebulon B. Vance and 'The Scattered Nation'*. North Carolina: The Wildacres Press, 1995.

Theorising Indian Diasporic Writings
A Brief Reflection

—Jaydip Sarkar

> "They change their sky, not their mind, who cross the sea"...
> Horace, *Epistles* I.11.27 (qtd. in Allatson and McCormack 217).

In the dying decades of the twentieth-century a term, which was till then largely unfamiliar to the lower-middle class students and scholars hailing from relatively humble origins, was floating freely (perhaps, to an extent, rampantly) in the academic atmosphere of a provincial South-Asian University. The word 'diaspora' was a recent incorporation in the pedagogic lexicon of the Humanities but by the time we had migrated from our *muffaswil* (that is, sub-urban) homes in pursuit of higher degrees and had settled down as outsiders in the university-campuses located—predominantly—in various metro/cosmo-polises, the word had turned into an (quint)essential signifier, which distinguished the grain from the chaff, and the scholar from the simpleton. Like *the Beatles* or Badal Sircar, 'diaspora' was a significant touchstone endowed with a heavy cultural capital. Not to have known or heard about it was an irredeemable disqualification which significantly impeded one's possibility to claim their position in intelligentsia.

Originating as a compound word that is etymologically indebted to a pair of Greek words 'dia' (meaning 'across') and 'speirein' (that is, 'scatter'), 'diaspora'—as a theoretical concept—has been subjected to various introspections, elucidations and reflections. For William Safran, the "specific meaning" of Diaspora, historically speaking, has denoted the "exile of Jews from their historic homeland and their scattering" (83). And, for Robert Garland, the diasporic condition has originally been an inextricable component of the ancient Greek polis—though he confesses, "[T]he investigation of diaspora as historical phenomenon in the Greek (and Roman for that matter) world continues to be sparse" (Garland xvii). While theorists like Steven Vertovec and Walker Connor are of the opinion that the term 'diaspora' is intimately associated with the materiality of displacement and can allude to any "deterritorialised" or "transnational" populace—that is, "that segment of people living outside the homeland" (Connor 16). For someone like Judith T. Shuval, the diasporic experience is "a *social construct* (emphasis mine) founded on feeling, consciousness, memory, mythology, history, meaningful narratives, group identity, longings, dreams, allegorical and virtual elements all of which play an important role in establishing a diaspora reality" (43) To quote James Clifford, 'diaspora' has become a 'travelling term' (302), holding heterogeneous significances/ diverse implications that cannot be contained within the limits of a strategic and unproblematic definition.

In the introduction to *Tracing an Indian Diaspora: Contexts, Memories, Representations*, **Parvati** Raghuram and Ajaya K. Sahoo note that in the academic debates in India, the notion of 'diaspora' was rarely deployed until the closing decade of the 20th century (Raghuram *et al.* 1-20). In 1989, for instance, *Sociological Bulletin* — the official journal of the Indian Sociological Society, New Delhi — brought out a special issue on the theme of 'Indians Abroad' (38. 1, March 1989) in which eight out of nine articles focused on Indian communities abroad, but not a single one referred to them as 'diasporic'. The contributors, rather, used words like 'Indian immigrants' or 'overseas Indians'. As such, it was only in 1994 that an 'International Conference on Indian Diaspora' (could be and) was organised by the University of Hyderabad. The objective of the conference was to establish a centre which would be devoted exclusively to the study of the Indian diaspora, and it was at this conference that terms such as 'diaspora' and 'transnational Indians' came to be first and liberally used (Nadarajah 1994). The demands for the organised study of the 'Indian diaspora', their expectations, their contributions and scope of collaboration in various sectors of society, resulted in the establishment of the *Centre for the Study of Indian Diaspora* under the 'Area Studies

Programme' of the University Grants Commission (U.G.C.) in 1996 at the University of Hyderabad.

The presence of Indians in South-east Asia has a long history extending to the period before the so-called 'Christian-era'. The journey of Indians has continued from the pre-modern, through the colonial, into the contemporary age of globalisation. However, the proper roots of the contemporary Indian diaspora could be traced to the period of colonial domination by the English imperialists and the exploitation of cheap indentured labour from the Asian subcontinent in different parts of the colonial-empire. In the nineteenth century, the English instituted indentured labour — a 'new form of slavery' (Tinker 1). The 'indentured "coolies" were half-slaves, bound over body and soul by a hundred and one regulations' (Joshi 44). In 1884, the English consul in Paramaribo, Suriname, stated that 'the Suriname-planters [...] found in the meek Hindu a ready substitution for the negro slave he had lost' (Emmer 187). Nevertheless, what we conventionally understand as the 'Indian diaspora' today is a predominantly "border diaspora" (Mishra, *The Diasporic* 422) — constituted by professionals and skilled labourers who have moved and settled in the U.S.A. and other first world countries like the U.K., Canada, and Australia — especially in the later-decades of the twentieth century. Considerably impacted by the advent of electronic and satellite communications, recent diasporic trends have given a completely new dimension to the nature of connectedness between the host land and the lost homeland, something unthinkable in earlier times.

Yet, one cannot deny, that any diasporic experience is inevitably marked by a consciousness of displacement, loss and nostalgia. In the words of Vijay Mishra, irrespective of their historico-cultural conditions and contexts, "all diasporas are unhappy, but every diaspora is unhappy in its own way" (*The Literature* 1). Referring to Avtar Brah's conceptualisation of "homing desire", Mishra argues that the universal attribute of the diasporic imaginary is a persistent and unfailing realisation that "against one's *desh* (that is, 'home country') the present locality is *videsh* ('another country')" (*ibid.* 5). The consolidation of a real/

imagined homeland in consciousness (that is distinct from the *host-land*), which is neither redeemable in reality nor ethically substitutable, is the root of a growing sense of incompleteness which significantly corresponds to trauma, mourning and melancholy. It is thus unsurprising that the literary tradition of the Indian diaspora is chiefly preoccupied with the stated contentions of displacement, trauma, memory, mourning, and melancholy, among others.

Major English Indian writers such as Amitav Ghosh, Salman Rushdie, Anita Desai, Bharati Mukherjee, Anjana Appachana, Anita Nair, Jhumpa Lahiri, and Chitra Banerjee Divakaruni have become prominent writers in the Indian diaspora writing tradition. These writers have "attempted works on [their] lived experiences by adopting an interdisciplinary approach, drawing mainly from cartographical, historical, economic, political, ethnical, and ethnological sources. Their fiction chiefly narrates the causes that trigger diasporic movement, or a series of movements, the unrelenting connection between host land and homeland, the emergence of complex diasporian identities constructed from the negotiation of cultural values carried from the homeland, and the generational differences and the multicultural environment of host societies" (Chatterjee and Chatterjee 8).

Diasporic phenomena, namely, rootlessness, nostalgia, memory and alienation are the key issues in Amitav Ghosh's novels, especially *The Shadow Lines* (1988) and *The Glass Palace* (2000). In his novels, Ghosh uses the flashback technique in order to intensify the characters' chase for having their own identities in alien lands. The thread which links the past and the present of his characters is 'memory'. In *The Shadow Lines*, the glorious memories of Calcutta and Dhaka are beautifully pictured by the characters longing for their lost homelands. The partition of Bengal and the resultant trauma are widely depicted in the novel. Tha'mma's memorising of the old family house in Dhaka stands as a wholesome framework of attachment of *deep-rooted-ness*. It remains a home for the grandmother, even after partition, and she longs to see it again. In *The Glass Palace* also, thoughts of home are not something to be merely remembered as an abstract construct but represented as a cultural tool of negotiation for new cultural encounters. The past is remembered not as a dead, remote period, but as flowing on into the present.

In his novels, Salman Rushdie, in order to maintain the cultural traditions and native identity that he left behind, advocates "a set of ethnic particularities that embody national mythology" (Chiang 33). In "Imaginary Homelands" (1991), he himself aptly describes what might be one of the most potent motivations behind the use of myth-making by diasporic Indian writers, whose physical and cultural alienation from India means that it is impossible for them to recover precisely that which was lost, and that they will, in response, "create fictions, not actual cities or villages, but invisible ones, imaginary homelands, Indias of the mind" (428). His *Midnight's Children* (1981) is a product of reminiscence as much as of myth-making.

In the novel *The Namesake* (2003), Jhumpa Lahiri describes the struggle and hardships of a Bangladeshi couple who immigrated to the United States to live a peaceful life. This novel reveals the concepts of cultural identity, tradition, uprooting, and family expectations. In fact, in all her novels, nostalgia, memory, longing, and loss are prominent themes.

Anjana Appachana is a diasporic novelist who resides in the United States of America, and has received the *O' Henry Festival Prize*. She has written *Incantations and Other Stories* (1991), a collection of short-stories, and a novel—*Listening Now* (1997). She deals with the issues faced by Indian women in their homeland and abroad. In *Listening Now,* she analyses three-generation women's problems and how they sustained with the help of their friends and relatives. Her collections of short stories portrayed the perfect description of traditional and modern women. In her short stories, she describes the mother as a traditional figure.

Chitra Banerjee Divakaruni is another multi-faceted diasporic writer who resides in the U.S.A. Her short-story collection *Arranged Marriage: Stories* (1995) brought for her the *American Book Award* in 1995. Her works are usually set in the U.S.A. and India. Her principal focus is on the experiences of

South Asian migrants. She beautifully presents inter alia (among other things) the matrix of diasporic consciousness like alienation, rootlessness, loneliness, nostalgia, cultural conflict, questioning, etc., in her novels. She explores and highlights concerns for racism, economic disparity, miscarriage, divorce, longingness, homesickness, disappointments, and so on. Her characters are caught physically between the two worlds which challenge their belongings to either location. To keep hold of the values of the homeland in the new atmosphere of the adopted land often leads to mental conflict, dilemma, and unanswered questions which ultimately lead to identity crisis. The metaphor of 'Trishanku' has been commonly used to define people who live in a state of 'in-between-ness' (or more precisely, the immigrants). In general, the migrants are caught in the crisis of identity as an intuitive understanding of their native culture unavoidably comes into conflict with their rational understanding of a foreign culture. In an alien environment, they try to scrutinize and re-evaluate the tradition and culture of their homelands. In her novel, *The Mistress of Spices* (1997), she has constructed the story of dreams, desires, hopes, and expectations. Tilo, the main female character, was born in a faraway place and she travels through time to Oakland, California. The author of this novel creates this Tilo character as the successful survivor in a new place. Chitra narrates Tilo as a brave girl who breaks the rules and helping the other female migrant characters through their twists of trouble. Amit Chaudhari, in his novel *Afternoon Raag* (1993), portrays the lives of Indian students in Oxford. These writers also depicted the positive aspect of displacement. There are benefits of living as a migrant, the opportunity of having a double perspective of being able to experience diverse cultural modes.

Meera Syal, Hari Kunzru, Sunetra Gupta, Jhumpa Lahiri, and other second-generation Indian writers have faithfully tested the lives of first and second-generation immigrants in the United States. Like Meena in Meera Sayal's *Anita and Me* (1997) and Gogol in *The Namesake*, the children of diaspora are often stranded between two disparate cultures. The complicated contentions regarding race, owing to their 'natural' brown skin, impede/

perplex their pre-consideration of the host-Nation as 'home'. Simultaneously, the mythologised homeland, often (feignly) constructed around the problematic paradigm of post-memory, appears to be an unidentifiable, unfamiliar land that can be inherited but not lived in.

The list of diaspora writers is long and detailed and it is perhaps impossible to contemplate or attempt a comprehensive and exhaustive study of the literary tradition of the Indian Diaspora within the limited scope of an overview. The thematic contentions of displacement, emigration, homelessness and loss, although conventional and repetitive to a degree, are often revised and re-interrogated through diverse textual tropes and metaphors and such novelties in treatment have substantially enriched the cultural repertoire of the diasporic.

Works cited:

Allatson, Paul, and Joe McCormack (eds.). *Exile Cultures, Misplaced Identities*. Amsterdam: Rodopi B.V., 2008.

Chatterjee Nilanjana, and Anindita Chatterjee. *Re-theorising the Indian Subcontinental Diaspora: Old and New Directions*. Newcastle-upon-Tyne: Cambridge Scholars Publishing, 2020.

Chiang, Chih-Yun. "Diasporic Theorising Paradigm on Cultural Identity." *Intercultural Communication Studies* XIX (2010): 29-46.

Clifford, James. "Diasporas". *Cultural Anthropology: Further Inflections: Towards Ethnographies of the Future* 9.3 (August 1994): 302-08.

Connor, Walker "The Impact of Homelands upon Diasporas". *Modern Diasporas in International Politics*. Ed. Gabi Sheffer. New York: St. Martin's, 1986. 16-46.

Emmer, Pieter C. "The Meek Hindu: The Recruitment of Indian Indentured Labourers for Service Overseas, 1870–1916". *Colonialism and Migration: Indentured Labour before and after Slavery*. Ed. Pieter C. Emner. Leiden: Martinus Nijhoff Publishers, 1986. 187-207.

Garland, Robert. *Wandering Greeks: The Ancient Greek Diaspora from the Age of Homer to the Death of Alexander the Great*. Princeton: Princeton University Press, 2014.

Joshi, P.S. *The Tyranny of Colour: A Study of the Indian Problem in South Africa*. Durban: E.P. and Commercial Printing Press, 1942.

Mishra, Vijay. "*The Diasporic Imaginary*: Theorising the Indian Diaspora". *Textual Practice* 10.3 (1996): 421-47.

---. *The Literature of the Indian Diaspora: Theorising the Diasporic Imaginary.* New York and London: Routledge, 2007.

Nadarajah, Manickam. "*Diaspora and Nostalgia*: Towards a Semiotic Theory of the Indian Diaspora". Paper presented at the *International Conference on Indian Diaspora*, University of Hyderabad, 1–2 November 1994 <https://www.academia.edu/7972656/Diaspora_and_Nostalgia_Towards_a_Cultural_Theory_of_Indian_Diaspora>

Raghuram, Parvati, et al. (eds.). *Tracing an Indian Diaspora: Contexts, Memories, Representations.* New Delhi: Sage Publications, 2008.

Rushdie, Salman. "Imaginary Homelands." *The Post-Colonial Studies Reader.* Eds. Bill Ashcroft, Gareth Griffiths, and Helen Tiffin. New York and London: Routledge, 2006. 428-34.

Safran, William. "*Diasporas in Modern Societies*: Myths of Homeland and Return". *Diaspora: A Journal of Transnational Studies* 1.1 (Spring 1991): 83-99.

Shuval, Judith. "*Diaspora Migration*: Definitional Ambiguities and a Theoretical Paradigm". *International Migration* 38.5 (2000): 41-56.

Tinker, Hugh. *A New System of Slavery: The Export of Indian Labour Overseas 1830–1920.* Oxford: Oxford University Press, 1974.

Carving out Niches for Themselves
An Overview of Select Indian Novelists of the Diaspora

– Pinaki Roy

> "There was a time when Indians who had been abroad and picked up some simple degree or skill said that they had become displaced and were neither of the East nor West. In this they were absurd and self-dramatising: they carried India with them, Indian ways of perceiving. Now, with the great migrant rush, little is hard of that displacement. Instead, Indians say that they have become too educated for India. The opposite is usually true: they are not educated enough; they only want to repeat their lessons. The imported skills are rooted in nothing; they are skills separate from principles".
>
> —V. S. Naipaul in *India: A Wounded Civilisation* (qtd. in Naipaul 77).

It is not for the first time that the Indian intellectuals and writers (especially the novelists) of the Indian diaspora have been outrightly criticised. (Direct or indirect) support for Naipaul's unflattering 1976-assessment of the West-settled Indians can be noticed—over the years—in opinions of and overviews by, for example, S. Srinivasan, Mukesh Williams, Madhu Tyagi, Brij Lal, and Uma Parameswaran. However, Naipaul's tirade notwithstanding, it is an incontrovertible fact that the (English) writings by members of the (Indian) diaspora—especially the novels—have come to dominate the late-20th and early-21st-century literary milieus: so much so that Arianna Dagnino has identified the periods as the centur[ies] of exile, (im)migrants, postcolonial, and [Indian] diasporic writing[s] par excellence" (148). The perceived 21st century-*omnipotence* and *omnipresence* of the Indian (English) diasporic writings—the novels, above all—have *naturally* led Malati Mathur to marvel at the wide coverage of such writings; how they 'cover […] every continent and part of the world' (Sarwal 327). Uma Devi and Nagalakshmi, however, point out two important 'categories' or 'sections' of diasporic novelists:

> "One category includes those who have spent part of their lives in India and brought their heritage assets abroad. The other [category comprises] [...] those who [have] gr[own] up outside of India. They just dream of their own country from outside, like a strange place where they started. The writers in the first group ha[ve] actual displacements, while those in the second group f[ind] themselves uprooted. [...]. When these writers portra[y] [...] immigrant characters in their novels, they examin[e] the themes of displacement, alienation, assimilation, and cultural adaptation" (1909).

This 'categorisation' seems to follow Amba Pande's dividing the 'Old' and 'New' diasporas into two groups — the former consisting of indentured labourers, former convicts, free migrants, traders, government employees, and professionals, and the latter of skilled and semi-skilled workers, businessmen, students, and political diaspora (3-4). However, this 'division' by Pande somewhat problematises the identification of the so-called 'New Diaspora' Indian novelists: for example, Jhumpa Lahiri (b. 1967), Kavita Daswani (b. 1971), and Kiran Desai (b. 1971) — perceptively — do not fit into any of the 'groups' that comprise the 'New Diaspora' which have been listed by Pande. Yet they demonstrate the same diasporic consciousnesses in their respective novels as those of the other 'members'. William Safran's definition further complicates the issue. Terming 'diaspora' as a 'part of transnational and transpolitical ethnoscape', he writes about how the individuals belonging to the so-called 'New Diaspora' have, in time, 'dissolved completely into their *hostland* societies', and they and their descendants have 'little if any memory' of their *homeland* — that is, the *country-of-origin* (Ben-Rafael and Sternberg 75-76). One can, therefore, wonder whether the 'memories' and 'nostalgia' shown by the 'New' diasporic novelists are to be assessed as their 'genuine' feelings, or they are merely 'producing' them for writing their novels. Do they 'honestly' demonstrate — as Meenakshi Mukherjee almost dismissively writes in *The Perishable Empire* — 'the anxiety of Indianness' (181)? It is question that is quite complicated, and therefore, hard to answer.

Minutely assessed, the themes of 'displacement', 'alienation, assimilation and 'cultural adaptation' seem to permeate different novels written by such litterateurs as Kamala Markandaya (1924-2004), Anita Desai (b. 1937), Bharti Krichner (b 1940), Bharati Mukherjee (1940-2017), Salman Rushdie (b. 1947), Meena Alexander (1951-2018), Rohinton Mistry (b. 1952), Shashi Tharoor (b. 1956), Kunal Basu (b. 1956), Amitav Ghosh (b. 1956), Chitra Banerjee Divakaruni (b. 1956), Anita Rau Badami (b. 1961), Shauna Singh Baldwin (b. 1962), Amit Chaudhuri (b. 1962), Sunetra Gupta (b. 1965), Anjali Banerjee (b. 1965), Anita Nair (b. 1966), Jhumpa Lahiri, Hari Kunzru (b. 1969), Kavita Daswani, Kiran Desai, Vineeta Vijayaraghavan (b. 1972), Anjana Appachana (b. 1972), and so on.

Here, I am deliberately keeping Vidiadhar Surajprasad Naipaul (1932-2018), Moyez G. Vassanji (b. 1950), and Shani Mootoo (b. 1957) out of the 'list'. Naipaul was born to Trinidadian parents whose connection to India ended back in the 1880s', and, as an *Outlook-Books*-article of 3 February 2022 mentions, Naipaul has never claimed himself to be an Indian or has ever demonstrated any palpable pro-India-feelings[1]. Similarly, Shani Mootoo was born in Dublin to Trinidadian-parents, and though she has written novels like *Cereus Blooms at Night* (1993), *Valmiki's Daughter* (2008), *Moving Forward Sideways like a Crab* (2014), and *Polar Vortex* (2020), but her so-called 'Indianness' is highly problematised by the circumstances of migration. Understandably, Sebastian Schneider, in his 2008-e-essay "Challenging the Cultural Mosaic", refuses to call Mootoo's fiction anything more than 'Caribbean(-Canadian) or South Asian(-Canadian) literature' (Schneider). The same logic or reason has not permitted me to keep M.G. Vassanji, the well-known Kenyan-Canadian writer of nine wonderful novels published between 1989 and 2019, away from my analysis. Vassanji, of course, was born to Indian immigrant-parents in Kenya and raised in Tanganyika, but his ancestors had migrated to Kenya, and he to the U.S.A. (and, thereafter, to Canada) *so* early that it is difficult to imagine that he would be consciously (or unconsciously) 'flaunting' his 'Indian roots'. Understandably, only one of his novels — *The Assassin's Song* (2007) — is set in India.

It is not that the 'list' of Indian diasporic novelists that I have prepared is exhaustive. Now and then, novels and memoir/fictionalised-history-based-novels (by the expatriate Indian writers) like Rajiv Mohabir's *Antiman: A Hybrid Memoir* (2019), Sunjeev Sahota's *China Room* (2021), Sonia Falerio's *The Good Girls: An Ordinary Killing* (2021), Sanjena Sathian's *Gold Diggers* (2021), and Nawaaz Ahmed's *Radiant Fugitives* (2021) attract attention, are numerously purchased, and, thereafter, repeatedly read. Another important name — almost 'censurably' underrated — is that of Jacqueline Singh's whose 1992-novel *Seasons* earned rave reviews. The San Francisco-based Singh (1925-2019) might have also published several (other) critically-acclaimed novels and short-story-collections like *Dee Kay and the Mystery of the Laughing Nataraj* (1980), *Fat Gopal* (1984), *Uncle's Concubine and Other Stories* (1993), *Case of the Shady Sheikh and Other Stories* (1993), *Home to India* (1997), and *Majra* (2015), but she still remains a relatively-unknown novelist in her country-of-origin (C.O.O.). Nevertheless, as Bed Prakash Giri says, Rushdie, Mistry, Ghosh, Lahiri, and Desai, to name a few, are *'better known-*authors' of the 'diaspora/ Anglophone postcolonial literature' (243), and, hence, the writer of the present essay proposes to limit himself to reviewing only the 'better-known' names listed above.

Even a casual glance at the list of the 23 'better-known names' I have mentioned above immediately reveals some of the so-called 'paradigms' and/or 'nuances' of novels published in recent years by writers of the Indian diaspora. These are, however, common to the novels published by the 'Old' — or, specifically speaking, 'First Generation' — Indian diasporic authors (with most of their education formally completed in India) and those by the 'New' (or the 'Second Generation') Indian diasporic authors (most part of whose formal education has been completed in the West). One may here recall how Avtar Brah has consistently refused to recognise or support the notion(s) that the so-called 'Second Generation' Indian diasporic authors are the 'perceived' victims of 'culture-clash' or that they 'suffer from *in-between-ness* or 'identity-conflict' (41-42). She writes that there is no 'single identity' that is 'carried' by the 'Second Generation'-Asians (including the Indian novelists) settled in the West (*ibid*. 42), and, hence, the (perceived) 'conflict' simply does not exist.

Returning to the issue of 'paradigm': first of all, it could be noticed that in the field of Indian English diasporic novels (written by both the 'Old' and 'New' diasporic litterateurs), the female writers dominate in numbers. Sixteen of the twenty-three names listed above are those of females'. It is understandable why the 21st-century (diasporic) novels—almost routinely—have strong female characters, and are usually centred on exploration and reinterpretation of feminist-themes. Most of the female characters, moreover, are shown to be unmarried, or, even when married, (perceptively) live life almost on their own terms. Although Banerjee has strongly argued in *Incarcerated Female Subalterns in select Indian Diasporic Novels* that the supposedly-'free' (female) characters (usually) remain tied hopelessly to the Indian traditions in the end (19-35), the *female-centred*-ness of these novels is undeniable. In contrast, the male Indian novelists of the diaspora—especially Rushdie and Ghosh—deal with history, myths, and unrequited love as their general themes.

Second, many of these (Indian diasporic) writers are either Bengalis or have distinct Bengali-roots (like that of Kiran Desai's). Of the twenty-three 'better-known names', ten litterateurs are either Bengali (or are connected to Bengal). They are Anita Desai, Bharati Mukherjee, Kunal Basu, Amitav Ghosh, Chitra Banerjee Divakaruni, Amit Chaudhuri, Sunetra Gupta, Anjali Banerjee, Jhumpa Lahiri, and—to repeat—Kiran Desai. This information seems to account for the surfeit of memorable Bengali characters (like 'Tara Lata Gangooly', 'Tara Chatterjee', 'Anjali Chatterjee', 'Basudha Chatterjee', and 'Gogol') in the fast-expanding pool of appreciable (fictional) diasporic Indians.

Third, almost all the litterateurs listed above (with the exception of three) are still alive, and their average age is approximately 63.5 years. This, in fact, indicates the comparative 'newness' (and the consequent—if I am permitted to use the term –'immaturity') of the Indian English diasporic novel as a literary-genre. Whereas the general fictional writings (especially the novels) could be of any theme *under the sun* — something horrible, or terrible, something fantastic or imaginary, something lovely, passionate or sexy, or something mysterious or intriguing or suspicious or historically-important or expressions of wish-fulfilment, the diasporic Indian novels have — sometimes, very objectionably — straightjacketed themselves into what Pande summarises as 'in-between-ness', 'anxiety', 'migrancy', 'hyphenated existence', 'concern about forming new identities', 'consciousness regarding the differences between the *home-land* and *host-land*', 'nostalgia', 'patriarchal domination', and 'stereotypical representation' (1-10). As the Indian (English-writing) diasporic novelists usually (and strictly) confine themselves to employing only these 'features' in their publications, the coverage of their novels become restrictive, and they sometimes become repetitive and monotonous.

Fourth, the so-called 'homeland-myths' or 'the repeated demonstration of desires and readiness to return to countries of origin' are — obtrusively or unobtrusively — present in most of these novels, especially those written by the Indian diasporic litterateurs with 'roots' in Bengal. These 'myths' are, frankly, challengeable. One might cite here the observation of William Safran's who, in his 1991-essay, writes, "An Indian homeland has existed continuously and that homeland has not been noted for encouraging an 'ingathering'. [...] The homeland myth is not particularly operative where the Indian diaspora is in the majority [...], or where it constitutes a large, well-established, and sometimes dominant minority [...]" (88-89). One might, in this respect, wonder whether the *myths of homeland* are *really* believed in by their writers, or whether the novelists merely use them, as Safran notes, as 'defence mechanisms against slights committed by the host-country', and the exploration of these myths do not 'lead [...] [the writers] to prepare for the actual departure to the homeland' (94).

This debate, in turn, highlights the fifth (characteristic) similarity among the Indian (English) diasporic novelists. All the authors whom I have listed based on theory popularity, readership, and 'acceptability' in India, are settled in the West—in especially three countries where the Indians—ethnographically speaking—live as 'very influential minorities': the U.S.A., the U.K., and Canada. They have long become citizens of these so-called 'First World Countries'. Without any visible and 'viable" urge to return to their country-of-origin, they are permanently settled in the U.S.A./ the U.K./Canada, and nostalgically write about the Indian traditions, early life back in the country, and, sometimes, about their own 'Indianness', which several critics and numerous readers have found 'unconvincing'. There are *good reasons* for that. In 2022, there are, approximately, 4.5 million Indians living in the U.S.A.[2], 1.76 million in the U.K.[3], and 1.6 million in Canada[4]. Hence, as per Safran's views, the 'myths of homeland'—present in a dispersed manner in these people's writings—would be liable to be 'rejected' or 'dismissed'. That most of these writers are working as academicians or professors at different American, British, and Canadian universities or colleges is another similarity between them—the last one. These instances of employment also reveal why these authors would never, under normal circumstances, return to their so-called 'homeland'.

Among the Indian novelists of the diaspora, only Vikram Seth (b. 1952): the celebrated bi-sexual novelist of *The Golden Gate* (1986), *A Suitable Boy* (1993), and *An Equal Music* (1999) , and the former Indian civil-servant and present Thiruvananthapuram-M.P., Shashi Tharoor—the writer of *The Great Indian Novel* (1989), *Show Business* (1992), and *Riot* (2001)—have returned to India—Seth to his ancestral house in Noida (Uttar Pradesh) and Tharoor to Thiruvananthapuram (Kerala)—and that too, not permanently. Seth and Tharoor also differ from almost all the (English-writing) novelists of the Indian diaspora in terms of the themes and contents of their respective novels. Tharoor's *The Great Indian Novel*, for example, satirically connects events and characters from the *Mahabharata* (c. 400 B.C.) to the period of Indian independence and the various socio-economic-political incidents happening in the country until the 1970s'. In *Show Business*—identifiably drawn on the 26 July 1982-spleen-injury of the Hindi film-actor Amitabh Bachchan's (b. 1942)—he connects the Mumbai film-industry and its various 'aspects' to politics and religion, while in the somewhat-grim *Riot*, he explores the circumstances surrounding the murder of the 24-year-old U.S.-student and health-programme-volunteer, Priscilla Hart, in a communally-divided India of 1987. Seth's *The Golden Gate* is a *novel-in-verse* that is set in San Francisco of the 1980s', and focuses on the different love-and-marriage-related developments between the characters like 'John Brown', 'Janet Hayakawa', 'Elizabeth Dorati', and 'Philip Weiss'. In *A Suitable Boy*, set in different Indian cities (including New Delhi, Kolkata, Lucknow, and Patna) after independence, the university-student 'Lata Mehra'—sister to 'Arun Mehra' and daughter to the domineering 'Rupa Mehra'—finally marries 'Haresh Khanna', a shoe-businessman, choosing him over 'Kabir Durrani' and 'Amit Chatterjee', a U.K.-returned poet. *An Equal Music*, Seth's last novel to be published till date, is distinctively autobiographical (just like his *A Suitable Boy*, where 'Haresh Khanna', like Vikram Seth's own *Bata India*-employee-father, Premnath Seth, is associated with shoe-trading)—as per his various confessions—and deals with the secret and later-in-the-life-love-affair between the violin-player Michael, and Julia, his beloved-from-his-student-days. In these novels by Seth and Tharoor, the usual diasporic-themes of 'anxiety', 'lack of identity', 'hyphenated existence', and 'in-between-ness' cannot be noticed, making the two writers 'exceptions' in the list. Childs and Storry do not put emphasis on Seth's and Tharoor's so-called 'diasporic consciousnesses'—they rather praise them for their 'exciting' Indian English-fiction on themes like decolonisation, migrant identity, and colonial relationships (373). Meenakshi Sharma, in addition, rereads Seth's and Tharoor's novels for their being history-based 'narratives on/of India'—the 'indigenousness' making them important postcolonial narratives (Pandey 125-40).

In her 2017-publication, Jasbir Jain names Govindas Vishnoodas Desani (1909-2000), Raja Rao (1908-2006), Santha Rama Rau (1923-2009), and Kamala Markandaya as being 'among the earlier Indian diasporic writers producing novels in English' (1-2). Adding Sankarankutti Menon Marath (1906-2003), Balachandra Rajan (1920-2009), and Victor Anant (1928-99) to the list, Sudesh Mishra finds both an 'insider's intimacy' and an 'outsider's curiosity', as well as an intense desire to 'consciously engage with the country-of-origin' in the novels by these earliest Indian diasporic writers (Mehrotra 282). Gopika Shankar U., in a 2019-*e-article* have summarised the following features of the Indian {English] diasporic literature, including those of the diasporic Indian novels in English, which usually are not found in the early writers:

> "[Indian] [d]iasporic literature [including the Indian diasporic novels in English] is [/are], time and again, approached from the perspectives of nostalgia, loss and longing. While past and rootedness or rootlessness are often the central themes in many diasporic texts, they are not limited to such themes alone. They convey much more, and can even emerge as complementary readings to sociological studies on diaspora. From portraying culture shock and spatial shock, to examining minute details of identity politics, to illustrating generation gap to reverse culture shock and globalisation, diasporic literature juxtaposes the real and the imagined in a telling manner"[5].

Literary historians, critics and researchers — while identifying the dominant ideologies in diasporic writings — are widely divided among themselves over/regarding the approximate time-period when the Indian (English) diasporic writings began to leave their marks. The researcher, Suman Rani, for example, refuses to recognise G. V. Desani's and Ved Mehta's (1934-2021) as 'early Indian diasporic novelists' *proper*. She has her own reasons:

> "G. V. Desani's [...] *All about H. Hatter* (1948) and Ved Mehta's [...] *Delinquent Chacha* (1969) [...] [bear] the first references of immigrant experience in Indian English literature, [and] yet they lack [...] the depiction of life-struggles or despair of the Indian immigrants [in the West]. Thus *The Nowhere Man* (1972) by Kamala Markandaya and Bharati Mukherjee's *Wife* (1975) are considered [by critics and readers alike] to be among the first few novels which depict the discrimination, disappointment, despair and isolation faced by Indian immigrants who are living in foreign contexts. Hence, the [approximate time for] establishment of diasporic Indian English literature as an independent genre of Indian English writings is regarded [by critics] at the end of 1980s'" (Rani 254).

Indeed, Raja Rao's *Kanthapura* (1938), Santha Rama Rao's *This is India* (1953), Menon Marath's *The Wound of Spring* (1960), Anant's *The Revolving Man* (1959), and Rajan's *Too Long in the West* (1961) might be among the earlier Indian diasporic novels in English, but all of them have almost similar conclusion(s). As Mehrotra summarise, in almost each of these novels, the principal characters return from the West to India (282-83) towards the end. Perhaps *The Open University-Making Britain*-assessment of Santha Rama Rau (available, on *https://www.open.ac.uk/researchprojects/making britain/content/santha-rama-rau*) could be recognised as a paradigm for understanding these early diasporic-authors' writings:

> "In her book on Santha Rama Rau, Antoinette Burton describes 'the modicum of fame [she] achieved' as resulting 'mainly from her success at being recognized as an authority on India on the eve of independence' [,,,]. To the 'West', she offered an 'insider's view' of Indian culture, countering stereotyping and Orientalist misrepresentations, especially in *This is India*".

Many of Kamala Markandaya's (that is, Kamala Purnaiya Taylor's) 11 novels—published principally from New York and London between 1954 and 2008 (posthumously)—seem to set the tone, with some exceptions, for the (post-Indian-independence) diasporic fictional narratives. There is, at least, one prominent Western character in almost each of her novel—for example, Dr. Kennington in *Nectar in a Sieve* (1954), Caroline Bell in *Possession* (1963), Helen in *The Coffer Dams* (1969), Mrs. Pickering in *The Nowhere Man* (1972), and Sophie in *The Golden Honeycomb* (1977). Importantly, Markandaya—a journalist who went to England to settle down permanently after the Indian independence—is interested, in her novels, more in bringing the Western characters to India that writing about the vice versa. Uma Parameswaran writes that Markandaya's novels are more important for their projections of the 'diasporic realities' and the conspiracies that the diasporic writers usually encounter in the West (Fludernik 55) than her feminism and employment of resilient female characters—an issue on which there are several critical studies, including those by, for instance, Sharat Srivastava (1996), Lakshmi K. Sharma (2001), Urmila Sharma (2005), Sudhir Arora (2006), and Chandra Singh (2007), to name a very few.

Though junior to Markandaya by sixteen years, Bharti Krichner—presently an inhabitant of Seattle (Washington)—also belongs to the so-called 'Old Diaspora'-group. She has, along with her 8 novels (including the critically-acclaimed *Shiva Dancing*, 1998, *Darjeeling*, 2002, and *Season of Sacrifice*, 2017), produced a number of cookbooks as well. Sachin Salunkhe might have found, in Krichner's (novelistic) oeuvre, a representation of the 'psychological and emotional trauma and rehabilitation with a negation of origin' (36), but the usual themes of modern diasporic litterateurs are not easily noticeable in most of her publications.

Anita Desai—born in Mussoorie (Uttarakhand) to the Bengali engineer D.N. Majumdar and his German wife Toni Nimé, and presently working as the *(Emerita) John E. Burchard Professor of Humanities* at the *Massachusetts Institute of Technology*—is senior to Krichner by three years, and, identifiably, enjoys more popularity and readership than her's. Writer of 18 unforgettable novels and short-story-collections—published between 1963 and 2011, and winner of 7 prestigious international awards/prizes/accolades (from 1978 to 2014), Anita Desai, mother to the 2006-*Man Booker Prize*-winning novelist Kiran Desai, is best known for her concern with the 'motivation, conscience, and psychic tension of her characters' who are 'hypersensitive females' (Bhatnagar and Rajeshwar 115). Almost all the leading female characters in her famous novels like *Cry, The Peacock* (1963), *Voices in the City* (1965), *Bye-bye Blackbird* (1971), *Where Shall We Go This Summer?* (1975), *Fire on the Mountain* (1977), *Clear Light of Day* (1980), *The Village by the Sea* (1982), and *In Custody* (1984) distinguish themselves by their psychological turmoil, resilience, and deep insights. In contrast, the 'diasporic angst' is less obtrusive in her characters, though it is present much in (her New York-dwelling-daughter) Kiran Desai's *The Inheritance of Loss* (2006), which won the *Man Booker Prize* for her in 2006.

Kiran Desai's first novel, *Hullabaloo in the Guava Orchard* (1998)—based on the real-life 'misadventures' of Kapila Pradhan (b. 1961) of Nagajhara, Odisha—did not create much readership despite its winning the *Betty Trask Award*—1998. Her contribution, following her winning the *Man Booker Prize*, seems to have ended abruptly. Understandably, in an article published in *The Hindu*, 5 February 2017 (which is available on *https://www.thehindu.*

com/books/Two-alone-two-together/article17194613.ece) the journalist Sudipta Datta has not painted a very-flattering picture of Kiran Desai's over this particular issue. However, the innate brilliance and poignancy of Kiran Desai's *The Inheritance of Loss* has led to the publication of some appreciatory works on her—for example, by Nilanshun Agarwal (2013), Kamal Kumar Raul (2015), Archana Bhattacharjee (2016), K. Kavitharaj (2018), and Sarbjeet Cheema (2021).

With Bharati Mukherjee's name ends the so-called 'list of Old or First-generation Diasporic Indian writers writing in English'. Ahmed Salman Rushdie is usually not grouped by literary historians into the 'Old Diaspora'-section; he might be, rather, identified as belonging to—if anything like that exists at all—the 'Middle Diaspora'-group: indicative of his itinerant-status— journeying constantly to his country-of-origin and going back to his 'hostland'. If Anita Desai's characters like 'Amla' (*Voices in the City*), 'Sita' (*Where shall we go this Summer?*), 'Nanda Kaul' (*Fire on the Mountain*), and 'Tara Das' (*Clear Light of Day*), for instance, are intimately tied to web-like familial relationships and so-called 'feminine-duties', the (former and late) University of California-professor Bharati Mukherjee's fictional females like 'Tara' (*The Tiger's Daughter*, 1971), 'Dimple Dasgupta' (*Wife*, 1975), 'Jasmine'/'Jyoti'/ 'Jane'/'Jase' (*Jasmine*, 1989), 'Tara Chatterjee' (*Desirable Daughters*, 2002), 'Tara Lata Gangooly' and 'Tara Chatterjee' (*The Tree Bride*, 2004), and 'Anjali Bose' (*Miss New India*, 2011) are less 'family-oriented', and more fiery and feisty—though they too, towards the conclusion of the novels, are ultimately subsumed into the 'traditional Indian' patriarchal system which— interestingly—operates in the U.S.A. as well (most of Mukherjee's novels are set in the U.S.A.—the country to which Mukherjee herself migrated in the early 1960s'). Nagendra Kumar writes other than exploring the 'problems of expatriation and immigration' in her novels (17), Mukherjee usually creates 'strong female characters' who usually belong to the so-called 'upper-strata of society' and are quite 'Americanised' (*ibid.* 20-21). Markose Abraham, in addition, reads the (fictional prose) writings of Mukherjee's and Bernard Malamud's for their exploration of '[t]he picture of the immigrant[s] caught in a Sisyphean cycle of insecurity, isolation, and dehumanisation' and how the immigrants, 'treated as [...] commodit[ies]' in the West, feel like 'losing their own personalities' (9).

Uma Parameswaran (b. 1938)—a former professor of English of the University of Winnipeg (Winnipeg, Manitoba, Canada) who was born in Chennai and raised in Jabalpur—should have been also included in the so-called 'group' of Mukherjee's: her fictional-prose-oeuvre comprises *The Sweet Smell of Mother's Milk-Wet Bodice* (2001), *Mangoes on the Maple Tree* (2002), *Cycle of the Moon* (2010), and *Maru and the Maple Leaf* (2016). However, in the 21st-century-academic world, she is—arguably—known more for her works of non-fiction and literary-criticism than for her novels, and, hence, she has not been extensively reviewed in this essay.

The 'in-between-ness', 'anxieties', 'cultural-hybridity', and other characteristic features, which are usually associated with diasporic writings, are not overtly present in most of the 12 novels published by Salman Rushdie (presently associated with the University of New York) between 1975 and 2019. His usual focuses—in novels like *Grimus* (1975), *Midnight's Children* (1981), *The Moor's Last Sigh* (1995), *Fury* (2001), *Shalimar the Clown* (2005), *The Enchantress of Florence* (2008), *The Golden House* (2017), and *Quichotte* (2019)—include the employment of magic realism, and, as C. A. Sorowarthy writes, 'politics, history, nation and the self"(4). Pradip Dey, in addition, comments, "Rushdie, like [Bertolt] Brecht, intentionally breaks the hold of mimetic forms, well-structured plot and lifelike characters who make free choices and demand sympathy from the readers" (91). Nevertheless, the biting satire that often underlies Rushdie's novels (which do not deal with the 'diasporic confusions' or hybridity though some of them, like *Fury* and *Shalimar the Clown*, are set in the West) has often had landed him into trouble: in the past, other than minor but disturbing incidents, he was, in 1989, sentenced to death *in absentia* by the Iranian politician-and-religious-leader Ayatollah Khomeini (1900-89), and was near-fatally stabbed at Chautauqua (New York) in August 2022. But his diasporic and magic-realistic voice has consistently refused to be silenced.

Meena Alexander—as Rama Nair writes—'ha[s had] unwittingly broken out of the traditional patriarchal mould of an Indian society', but the 'questions of identity, displacement, and rootlessness persist' (Khan and Das 74) in the characters that she creates/employs in her two novels *Nampally Road* (1991) and *Manhattan Music* (1996)—which she wrote even as she taught English-literature at Hunter College, New York, and the City University of New York Graduate Centre before succumbing to uterine cancer at the age of 67 years. In Alexander's 1991-novel, the apparently-self-confident 'Mira Kannadical', after returning to Hyderabad from England, has what the writer herself published in 1999 as 'The Shock of Arrival', while *Google Books* describes the plot of *Manhattan Music* as: "Sandhya Rosenblum, an immigrant from India married to an American Jewish man, tries to make sense of her life in a time of turbulence. In this sweeping novel set in Manhattan and India, Alexander lyrically and poignantly explores crossing borders, the Indian diaspora, fanaticism, ethnic intolerance, interracial affairs and marriages, and what it means to be an American today"[6]. In both the novels, however, both the female protagonists makes their diasporic personality felt and thoroughly noticed.

Younger to Alexander by a year, Rohinton Mistry—a Parsee born in Mumbai and elder-brother to the Indian litterateur Cyrus Mistry (author of the play *Doongaji House*, 1978, and the novels *The Radiance of Ashes*, 2005, and *Chronicle of a Corpse-bearer*, 2013)—migrated to Canada in 1975, where the former economist and philosopher is presently settled in Toronto (southern Canada), as a full-time-writer. Though Rohinton Mistry rose to prominence for his 1987-collection-of-short-stories *Tales from Firozsha Baag*, his three novels—*Such a Long Journey* (1991), *A Fine Balance* (1995), and *Family Matters* (2002)—earned for him both accolades and brickbats. Focussing on the prominent 21st-century Canadian writers, one of the (central Canada-based) *University of Athabasca*'s webpages thus describes the contents of Mistry's novels:

> "Mistry's first novel, *Such a Long Journey*, brought him national and international recognition. The book concerns an ordinary man who

becomes involved in the politics surrounding the Bangladesh separatist movement in India and Pakistan. [...] [His] subsequent novels have achieved the same level of recognition as his first. His second novel, *A Fine Balance*, concerns four people from Mumbai who struggle with family and work against the backdrop of the political unrest in India during the mid-1970s'. *Family Matters* [,] [the third novel] [,] describes the members of a blended family who are trying to cope with the failing health of their father. In the meantime, the father relives his past, a past beset by thwarted love and crushing social strictures. Mistry's fiction deploys a precise writing style and a sensitivity to the humour and horror of life to communicate deep compassion for human beings. His writing concerns people who try to find self-worth while dealing with painful family dynamics and difficult social and political constraints. His work also addresses immigration, especially immigration to Canada, and the difficulty [that the] immigrants face in a society [...] [which] recognises their cultural differences and yet cannot embrace those differences as being part of itself"[7].

Pramod K. Nayar, in a 2004-critical study, adds that 'clash of generations', 'existence of neighbourhood tensions', 'outright criticism of government's perceived anti-citizen-politics', and 'employment of a dystopic look at India' (Dodiya xi-xiii) are the additional features that, actually, serve to make Rohinton Mistry's novels 'poignant', and, yet, 'unputdownable'.

Kunal Basu (whose short-story "The Japanese Wife", 2008, gained for him a worldwide recognition) — born in Kolkata and a former lecturer of Jadavpur University — migrated to Montreal (Canada) in 1986, and taught management for thirteen years at McGill University. Thereafter, in 1999, he migrated to the U.K., and for the last twenty-three years, he is employed as a professor of management at *Said Business School*, University of Oxford. His six novels (till date) — *The Opium Clerk* (2001), *The Miniaturist* (2003), *Racists* (2006), *The Yellow Emperor's Cure* (2011), *Kalkatta* (2015), and *Sarojini's Mother* (2020) — are steeped, mostly, in history, and have been succinctly described by Charne Lavery as 'exploring Indian ex-centric links across a range of periods' (13). Brian Hamnett almost echoes (294) Lavery's assessment, but fails to notice the presence of several other serious issues in Basu's oeuvre, including rebellions, addictions, and intrigues (*The Opium Clerk*), the morality of art and sexuality (*The Miniaturist*), complexion-consciousness and innate imperialistic tendencies

(*Racists*), Orientalism, journeying, and transcultural amour (*The Yellow Emperor's Cure*), the shadiness of intellectual world, South Asian-migrations, and affection (*Kalkatta*), and, finally—as is found in most of the diaspora-novels—the angst of migration and identity (*Sarojini's Mother*).

The social-anthropologist Amitav Ghosh and Chitra Banerjee Divakaruni are of the same age as Basu's, and with Jhumpa Lahiri, eleven years their junior, they (symbolically) form the so-called 'Bengali Trio', all settled in the U.S.A., (in the group of expatriate Indian writers in English) who have attracted—perhaps—the most intense critical attention for the different themes and focuses of their novels. While Amitav Ghosh is presently employed as a Senior Editor of *Little, Brown, and Company* (Boston), Chitra Banerjee Divakaruni works as the *Betty and Gene McDavid Professor of Writing* at the University of Houston (Houston, Texas), while Lahiri is the *Millicent C. McIntosh Professor of English* at Barnard College of Columbia University, New York. Though Brian Hamnett puts particular emphasis on the historical representations of different important events as the most important characteristic feature of Amitav Ghosh's novels (294, 297), he shows in them the same 'in-between-ness', 'diasporic confusion', 'angst', 'socio-cultural hybridity', and provides the same 'snippets' of 'unpalatable diasporic Indians' experiences in the West' as are usually found in Divakaruni's novels like *The Mistress of Spices* (1997), *Sister of My Heart* (1999), *The Vine of Desire* (2002), *Queen of Dreams* (2004), *One Amazing Thing* (2010), *Oleander Girl* (2013), and *Before We Visit the Goddess* (2016) and Jhumpa Lahiri's three excellent fictional-prose-narratives: *The Namesake* (2003), *The Lowland* (2013), and (with a difference, her latest-novel) *Whereabouts* (2021). Thus the predicaments of the unnamed (male) narrator's in Ghosh's *The Shadow Lines* (1988), Antar's (in *The Calcutta Chromosome*, 1995), Piyali Roy's (in *The Hungry Tide*, 2004), (the American) Zachary Reid's (in *Sea of Poppies*, 2008), and (the Brooklyn-resident) Dr. Dinanath Dutta's and Piyali Roy's (in *Gun Island*, 2019) while inhabiting the West in general, and the U.S.A. and the U.K. in particular, are not very much unlike those of Tilottama's (in Divakaruni's *The Mistress of*

Spices), Anjali Chatterjee's and Basudha Chatterjee's (in *Sister of my Heart* and *Vine of Desire*), Korobi Roy's (in *Oleander Girl*), and Bela's (in *Before we visit the Goddess*), or Nikhil 'Gogol' Ganguly's (in Lahiri's *The Namesake*) and Gauri Sarkar's (in *The Lowland*). While Rajesh Nair notes how Lahiri 'chronicles dislocation and social unease in a fresh manner', convincingly explores the culture-clash-caused 'inner turmoil' of her important characters, and demonstrates a keen awareness 'of ethos of Indian culture and sensibility' (Sree 177), K. Sandhya praises Divakaruni's narratives for the value that they give to human relationships even when such relationships are at stake in the West (*ibid*. 210). Moreover, Ganapathy-Dore finds how the novels of Divakaruni's and Lahiri's 'deal with the transplantation of domicile from the women's point of view' (74).

Whereas Shauna Singh Baldwin, the Canadian-born American novelist of Indian origin (presently living in Milwaukee, Wisconsin), firmly ensconced herself in the field of Indian Writing in English (including the Literature produced by the Indian novelists of the diaspora) through her magnum opus *What the Body Remembers* (2000)—focusing on the pathetic, skin-cringing, Indian Partition-time-experiences of 'Roop', 'Satya', and their husband 'Sardarji' in a milieu of Hindi-Muslim-Sikh interracial-tension—and *The Tiger Claw: A Novel* (2004) on the Second World War-time espionage and Nazi-execution of the English-Indian spy Noor Inayat Khan (1914-44; the great-great-granddaughter of King Tipu Sultan or Fateh Ali Sahab Tipu, 1751-99, of Mysore), Anita Rau Badami—also settled in Vancouver (Canada, to where she migrated from Rourkela, Odisha, at the age of 30 years)—explores the difficulties faced by the immigrated Indians in the West in her four novels, published between 1996 and 2011. Another of *University of Athabasca*'s webpages thus summarises the contents of her novels:

> "[…] [Badami's] M.A.-writing-project became her first novel, *Tamarind Mem* (1996), which deals with relationships in Indian families and the cultural problems when family members go abroad. […] Her second novel, *The Hero's Walk* (2001) begins with an ordinary man, Sripath and the sudden death of his estranged daughter in Vancouver. He and his family

are conflicted about the death and the arrival of the orphaned granddaughter, Nandana, who comes to live with them in India. This experience is the catalyst for the transformation of Sripath in the rest of the story from an ordinary man into a committed individual. [....] [Her] third novel, *Can You Hear the Nightbird Call?* (2006), was inspired by events surrounding the *Golden Temple Massacre* (1-8 June 1984), the assassination of [the Indian Prime Minister] Indira Gandhi (31 October 1984), and the Air India Flight 182-Bombing (23 June 1985). The narrative traces the lives of three Indian women through fifty years of life in India and Canada. At the beginning of this book we see Sikhs, Muslims and Hindus all living in one village in Punjab in northern India. But then we also see the conflicts among ordinary people caused by the events mentioned above. [...] [Badami's] fourth novel, *Tell it to the Trees* (2011), is set in [...] [Merritt, British Columbia] where the Dharma-family live in dysfunctional relationships. The father, Vikram, is an abusive tyrant who drives his wife, Helen, to eventually try to escape him, only to die in a car accident. Vikram goes back to India to find another wife, Varsha, whom he can control. The physical and emotional abuses result in the death of Anu, a house-guest, whose body is found outside the house in a snow bank. [...] [Readers] realise that the children have been damaged beyond help. The wealth of different characters in this narrative provides varying perspective on this family drama and the dark secrets each of them hides"[8].

Several critics have also recalled, with reverence, Baldwin's and Badami's contributions to the maturing of the 'Sikh Studies' in the West, and about how the two writers have 'enlarged and deepened the field of adult fiction [by] adding a useful and poignant gender perspective' (Hawley 353).

With 'Amit Chaudhuri' and 'Hari Kunzru' ends the list of the names of the 'well-known' male novelists of the Indian diaspora in English. They, however, do not belong to the same age-group. While Chaudhuri, presently teaching at *Ashoka University* (New Delhi) as a Professor of English (after his 2006-21-teaching-stint at the University of East Anglia, Norwich, England), is just above sixty years old (in October 2022), Hari Mohan Nath Kunzru—son of a *Kashmiri Pandit*-father and an English mother, and the present Deputy President of the *English P.E.N.*—is fifty-three. From his very first novel—*The Impressionist* (2002)—onwards, Kunzru has clarified that confusions, anxieties, and questions of identity would be some of the consistent and major themes of his novels. His second novel, *Transmission* (2004), is about how the U.S.-immigrated Arjun Mehta, with several doses of unpalatable experiences in the host-country, transmits a fatal computer-virus through e-mails in order to retain his job. His fourth novel to be published, *Gods without Men* (2011) (*My Revolutions*, 2007, is his third novel) takes place in south-western U.S.A., and deals with the unpalatable, near-fatal experiences of 'Jaz' and 'Lisa Matharu' during a family-trip. *Memory Palace* (2013) is paints a dystopic future-land where memorising is banned, while *White Tears*, first published by *Knopf-Doubleday* in March 2017—as *Good Reads* reviews on *https://www.goodreads.com/en/book/show/30780283-white-tears*, "is a ghost-story, a terrifying murder mystery, a timely meditation on race, and a love letter to all the forgotten geniuses of American music". His latest novel till date—*The Red Pill* (2020)—juxtaposes history and existentialism. While Kunzru has seven novels to his credit—published between 2002b and 2020—Amit Chaudhuri has written seven too: *Afternoon Raag* (1993), *Freedom Song* (1998), *A New World* (2000), *The Immortals* (2009), *A Strange and Sublime Address* (2012), *Odysseus Abroad* (2015), and *Friend of My Youth* (2017)—all of which deal with the themes of exile, returning, confusions, and searches for identities—which usually permeate the Indian diasporic novels. Peter Childs, importantly, says that novelists like Chaudhuri and Kunzru might not have met with spectacular commercial successes, but they have—through their respective novels—contributed mellifluously to the ever-expanding genre of postcolonial novels through their employment of themes like 'decolonisation and diaspora' (Shaffer 220-21).

Sunetra Gupta, the 57-year-old litterateur with five critically-acclaimed diasporic novels to her credit (*Memories of Rain*, 1992; *The Glassblower's Breath*, 1993; *Moonlight into Marzipan*, 1995; *A Sin of Colour*, 1999; and, *So Good in Black*, 2009), is actually employed as a professor of theoretical epidemiology at the Department of Zoology, University of Oxford. The winner of the 1996 *Sahitya Akademi Award*, Gupta—in her very first novel on the familial misfortunes and love-affairs of the Kolkata-born-London-settled-protagonist Moni—sets the tone for the other four fictional-prose-narratives to follow. *Kirkus Review*, in April 1992, thus reviews *Memories of Rain*:

"Moni's sensibility—formed by the poetry (both English and Bengali) of anguished passion, darkness, and death—is the basis for gorgeous prose that flickers between romantic longing and exquisite detail. Gupta is impossible to quote briefly. In her sinuous sentences past and present, London and Calcutta, reality and shadow and the painful phrases of Tagore songs melt into one another in long continuous streams. A rare shimmering dream of a book"[9].

Sachin Salunkhe credits Gupta for the ease and élan with which she employs such Indian diasporic-novel-writing-themes in her various publications like the 'trauma of cultural dislocation', the 'identity-crisis due to in-between-ness', the 'displacement', and the 'diasporic feelings of different characters in the host-lands' (Salunkhe 18).

Of the same age as Gupta's, Anjali Banerjee (lawyer and University of California-alumnus)—who was born in Kolkata and grew up in Manitoba (Canada) and California (U.S.A.), presently resides alternatively at Pacific Northwest and Washington. She has written a total of nine novels until 2022, but, strangely—comparatively speaking—is yet to find the prominence of—for example—Gupta's or Lahiri's. Her own website (*https://anjalibanerjee.com/bio*) thus describes her books, which are yet to find a substantive body of lengthy critical assessments:

"*Romantic Times* magazine [...] [has given Anjali Banerjee's novel], *Enchanting Lily* (2012), a top rating of 4.5 stars: 'This is a wonderful story with lovable characters who are trying to start fresh after tragedy touches their lives. Readers will fall head over heels for a four-legged character who almost upstages the two-legged leads'. Of her novel, *Haunting Jasmine* (2011), Melinda Bargreen of *The Seattle Times* wrote, 'Banerjee invites the reader into her colourful, hopeful world, one in which the Northwest island tides coexist with the ghost of Julia Child, Charles Dickens's mirror, and a sari or two'. *The Philadelphia Inquirer* called her young-adult novel, *Maya Running* (Wendy Lamb Books/Random House, 2006) 'beautiful and complex' and 'pleasingly accessible'. *The Seattle Times* praised Banerjee's 2005-novel, *Imaginary Men* (Downtown Press/Pocket Books), as 'a romantic comedy equal to *Bend it like Beckham*'. *Zoo Break Productions* acquired film rights to her 2006-middle-grade novel, *Looking for Bapu*. Post-production just wrapped up for the feature-length film titled *Finding Bapu*."

In the John Stephens *et al.*-edited e-book *The Routledge Companion to International Children's Literature* (New York and London:

Routledge, 2017), Anjali Banerjee has been appreciated as an important writer of children-fiction and young-adult-stories, while *Looking for Bapu* has been appreciatively mentioned for 'its value as a multicultural text that can foster better understanding and harmony between cultures'. In addition, Pathak, Dabir, and Mishra mention her name for her 'immense contribution' to the genre of postcolonial Indian English fiction (vii).

If Salman Rushdie, in the first chapter of his *Imaginary Homelands*, outrightly refuses to rely on the 'accuracy' of memory of diasporic characters (Rushdie), there too are high chances that the diasporic memories of—for example—Gupta's or Banerjee's characters regarding their homeland or country-of-origin would be faulty, and, yet, from their 'memories', readers can assess how perplexed the diasporic characters sometimes feel in the West. These perplexities, changing into angst, are percolated into the various novels by the Indian expatriate writers. However, Antonia Navarro-Tejero (of the University of Cordoba, Spain) cannot help mentioning:

> "Expatriate representation has been questioned on several counts. Most expatriate writers have a weak grasp of actual conditions in contemporary India, and tend to recreate it through the lens of nostalgia, writing about 'imaginary homelands'. Distancing lends objectivity, but it can also lead to the ossification of cultural constructs, and even if memory is sharp and clear, the expatriate is not directly in contact with the reality of India. The East/West confrontation, or the clash between tradition and modernity, is the impulse behind the works of acclaimed migrant writers, such as Meera Syal, Anita Rau Badami, Shauna Singh Baldwin, Uma Parameswaran, Chitra Banerjee Divakaruni, Anjana Appachana, and Kiran Desai"[10].

Though the name of Anita Nair's (presently a highly-successful 56-year-old feminist-novelist settled in Bengaluru) is sometimes classified into the group of 'diasporic writers'—for example, by Sasikala Alagiri (64) and Pravina Shukla in her *The Grace of Four Moons* (53)—her direct association with the West ended with the completion of the period of her fellowship from *The Virginia Centre for the Creative Arts*, Amherst, in the late-1990s'. Nevertheless, her novels like *The Better Man* (2000), *Ladies Coupé* (2001), and *Mistress* (2005) are important contributions to the genre of *Indian English Fiction by Female Writers,* and often reveal themes which are usually found in the Indian diasporic novels. Along with Manju Kapur (b. 1948), Nair—right now—is one of the more sought-after female litterateurs in the 21st-century India.

The overview of the 'well-known' Indian English novelists of the diaspora concludes with references to the works of Kavita Daswani (a 51-year-old journalist who grew up in Hong Kong and presently works as a journalist in Los Angeles), Vineeta Vijayaraghavan (an employee of the New York-based consulting-firm *Katzenbach Partners, L.L.C.,* who was born in India and completed her education from Harvard University), and Anjana Appachana (a resident of Tempe-Arizona, and an alumnus of Jawaharlal Nehru University and Pennsylvania State University). They, along with Kiran Desai, form the so-called 'young brigade' of the Indian English diasporic novelists' who have carved out firm niches for themselves in the 21st century literary-world. What, however, needs to be mentioned that both Vijayaraghavan and Appachana—like Kiran Desai, and unlike Daswani—have an extremely limited novelistic 'oeuvre' (if that could be called 'oeuvre' at all) that consists of hardly one or two novels. For example, Appachana—so far- has published one collection of short-stories *Incantation and Other Stories* (1991), and the novel *Listening Now* (1997), which has been very well-received throughout the English-literary-world and in India. *Google Books* thus reviews the contents of the novel:

> "*Listening Now* unfolds through the intensely personal worlds of seven characters. First, there is the child Mallika, brimming with romantic fantasies and bemoaning the lack of passion in the lives of her mother, Padma, and her mother's contemporaries—women whom she nevertheless loves fiercely. Mallika renders her fantasies through a highly wrought imagination, re-creating for the readers the events that came to devastate her childhood. Then, we revisit the events Mallika has described as they are retold from the points of view of Padma and Padma's sister, mother and friends. The story that slowly emerges is not the same as the one Mallika told. For the world of these women is one where secrets grow like fungus, where guilt roots and ripens, where anger burns and smoulders. Every one of them carries the burden of secrets that may or may not be known by the others—some secrets obvious, others subtler and more

insidious—and that have for them become a way of life. And so they tell their stories, stories by no means as prosaic as the child Mallika believes. Layer after layer of concealing silence is relentlessly peeled off, till, at last, the truth behind the greatest secret of all is laid bare—the story of Padma's love"[11].

Appachana has linked the patriarchal domination of women in India (and, in extension, in the Western nations as well) to the various problems that the Indian women novelists, including those of the diaspora, experience during their writings. She has been vociferous regarding this issue. *Goodreads*, in 1999, quotes her saying at an interview:

> "Writing is not deemed legitimate work by anyone. They assume that it can be put aside for anything and everything -- for housework, for house-guests, [and] for cooking. [...] Now tell me, how many people who work outside the house do you know who would take time off from their work to cook a meal or do groceries or laundry or look after house guests? None, right? [...] That is because they work outside the house and because they have a regular income which apparently legitimises their work"[12].

Appachana's exasperation is (perceptively) shared by Vijayaraghavan as well who, in her only novel so far—*Motherland* (2001)—adds the perspective of cultural differences that the Indian women face in the Western nations (which makes their task even more difficult). However, her 2001-novel, on its exterior, has a seemingly-different plot which makes such an outright interpretation of motives rather difficult. In her novel, she shows the same diasporic awareness of cultural differences and difficulties of having a fixed identity in the West as could be found in the novel of, for example, Kiran Desai. As *Encyclopaedia.com* reviews (*https://www.encyclopedia.com/arts/educational-magazines/vijayaraghavan-vineeta-1972*):

> "[Vijayaraghavan's] *Motherland* [...] tells the story of Maya, a fifteen-year-old Indian girl living in the U.S.A., whose parents ship her back to India for the summer when they begin to feel that she has become too steeped in American culture. They hope the time away, spent with Maya's mother's family, will allow her to develop an appreciation for her heritage and culture, and that it might also instil in her a more traditional mode of behaviour. [...] Maya is, of course, resentful of being banished for her vacation and arrives in India displaying a petulant attitude typical of many

teenagers. However, after an accident lands her in bed, Maya finds herself confiding the details of her life to her grandmother, a nurturing woman who cared for Maya when she was small and who has never quite gotten over her own maternal instincts toward the girl. Once Maya is well, her grandmother gives her a gift of a book in which she has chronicled the life Maya described, giving her the chance to see her own experiences with fresh eyes. Vijayaraghavan illustrates the cultural differences between the U.S.A. and India through Maya's eyes, while also showing how much Maya has changed in the eyes of her family in the few years that she has been away in the U.S.A."[13]

Kavita Daswani, like Anjali Banerjee, writes principally for the young-adults, and is particularly known for her 'chick-lit' novels—as described by Silvia Schultermandl (23). Her oeuvre—which predominantly 'explicates the diasporic experiences of the migratory subjects' (Salunkhe 11)—consists of eight (apparently-light-hearted) novels—*For Matrimonial Purposes* (2004), *The Village Bride of Beverly Hills* (2005), *Salaam, Paris* (2007), *Inde Girl* (2007), *Lovetorn* (2012), *Bombay Girl* (2012), *Betrayed* (2012), and *Kingpin* (2016)—whose funny exteriors conceal the umpteen numbers of problems that the young (diasporic) Indian women settled in the West—primarily in the U.S.A.—have to face every day, and many of those are concerned with their marriages. Prashant Sidnal has grouped the novelists in the age-group of Bharati Mukherjee's as 'Old Diaspora' novelists (17), while Lahiri and Daswani are 'New Diaspora'-writers, and her being a 'member' of the 'New Diaspora'-group has probably induced in Daswani—a (migrated) Sindhi and, therefore, a writer of the so-called 'double diaspora'-fraternity—to look at the 'problems' of the young West-settled Indian women in a 'new' way: she traces the 'roots' of the 'problems' of characters like 'Anju' (*For Matrimonial Purposes*), 'Priyanka Sohni' (*The Village Bride of Beverly Hills*), Tanaya Shah (*Salaam, Paris*) and 'Shalini Agarwal' (*Lovetorn*) to their marriages or their 'choices of being married'—something which has been repeatedly mentioned by Marian Aguiar in her (*e-book*) *Arranging Marriages: Conjugal Agency in the South Asian Diaspora* (2018). In addition, Erin Hurt notices how "[t]he protagonists in Kavita Daswani's novels [...] couple critiques of consumption with depictions of 'Indian heroines' cultural struggle in the diaspora in America' as well as 'alienation after colonialism'" (16).

In conclusion, one could notice how the Indian diasporic novelists—who usually focus on the different 'problems' that the Indians face in their Western-host-nations (where English is the predominant language) have consciously chosen to write only in English. One can understand—of course—how the supposed 'universality' of the language, and its 'marketability', and the issue of 'readership' are taken into account by these writers. But does the usage of English make them 'lest post-colonial'? Navarro-Tejero has an important observation. She writes:

> "A number of Indian [...] novelists made their debut in [...] [very recent times]. [...] These writers were born after Indian independence, and the English language does not have colonial associations for them. Their work is marked by an impressive feel for the language, and an authentic presentation of contemporary India, with all its regional variations. They generally write about the urban middle class, the stratum of society they know best"[14].

Their usage of 'English'—which is widely derided as 'the imperialists' language'—notwithstanding, the Indian novelists of the diaspora have contributed handsomely to the advancement of the genre of Indian English novel. They have been mercilessly criticised at different times, or have been dismissed as people who can write 'anything because they are settled in the West and have lots of money to spend and publish', but one cannot ever deny the spectacular recognition they have brought for the Indian Writing in English in the postmodern literary world.

Notes:

1. "Why has Naipaul been honoured?". *Outlook — Books* 3 February 2022. Accessed on 15 October 2022 <https://www.outlookindia.com/website/story/why-has-naipaul-been-honoured/282853/>
2. "Indian Population in the United States of America, 2022". *Find Essay.* Accessed on 16 October 2022 <https://www.findeasy.in/indian-population-in-united-states/>
3. "Indian Population in the United Kingdom, 2022". *Find Essay.* Accessed on 16 October 2022 <https://www.findeasy.in/indian-population-in-united-kingdom/>
4. "Indian Population in Canada, 2022". *Find Essay.* Accessed on 16 October 2022 <https://www.findeasy.in/indian-population-in-canada/>
5. Shankar U., Gopika. "Indian Diasporic Literature: *A verbal Journey through Time and Space*". *Diplomacy and Beyond Plus: A Journal of Foreign Policy and National Affairs* 15 March 2019. Accessed on 16 October 2022 <https://diplomacybeyond.com/indian-diasporic-literature-a-verbal-journey-through-time-and-space/>
6. "Google Books — About 'Manhattan Music' by Meena Alexander". *Google Books.* Accessed on 17 October 2022 <https://books.google.co.in/books/about/Manhattan_Music.html?id=fLogAQAAIAAJ&redir_esc=y>
7. "English-Canadian Writers: Rohinton Mistry". *Faculty of Humanities and Social Sciences,* Athabasca University-Online 12 February 2015. Accessed on 18 October 2022 <https://canadian-writers.athabascau.ca/english/writers/rmistry/rmistry.php>
8. "English-Canadian Writers: Anita Rau Badami". *Faculty of Humanities and Social Sciences,* Athabasca University-Online 12 February 2015. Accessed on 18 October 2022 <https://canadian-writers.athabascau.ca/english/writers/abadami/abadami.php>
9. "Kirkus's Review of Sunetra Gupta's Memories of Rain". *Kirkus Review* 1 April 1992. Accessed on 18 October 2022 <https://www.kirkusreviews.com/book-reviews/sunetra-gupta/memories-of-rain/>

10. Navarro-Tejero, Antonia. "Modern Indian Women Writers in English". *Literature Study Online.* Accessed on 19 October 2022 <*http://www.literature-study-online.com/essays/indian-women-book.html*>
11. "Google Books-Review of 'Listening Now'". *Google Books.* Accessed on 19 October 2022 Google Books <*https://books.google.co.in/books/about/Listening_Now.html?id=3ylaAAAAMAAJ&redir_esc=y)*>
12. "Goodreads—on 'Listening Now'. *Goodreads.* Accessed on 19 October 2022 <*https://www.goodreads.com/book/show/1155047.Listening_Now*>
13. "On Vineeta Vijayaraghavan". *Encyclopaedia.com.* Accessed on 19 October 2022 <*https://www.encyclopedia.com/arts/educational-magazines/vijayaraghavan-vineeta-1972*>
14. Navarro-Tejero, Antonia. "Modern Indian Women Writers in English". *Literature Study Online.*

Works cited:

Abraham, Markose. *American Immigration Aesthetics: Bernard Malamud and Bharati Mukherjee as Immigrants*. Bloomington: Author House, 2011.

Aguiar, Marian. *Arranging Marriages: Conjugal Agency in the South Asian Diaspora* (e-book). Minneapolis: University of Minnesota Press, 2018.

Alagiri, Sasikala. *Tradition and Modernity: Changing the Images of Women in selected Fiction by Manju Kapur and Anita Nair*. Hamburg: Anchor Academic Publishing, 2017.

Banerjee, Subhrasleta. *Incarcerated Female Subalterns in select Indian Diasporic Novels*. New Delhi: Authors Press, 2021.

Ben-Rafael, Eliezer, and Yitzhak Sternberg (eds.). *Transnationalism: Diasporas and the advent of a new (Dis)order*. Leiden: Brill, 2009.

Bhatnagar, Manmohan, and M. Rajeshwar (eds.). *The Novels of Anita Desai: A Critical Study*. New Delhi: Atlantic Publishers and Distributors, 2008.

Brah, Avtar. *Cartographies of Diaspora: Contesting Identities*. New York and London: Routledge, 1996.

Childs, Peter, and Mike Storry (eds.). *Encyclopaedia of Contemporary British Culture*. New York and London: Routledge, 1999.

Dagnino, Arianna. *Transcultural Writers and Novels in the Age of Global Mobility*. West Lafayette: Purdue University Press, 2015.

Dey, Pradip Kumar. *The Atlantic Critical Studies: Salman Rushdie's 'Midnight's Children'*. New Delhi: Atlantic Publishers and Distributors, 2008.

Dodiya, Jaydipsinh K. (ed.). *The Novels of Rohinton Mistry: A Critical Study*. New Delhi: Sarup and Sons, 2004.

Fludernick, Monika (ed.). *Diaspora and Multiculturalism: Common Traditions and New Developments*. Amsterdam: Brill—Rodopi, 2003.

Ganapathy-Dore, Geeta. *The Postcolonial Indian Novel in English*. Newcastle-upon-Tyne: Cambridge Scholars Publishing, 2011.

Giri, Bed Prakash. "The Literature of the Indian Diaspora: *Between Theory and Archive*". *Diaspora: A Journal of Transnational Studies* 16. 1 and 2 (2007): 243-53.

Hamnett, Brian. *The Historical Novel in 19th-century Europe: Representations of Reality in History and Fiction*. Oxford: Oxford University Press, 2011.

Hawley, Michael (ed.). *Sikh Diaspora: Theory, Agency, and Experience*. Leiden: Brill, 2013.

Hurt, Erin (ed.). *Theorising Ethnicity and Nationality in the Chick-lit Genre.* New York and London: Routledge, 2018.

Jain, Jasbir. *The Diaspora writes Home: Subcontinental Narratives.* Singapore: Springer Nature, 2017.

Khan, M. Q., and Bijay K. Das (eds.). *Studies in Postcolonial Literature.* New Delhi: Atlantic Publishers and Distributors, 2007.

Kumar, Nagendra. *The Fiction of Bharati Mukherjee: A Cultural Perspective.* New Delhi: Atlantic Publishers and Distributors, 2001.

Lavery, Charne. *Writing Ocean Worlds: Indian Ocean Fiction in English.* Cham: Palgrave Macmillan Switzerland, 2021.

Mehrotra, Arvind Krishna (ed.). *A History of Indian Literature in English.* London: Hurst and Company, 2003.

Mukherjee, Meenakshi. *The Perishable Empire: Essays on Indian Writing in English.* New Delhi: Oxford University Press, 2000. Rpt. 2005.

Naipaul, Vidiadhar S. *Vintage Naipaul.* London: Vintage Books, 2004.

Pande, Amba (ed.). *Women in the Indian Diaspora: Historical Narratives and Contemporary Challenges.* Singapore: Springer Nature, 2018.

Pandey, Surya Nath (ed.). *Writing in a Postcolonial Space.* New Delhi: Atlantic Publishers and Distributors, 1999.

Pathak, Vandana, Urmila Dabir, and Shubha Mishra (eds.). *Contemporary Fiction: An Abthology of Female Writers.* New Delhi: Sarup and Sons, 2008.

Rani, Suman. "Themes of Alienation and Displacement in Diasporic Writings, in relation to Indian Writers in English". *Journal of E.T. and I. Research* 5.5 (May 2018): 253-56.

Rushdie, Salman. *Imaginary Homelands: Essays and Criticism, 1981-91* (e-book). London: Vintage Books, 2012.

Safran, William. "*Diasporas in Modern Societies*: Myths of Homeland and Return". *Diaspora: A Journal of Transnational Studies* 1.1 (Spring 1991): 83-99.

Salunkhe, Sachin. *Indian Diaspora Writers.* Lucknow: Book Rivers, 2017.

Sarwal, Amit (ed.). *Bridging Imaginations: South Asian Diaspora in Australia.* New Delhi: Readworthy Press and A.I.I.R.N., 2013.

Schneider, Sebastian. "Challenging the Cultural Mosaic: Shani Mootoo's Out on Main Street". *C.O.P. American Studies* 9 (2008): https://copas.uni-regensburg.de/article/view/105/129

Schultermandl, Silvia. *Transnational Matrilineage: Mother-Daughter Conflicts in Asian-American Literature.* Muenster: Lit Verlag, 2009.

Shaffer, Brian (ed,). *A Companion to the British and Irish Novels, 1945-2000.* Oxford: Blackwell Publishing, 2005.

Shukla, Pravina. *The Grace of Four Moons: Dress, Adornment, and the Art of the Body in Modern India*. Bloomington: Indiana University Press, 2008.

Sidnal. Prashant. *Bharati Mukherjee, Chitra Banerjee Divakaruni, and Jhumpa Lahiri as the Women Writers of the Indian Diaspora*. New Delhi: Authors Press, 2018.

Sorowarthy, Chamsul Alom. *History and National Theme in the Novels of Salman Rushdie*. Lucknow: B.F.C. Publications Pvt. Ltd., 2021.

Sree, Sathupati Prasanna (ed.). *Indian Women Writing in English: New Perspectives*. New Delhi: Sarup and Sons, 2005.

Uma Devi, K.N., and M. Nagalakshmi. "Indian Diasporic Writers in Diasporic Literature: A Study". *Turkish Online Journal of Qualitative Inquiry* 12.8 (July 2021): 1908-12.

Coolie Diaspora
A Trans-Oceanic Border Crossing

— Auritra Munshi

> "The sea
> has locked them up.The sea is History.
> ...
> the lantern of a caravel
> and that was Genesis,
> the shit,the moaning:
> Exodus."[1]

Derek Walcott, the famous Caribbean writer, in his poem 'The Sea is history', referred to the history of the migration of the Africans who were treated as slaves; they were transported in slave ships and taken to the Caribbean shores thereby. Walcott resorted to Biblical myths in delineating the deplorable condition of the African slaves. Their journey was full of agony of thinking of their departed homeland and their impending future in the new island. The situation of the African emigrants mentioned in the poem resembles the theme of *Kala pani* crossings, which also deals with the tales of the sufferings of millions of men and women during their perilous voyage. They migrated from India willingly or unwillingly to French, Danish and Dutch colonies from the 1830s' onwards till the indentureship was abolished. There were so many reasons for their departure. As Judith Misrahi-Barak observes, "[S]tarvation, chronic debt, domestic violence, caste oppression and other such factors pushed the hopeful emigrants away from their villages" (74). However, Seascape—for them—was the inevitable medium for exodus to have their subjective visibility in the different location. During their journey, they developed a friendship among themselves on the boat which stripped them off their caste affiliation and brought them under a single identity, that of jahaji Bhai and jahaji bahins. The transoceanic crossing drove them to confront a series of traumatic and painful ordeals which shaped a collective memory and imagination. Emigrants were bound to sign over a contract called *Girmit* in which each and every individual emigrant was committed to work on the sugar plantation for five years or more.So, they were completely uncertain of their future and the possibility of returning to their homeland. They were deemed to be coolies or indentured labourers and so conformed to, in view of Marina Carter and Khal Torabully, the concept of 'Coolitude'[2]. So, the utopia of freedom they once dreamt of having across the continent had been turned into a new form of slavery in which they were under the constant surveillance of the *arkatis* or recruiters.In this system, their bodies were interpellated into the colonial subject and were the markers of servitude; they became a saleable commodity to the recruiters in the host land and entered into an industry called 'Coolie'.However, Ocean seems to be a palimpsest in the context of *Kala pani* Crossings which reveals the tales of power,violence, exchange, resistance and survival.

After the emancipation of the African slaves in the British Carribean in 1834, importation of Indian laborers to the Caribbean islands took place. Stephen Vertovec has listed the reasons of such immigration:

> "After abolition, by increasing calls for cheap, controllable labour from outside their respective colonies (even in times of actual low labour need), planters could ensure depressed agricultural wages within the colony and could mitigate against the possibility of the African ex-slaves becoming a proletariat class which might threaten production and profit by making demands and withholding labour"(2).

Indians were transported in overcrowded vessels, and the mortality rates of them were too high. Indentured labourers lived in the Carribean Islands and occupied the same space like that of the former African slaves, but there is a subtle difference between slavery and indenture. Because unlike slavery, indenture was for a fixed period, and their children were born free. As Morton Klass has observed, while many labourers were lured or misled by the recruiters, there were important factors which led them towards migration: "A few came for the adventure; a few to escape the law; a few because of family conflicts-but most came because food, money and employment were scared at home" (Klass 9).

Although the relocation of a large number of Indian men and women in the British Carribean island occurred, but the past of the indentured labour is neglected. Historians who are interested in the living and working situations of indentured labourers have placed far less attention on the affective consequences of their conditions. Most have participated in two debates: whether indenture was 'a new system of slavery', launched by Hugh Tinker; and whether it was a 'free' or 'unfree' system of labour. But it is not easy to ascertain the control of the impact of indenture on the labourers' psyche in these debates. Actually, Indian indentured workers played a vital role in the Caribbean's economic, social and cultural life during the period of indenture. But the labourers' own voices are seldom heard. Moreover, there have been conscious attempts at wiping out memories of indenture. So, Derrida, in *Archive fever: A Freudian Impression*, emphasises on the importance of the role of archive and archiving and thus justifies his demand by proclaiming:

> "It is to burn with a passion. It is never to rest, interminably, for searching for the archive right where it slips away. It is to run after the archive, even if there is too much of it, right where something in it anarchives itself. It is to have a compulsive, repetitive, and nostalgic desire for the archive, an irrepressible desire to return to the origin, a homesickness, a nostalgia for the return to the most archaic place of absolute commencement" (91).

He also believes that the archive is involved in a politics of power which raises selective history. Hence, Derrida says, "There is no political power without control of the archive, if not of memory. Effective democratization can always be measured by this essential criterion: the participation and the access to the archive, its constitution, and its interpretation"(4). Since, archive and power are interconnected; historians duty is to bring out the marginalized, unrepresented history. Paul Ricoeur in this connection states, "The fundamental objective of the good historian is to enlarge the sphere of archives, that is, the conscientious historian must open up the archive by retrieving the traces which the dominant ideological forces attempted to suppress" (16).

It is understood that the historians have their ethical responsibilities to defy the manipulative history and render voices to the abused and excluded. The experiences of the indentured labourers are embedded in the narratives which excavate unusual facts from beneath the debris of silence and bring out humanitarian aspects which were affected by the British colonial project of plantation economy.In this book chapter, I have taken up two *Kala pani* narratives such as Gaiutra Bahadur's *Coolie Woman: The Odyssey of Indenture* (2013) and Totaram Sanadhya's *Fiji Dwip Me Mere Ikkis Varsh* (1914), which was later translated into English as *My Twenty-One Years in the Fiji Islands* (1991) with a view to showing the indentured labourers' tough journey, containing the records of incidents of exploitation , violence in India and their host countries, and their quest for freedom. Of these two texts, *Coolie Woman* is a narrative made by Bahadur,the fourth generation emigrant, who investigates the years long buried ancestral history of her grandmother Sujaria, and the story is deemed as 'faction'[3] which refers to the admixture of fact and fiction. And *My Twenty-One Years in the Fiji Islands* is a fact brought to the fore by Totaram Sanadhaya who has direct experience of the oppression and sufferings of the Indian indentured labourers in Fiji. He has also revealed as to how the oppressive mechanism of patriarchy perpetuated in the Indian society which is one of the reasons of their willful exodus and how Coolitude made a vulnerable impact on the indentured labourers working in Fiji. Both of the texts have been written in different time span, but they intersect at the particular point which crops up the marginalized history of the indentured labourers' struggle. There is a dearth of creative and critical works on indenture in the Indian market, which is a stumble block for the dissemination of the knowledge about such kind of migration. Of late, the market providers are making the works published which help flourish this area further.

The 'Kala pani' (the 'dark waters') is a phrase which has its roots in ancient Buddhist and Hindu scriptures. These scriptural religions established each person's code of conduct. As Baudhayana's Dharmashutra implies, Crossing the *kala pani* is considered to be endemic or immoral. Traversing the ocean is indicative of losing one's own caste, which leads towards social exclusion and marginalization. The ocean as *Kala pani* conveys the sense of death in the literary sense. The sea-voyage, according to Baudhayana's Dharmashastra, denies the possibility of reincarnation, and also restrains one from performing prayers and funeral rites. Ocean was thought to be a terrible location for them as it was regarded as the abode of terrifying beasts and monsters. Brinda Meheta writes, "According to Hindu belief, the traversing of large expanses of water was associated with contamination and cultural defilement as the crossing led to loss of tradition, caste, class and a generally purified ideal of *hinduness*" (1). The *kala pani*-crossings brings out the history of transgression of the emigrated men and women. Disenfranchised Hindu men who were oppressed by the upper-class Hindu high-mindedness forged the majority of the indentured population. However, the Hindu women, who referred to a significant minority in the Carribean islands, had a hope to attain something by crossing the *kala pani* because they were caught into the claptrap of patriarchal oppression prevalent in India. So, Bahadur states, "To leave was to cross the *Kala pani*, "the dark water", of the Indian Ocean and therefore to lose caste, according to the strictures of Hinduism" (24). Hence, they sought to break down the confinement of the patriarchal structure and resorted to seascape to find liberty in the host country, connoting their survival stategy. And it resulted in the formation of an expansive diasporic community.

Against the backdrop of overt male chauvinism in the nineteenth and early twentieth century India, Gaiutra Bahadur's *Coolie Woman: The Odyssey of Indenture* (2013) develops a discursive framework for examining indentureship or post-indentureship experiences of female selves through the lens of exile and hybridity in order to make gender negotiations and feminist solidarity visible.The narrative of the story reveals how geographies constitute female subjectivity and how deeply they feel about their choices they make in an ambivalent world where female self, excluded from history, is susceptible to amnesia. Brinda Meheta defines *Kala pani* as "a gendered discourse of exilic beginnings that simultaneously reclaims and contests otherness by highlighting the traditional invisibility of female historical subjectivity in androcentric colonial and national narratives" (24). Gaiutra Bahadur belongs to the fourth-generation descedant of indentured Indian women who left Carribean islands for the U.S.A. in order to escape institutionalised 'cultural freeze' (Meheta 33). And she was pondering over that "leaving for countries with better-rooted traditions of feminism and greater opportunities for education and economic independence has meant that women in the second diaspora are transcending their history" (Bahadur 274). India appears to be a distant place, the place of ancestral origin, which is completely alien to Bahadur. So, it ignites Bahadur to find out the traces of her ancestral origin. She is in search of her great grandmother, Sujaria, and in so doing, she arrives at Bhurahpur in Bihar where Sujaria used to stay. She visited the village twice in 2005 and 2008 and came to realise that patriarchal mindset in rural India remained the same as it was. After observing the place in which Sujaria used to live, Bahadur understood what kind of hatred the common people of that place did possess for her grandmother. The grand old man who was 'the keeper of local memory' (*ibid*. 105) became harsh towards Bahadur too. He kept on looking at her dress and her untied open hair, which he thought to be an indication of her defiance. Although the reason of Sujaria's displacement remained unknown, Bahadur felt why Sujaria left the country and resorted to seascape; she sought to challenge the phenomenon of invisibility in the enveloping patriarchal environment. Being a fourth generation emigrant, Bahadur developed a negative impression in her mind about India. Sujaria, the great grandmother in the story, being the first generation emigrant, shows her independence, determination, courage, self- reliance and sexual independence, which have made her a worthy instance of emulation by her future generation. Although Sujaria was not content with her subjugation and oppression, she 'braved the treacherous waters of the Atlantic'(Mehta 4), and thus she forged an alternative lifestyle for herself. Bahadur went to Guyana and India for the sake of collecting the details of her grandmother, Sujaria, deeply buried and thus brought out and reinvented her struggle in a new world.

Bahadur portrays a grim picture of the nineteenth and early twentieth century India, which was rife with patriarchal oppression; it reduced the position of women. *Satidaha* or 'widow immolation', and dowry were prevalent in the Indian society. Several female figures, as Bahadur observed, had to undergo socio-cultural subordination in their homeland as widows, outcasts, prostitutes, runaway wives, and Vaishnavite pilgrims. It resulted in their social exclusion, marginalization and alienation. In order to flee abusive relationships, the mistreatment of the women caused them to migrate to far-off colonies. In Sahabad (Bihar), a large number of widows themselves came forward in search of recruiters in order to escape the difficult circumstances in which they were caught. Suicide or prostitution were the only options available to such widows. In Calcutta's red light districts, Lalbazar or Chakla Ghar, many women sought refuge. Premature marriage of a girl with an aged husband was a natural phenomenon of Indian society, which mostly occurred in the Upper Caste Hindu community. As a result, it increased the high mortality rates of elderly husbands, and thereby forcing women to assume widowhood. And the widowhood did not allow them to go for remarriage, and it also forbade them to engage in economic activity outside the home. As a matter of fact, young widows were basically seen as a burden, which led them to take different courses. Widowhood made them 'docile' bodies in India. Performing widowhood in India was a compulsory practice and the widows had to go through starvation, social ostracism, maternal dispossession and physical defilement. Such vehement torture compelled them to adhere to the attitude of 'Pativrata' to conform to the status of 'Grihalaxmi', or *Goddess of home*. Those who did not want to conform to their insular lived experiences, resorted to prostitution; it also led them to another kind of oppression and suffering.

The precarious condition where they usually lived in was unbearable for them and it consequently moved them to be lured by the recruiters to go across the *Kala pani*, and start their journey anew as indentured labourers. According to Indenture regulations, there should be at least forty women for every hundred men. Although maintaining the men and women ratio was quite challenging. So, the *arkatis* or recruiters allured women for having their better future and made false promises of marriage with a view to taking the advantage of their weakness and misery. They were also carried away by their false promises. Instead of freedom, they were caught in a new kind of bondage in their host land. Their journey through the boat was not secure enough as they were sexually harassed by the authoritative figures on the boat too: "The journey of indentured women from Calcutta (now Kolkata) to their respective colonies on ship was full of danger. These women could fall prey to the lust of crew members or the ship's surgeon or his junior compunder" (qtd. in Tewari 58). In her *Coolie Woman* (2013), Bahadur described how the confined coolie women made an effort to break any sort of social,cultural as well as political barriers. They embraced extra-marital or inter-community relationships in the Caribbean islands. As Bahadur has rightly pointed it out, "Coolie women could leave their husbands, and they could partner across caste. Relationship taboo in India became necessary and practical in indenture, because women were few" (120). Women on the plantation could choose their male partners to come out of their abusive relationships and they used to get such liberty because of unequal male and female ratio in the plantation. After their arrival in the new land, coolie women were exploited economically as well as physically. In actuality, the recruited indentured labourers were also involved in a variety of relationships on the plantations, both with other indentured men and women as well as with some of the landowners and their overseers. With their wealth and status, the overseers could seduce those indentured ladies. And as a result, there were more extramarital relationships. It caused anger to the rejected husbands, which led them to murder their wives brutally out of rage. Undoubtedly, the violence unsettled the moral principles enshrined in the Hindu marriages.

The murdering of wives on the sugar plantation often occurred due to sexual jealousy. Patriarchal mindset was prevalent in the plantation. Patriarchal resentment emerged due to the freedom women had in the plantation. For women, the plantation system offered a society that was largely free.The plantation system broke down the prejudices concerning inter-caste and inter-faith marriages. The male members of the community were challenged by the choices of couples, which served as the foundation for weddings in plantations. In the plantation, divorce was a frequent occurrence. Women frequently deserted their husbands in favour of better, more lucrative possibilities. Caste and religious barriers seldom existed in the plantation. In reality, Hindu ladies wedded Muslim men, a sweeper could wed a Brahmin, and women from the Indo-Caribbean region wed Black men.This resulted in the annihilation of caste or religion to a great extent.

In fact, the extramarital affairs of the coolie women with the overseers produced children. Bahadur, in her *Coolie Woman*, states:

> "[...] at another Davson plantation on the Berbice river, an overseer returned from England to find that the Indian man whose wife he had enticed years earlier had been emboldened to complain, again, to the authorities. When the man had first discovered the affair, he had beaten his wife then informed the local immigration agent. She had promptly left him, and the agent had referred the complaint to the manager. Not only had the manager failed to investigate, he had fired the Indian, an unindentured worker. The coolie had held onto his job by begging for it, and the woman had moved to a neighbouring village, where she ultimately gave birth to the new overseer's son, christened Adam" (188-89).

It is an example of how women exercised their limited freedom of choice in the new island.It also indicates how their freedom was purchased by the overseers: 'The overseers could and did ultimately purchase the women's freedom' (193). Bahadur, further, points out:

> "As soon as an overseer eyes a nice looking coolie girl, she must fall a prey to him with the assistance of a sirdar or driver, who plays a great figure in it... If the girl does not consent and exposes the matter, she with her whole family will be turned off the estate. Of course, some fault is found with them as an excuse" (*ibid.* 195).

It reveals the appalling situation of women in the new society, where they had the freedom to choose their life partners, but those choices were almost always predetermined. Bahadur depicts the condition of women in the new island where she states,

> "[t]he women seemed to occupy an uncertain middle ground between slavery and liberty, a kind of demilitarized zone where coercion and incentive intermingled. The consequences, both positive and negative, awaiting them and their families if they refused determined their choices" (*ibid.* 196).

In the new territory, the company was empowered to determine the marriage of the overseers: 'The Company had fired a Scottish overseer because he intended to marry a Creole widow' (*ibid.* 196). It points out the inhibition of the companies in respect of a white man marrying a Creole widow. Bahadur observes, "The Company didn't explicitly ban marriage, but it did reserve the right to decide when matrimony was wise for its overseers. Apparently, it wasn't wise if the bride wasn't white" (*ibid.* 196). Racial prejudices could be located in such instances. Overseers were also regulated by the system which led them, consequently, to go for numerous relationships. However, Bahadur also pinpoints 'the absurdity of marriage in the colony, but it also illustrates the forces that constrained Indian women during the indenture era' (*ibid.* 131). Bahadur mentions the difficulties faced by the woman who had been married off to an unknown person by her drunken father for money. She escaped her abusive husband and was in search of another suitable person as her life partner who could stand by her to protect her from the clutches of her drunken father. While she met Bronkhurst, a missionary-priest, she revealed her miseries: 'Sir, I am going to town, to see if I can find a man of my own caste, who would make me his wife, and support me, and deliver me from my cruel and drunken father' (*ibid.* 131). Bronkhurst tried to make her understand that she could not go because she did not have the pass to return to India. The young woman disobeyed the rules of her father, and 'returned to the plantation that day but, in the long run, married a man of her own choice' (*ibid*. 132). In this way, she expressed her freedom of choice,and thereby challenging patriarchy.

The Caribbean landscape became the confluence of various cultures which resulted in the formation of Cultural hybridity. It was developed further by the indentured women as they transformed the landscape into a place of new alliances and opportunities. It, consequently, changed their status from coolie women to business women, and thus they were capable of averting the mournful stories of their widowhood.Emigration tended to free them from the oppressive patriarchal socio-cultural and religious customs and strictures. They remembered India as their 'home' and a few were yearning to return to their home, but thinking about their vanished roots, they decided to live in their host land. A few were reluctant to go back to India out of fear as they had crossed the *kala pani* and got married outside the Hindu customs. It was supposed to be a criminal offence in the eyes of the Hindu scriptural religion. So, they decided to settle in the free atmosphere of the sugar plantation. Sujaria desperately tried to see her 'home' again, but never returned: "Perhaps she was wise enough to know the subtle tricks that nostalgia plays. Or, perhaps she had the good sense to realise that […] she belonged to the vast majority who stayed in the West Indies to build a future" (*ibid*. 224) outside India. In an attempt to recreate her family, Sujaria had to undergo several stages: from labourer to an unpaid milk seller's wife. She inoculated a sense of duty in her family as a powerful resistant matriarch "away from the exploitation and indignity of plantation where they might nourish themselves with institutions remembered from India and seek the consolations of religion, kin and identity" (*ibid*. 268). In India her name has remained alive in cultural rituals like the songs of wedding ceremonies, which usually pay homage to all the ancestors. Finally, Sujari's dream to see India was inherited to her great granddaughter Bahadur, who tried to crop up her story beneath the debris of silence and thus brought out the repression and suppression of the coolie women.

Totaram Sanadhya, in his autobiography *Fiji Dvip Me Mere Ikkis Varsh, 1914* ('My Twenty One Years on the Fiji Islands, 1991') portrays the oppressive history of the coolie men and women lived in Fiji and traces the possible reasons of their emigration from India. This autobiography is written with immense passion as he himself had the experience of indentureship. So, after the completion of his tenure of indentureship, he remained absorbed in making case studies in Fiji. He met indentured men and women, listened to their stories, took sensitive snapshots, and thus tried to bring out a grim picture of the sufferings of indentured laborers. He revealed how they were misled by the *arkatis* or recruiters with their false promises. After meeting indentured women in particular, he further observed that some women stated, 'The arkati fooled my poor husband, and I had to come along with my husband' (Sanadhya 69). He brings to the fore through his autobiography the marginalized voices of the women as to why they were forced to resort to seascape. There are certain excerpts which may be quoted to justify the point:

> "Many women said, 'My father-in-law, mother-in-law, husband and so forth died, and the close kin did not help at all. For this reason I went on a pilgrimage tour, and from that the arkati fooled me and brought me" (*ibid.* 69),

and

> "Some women also said, 'When I became a widow on the death of my husband, the people of the house began to argue and fight with me, and to give me troubles.Because of these troubles I left home.On my way, unluckily I was caught up in the trap of the arkatis. In the end I was forced to come here to bear unending troubles" (*ibid.* 69).

Sanadhya was quite critical of the case-ridden Indian society which compelled the marginalized to abort their homes and communities. Kelly points out, "Indeed, my 21 years makes very clear that starting points of difficulty and sorrow in India set the emigration in motion [...]" (19). It resulted in the increasing number of deserted women. Apart from showing the case of a woman called Lilia's harassment by the recruiters, he also revealed another story of Kunti. Kunti was duped by an *arkati* who sent her to Fiji. A white overseer and a *Sardar* (Leader of the coolies) attempted to rape her in a banana plantation. In an attempt to save herself, she jumped into the river and was protected by an Indian boy. Later, the story of Kunty was published in *Bharat Mitra*, an Indian newspaper, which helped the Indian Government probe into the case.

Sanadhya articulated his distrust of the official historiography which overshadowed the voices of the repressed. So, he said,

> "the explanations for the public servants and the written report of the commission do not reveal the real conditions of the foreign dwelling Indians and that one requires a 'subtle vision' to know immediately that the coolie system is only a new form of slavery" (Sanadhya 118).

Hence, he emphasised the micro-narratives which could provide an alternative history of the coolie men and women. However, after carefully archiving the facts,figures,opinions and official documents, he wrote letters to Gandhi, Gokhale for the legal aids to abolish the sufferings of the girmitiya.After his return from Fiji, he stayed at Dharamtala in Calcutta (now 'Kolkata') for a month and delivered thirteen speeches and distributed fifteen thousand pamphlets with the help of Marwaris. Thus he started campaigning against the indentureship. Totaram travelled from village to village in order to inform the real truth of the indenture system among the people. For Totaram, the emigration of women under the indenture system generated a bad image of India in Fiji. An indigenous Fijian commented to Totaram on the conditions of women on plantations:

> "[...] India is a bad country,whose women come to a foreign country, Fiji to do the work of labourers. Coming here, they suffer many outrages.If the outrages, which are done to your women were done to our women, then we would destroy to the roots the ones responsible" (*ibid*. 32).

He was hell-bent on abolishing the indenture system. He tried to put an end to the castism prevalent in India, which was exclusionary and created a problem for the rehabilitation of the returnees to India. His approach was humanistic at its core, which referred to the dissolution of caste and religious barriers. Hence, he said in his autobiography,

> "May I ask the speech-giving religious people of our country, what is the harm in mixing these people into the castes again? Oppressed by outrages of the home,fooled by the wicked arkatis, sent to a foreign country, what are the defects in this of these helpless people" (*ibid*. 73).

This text is the product of his direct experience of the indenture system in Fiji which helps Totaram Sanadhya depict the dehumanizing system of indentureship.And it also leads him to represent the oppressive social structure which Castism and gender discrimination offer. He tried his level best to stop the indenture system by making a consensus among the people regarding the ill effects of the system and thus brought this matter to the then Indian leaders also.

Coolie diaspora, which is related to the crossing of *Kala pani*, bears the connotation of a transoceanic border crossing. It does not remain confined only to the crossing of cartographical border, but it conveys the abolition of all sorts of barriers such as caste, race, culture and creed. Dismantling the discriminatory caste system looming large in India, Indian men and women chose ship as the vehicle of their retriever to save themselves from the dungeon. That transcending *Kala Pani* is synonymous with the emigrants' 'social death'[4] is known to them well. They still accepted it in order to find their liberty in the free ambience of the plantation. Although, their experiences on the boat and on the plantation were also miserable. Whether their journey was indicative of freedom or another form of slavery is a bone of contention. Since, lots of people from various class, caste and race migrated through the boat, it helped form the cross-cultural fusion. Thus, it broke down the racial absolutism and tended to shape inter-caste alliances, as well as 'dougla' consciousness in the plantation. Bahadur and Totaram brought out these factors in their works apart from revealing the dehumanising effect of 'Coolitude'. Both Totaram and Bahadur belong to the different generations and different time spans, but they intersect at the same point which revolves around the subjugation of the coolie men and women in the indentured system. Totaram himself is the victim of the recruiters' trap and has direct experience of such a vile system, and Bahadur, on the other hand, is the fourth generation descendant of indentured Indian women, who makes metaphorical as well as physical journey to India with a view to investigating the struggling history of her grandmother, Sujari ,which was eclipsed by the colonial historiography. Bhadur so takes recourse to imagination in order to make the story more than real, which attributes to her story the status of 'faction'. Totaram's autobiography is the historical documentation of the sufferings of the coolie men and women.A fictional and a non-fictional narrative have been taken up in this chapter in order to unveil the voices of the suppressed, which resound loudly from beneath the ruins of history. History demands creative indulgence on the part of the hisrorians in order to have both facts and fiction to reinforce the historical imagination and provide new dimensions to Indian history.

Notes:

1. "The Sea is History: Derek Walcott-1930 to 2017". *Poets.org*. Accessed on 13 June 2022 <https://poets.org/poem/sea-history>
2. The concept of 'coolitude' encompasses the experiences of first generation workers together with those of their descendants spread across the Caribbean, Pacific and Indian Ocean islands today. The symbolic value of the word lies in both the scope it gives us to interpret the specificities of the coolie experience and its use as a comparative tool. The concept called 'coolitude' has its various incarnations: the shared experience of the voyaging migrants, the walk from village to port town and the weeks spent on board ship.

It is indicative of cultural compromises and negotiations. See Marina Carter and Khal's Torabully's *Coolitude: An Anthology of the Indian Labour Diaspora* (London: Wimbledon Publishing, 2002).
3. Brij V. Lal coins the portmanteau word 'faction' which is a combination of 'fact' and 'fiction'.This coinage helps to resolve the gap which the mainstream history leaves behind by focussing on the marginalised history of the indentured labourer. Gaiutra Bahadur's *Coolie Woman* may be cited as an example of 'faction' in this connection.
4. 'Social death' refers to the condition of people not accepted as fully human by wider society. It is used by sociologist Orlando Patterson in his book *Slavery and Social Death: A Comparative Study* (1982). According to him, 'Social death' had both internal and external effects on enslaved people, changing their views of themselves and the way they were regarded by society. Slavery and social death can be linked in all civilizations where slavery existed, including China, Rome, Africa, Byzantium, Greece, Europe, and the Americas. I have opted Patterson's concept of 'Social death' in the context of crossing the *Kala pani* of the indentured labourers. Crossing the *Kala pani*, as Hindu religion implies, is indicative of the social exclusion of the indentured labourers. The texts I have taken up in this book chapter are instrumental in showing this issue. See Orlando Patterson's *Slavery and Social Death: A Comparative Study* (Cambridge: Harvard University Press, 1982, rpt. 2018).

Works cited:

Bahadur,Gaiutra. *Coolie Woman: The Odyssey of Indenture*. Gurgaon: Hachette India, 2013.

Barak, Misrahi Judith. "Indentureship, Caste and the Crossing of the Kala Pani". *Studies in Humanities and Social Sciences* 14 (2) (2017): 18-36.

Derrida, Jacques. *Archive fever: A Freudian Impression*. Trans. Eric Prenowitz. Chicago: The University of Chicago Press, 1996.

Kelly, John Dunham. 'Introduction' to Totaram Sanadhya's *My Twenty-One Years in the Fiji Islands and the Story of the Haunted Line*. Trans. John Dunham Kelly and Uttra Kumari Singh. Suva: Fiji Museum, 1991.

Klass, Morton. *East Indians in Trinidad: A Study of Cultural Persistence*. New York: Columbia University Press,1961.

Mehta, Brinda. *Diasporic (Dis)locations: Indo-Caribbean Women Writers Negotiate the Kala Pani*. Kingston: University of the West Indies Press, 2004.

Ricoeur, Paul. *Memory, History, and Forgetting*. Chicago: The University of Chicago Press, 2004.

Sanadhya, Totaram. "Fiji Dwip Me Mere Ikkis Varsh". *Samay*. Accessed on 19 November 2021 <*https://hindisamay.com/lekhak/totaram-sanadhya.htm*>

Tewari, Archana. "Indian Indentured Women in the Caribbeans and the Role Model of Ramayana's Sita: *An Unequal Metaphor*". *Women in the Indian Diaspora: Historical Narratives and Contemporary Challenges*. Ed. Amba Pande. Singapore: Springer, 2018.

Vertovec, Steven. *Hindu Trinidad: Religion, Ethnicity and Socio-Economic change*. Basingstoke: Macmillan Education, 1992.

Portrait of India in Chitra Banerjee Divakaruni's Fictional World

—Lata Dubey

It requires no validation when someone observes that among the 21st-century Indian litterateurs of the diaspora, Chitra Banerjee Divakaruni (b. 1956)—presently employed as the *Betty and Gene McDavid Professor of Writing* at the University of Houston (Houston, Texas, U.S.A.)—is one of the more critically-acclaimed and numerously read novelists. Other than her novels (and it not an exaggeration to say that the themes of her fictional-prose-publications provide a paradigm for interpreting the nuances or features of most of the novels by other expatriate Indian writers), she also writes short-stories and adult fiction, and is a social activist. Chitra Banerjee Divakaruni—who is married to S. Murthy Divakaruni (a petroleum-engineer, and Director, Special Projects, University of Houston)—is primarily known for her striking exploration of the immigrant-experiences, particularly that of Indian women. Divakaruni's prolific oeuvre include the best-selling novels like *The Mistress of Spices* (1997), *Sister of My Heart* (1999), its sequel *The Vine of Desire* (2002), *The Queen of Dreams* (2004), *The Palace of Illusions* (2008), *One Amazing Thing* (2009), *Oleander Girls* (2012), *The Forest of Enchantments* (2019), and *The Last Queen* (2021). There is sufficient testimony to the popularity of the novelist as her works have been widely published, anthologised, and translated. She is also a popular author of young adult-fiction that includes *Neela: Victory Song* (2002), and the trilogy *Brotherhood of the Conch*-series: *The Conch Bearer* (2003), *The Mirror of Fire and Dreaming* (2005), and *The Shadowland* (2009).

Born in Kolkata, India, Divakaruni moved to the U.S.A. in the late 1970s' to attain a Master's degree in English at Wright State University (Fairborn, Ohio), followed by a Ph.D. at the University of California, Berkeley. The heart-felt and the first hand experiences as an immigrant inspired her to write. "I did not think I had a story to tell!", she writes on her blog, "Moving to a very different culture and learning to live on my own made me see the world much more clearly. [...] I thought about India more than I had ever before. I realised what I appreciated about it, the warmth the closeness of extended family, the way spirituality pervades the culture" (qtd. in Sekhar). On the one hand, she proudly reminisces her cultural strength; and, on the other, she is acutely cautious of the problems with regards "to how women are often treated." In her short-story-collection, *Arranged Marriage*, and, later, in novels like *The Mistress of Spices*, *Queen of Dreams* and *Oleander Girl*, she would go on to delineate characters who had undergone experience of culture-shock, and they had made earnest effort to create new identities for themselves while relationship the most precious assets of their homeland and culture. As is revealed by various biographical works on Divakaruni, her (Bengali) mother was a predominant influence in her life. Naturally, the mother-figures in *Arranged Marriage* (especially those of mothers who try to strike new bondings with their young sons) are easily-observable examples. In *Sister of My Heart*, one encounters the instances of mothers-in-intense-action in figures of those who raise the protagonists Sudha and Anju while concentrating on physical beauty, studies, and mythological stories. In *Oleander Girl*, Karobi's mother dies at child-birth but keeps haunting her daughter during the latter's journey from Kolkata to New York to discover the secret that lies buried underneath Anu's life. Another example is that of *Before We Visit the Goddess*, which is a novel about three generation of women—grandmother, mother, and daughter—and about what they learn, both positive and negative, from one another.

Chitra Banerjee Divakaruni has constantly concentrated on the lives of immigrant women who are fraught with emotional anxieties and fettered with cultural shackles, and her novels are usually centred on the issue of immigrant conflict that is precisely the clash between acquired values *vis-à-vis* the adopted ones. The trials and tribulations stemming from the duality of immigration—that is the pain resulting from leaving the homeland as well as the excitement of settling down to a new place—lend voice to the inner-conflict that her characters routinely face. One could observe that the representative inhabitants of her fictional world are the protagonists of *Sister of my Heart, Oleander Girls,* and *Before We visit the Goddess,* among some others.

One of the most predominant trends in post-independence Indian (English) fiction is the portrayal of India and its vast multitudinous-ness, and of its vibrant and enduring culture. The image of India gets wonderfully expressed through the fictional works of Indian English writers, including in those by Divakaruni.

Divakaruni's fictional oeuvre truly reverberates and resonates with portrayal of India. Her themes include immigration, myth, and culture, along with magical realism. Indian culture gets delineated in relation to its belief practices, way of life and art. Culture broadly encompasses all the steps in an individual's development that may have been acquired from her/his group by conscious learning or by a conditioning process, beliefs and multivalent modes of conduct. As the food and culture is a defining feature of diaspora, a strong sense of connection to a homeland is conjured up through cultural practices and ways of life. These issues and aspects are omnipresent in Divakaruni's narratives.

Divakaruni's novels, above all, engage with women's issues and predicaments. The female protagonists in/of her novels — though eager to embrace the new culture — still cling to their old values and traditional beliefs. They assimilate the features of and adopt themselves into new countries/ cultures, and, in the process, forge new identities away from their homeland. The familiar Indian background — particularly religion, food and clothes — find their way in the writings of immigrant writers, most so in Divakaruni's novels. The works of contemporary Indian English women writers like Bharati Mukherjee, Jhumpa Lahiri, and Kiran Desai — like Divakaruni — also engage with the Indian immigrant experiences. Divakaruni's fictional-prose-writings, in particular, concentrate on the broad cultural issues which stem out of her own heartfelt and first-hand experiences and observations of her *host-lands* and *homeland*. The angst, deepest fear, and trauma faced by her female-protagonists both in India and abroad show them emerge in many cases stronger, bolder and self-reliant women of substance. It also deserves mentioning here that most of her fictional women are grounded on her own autobiographical inputs. The popularity that she has achieved through this has led to her books' being translated into multiple languages including Bengali, Hebrew, Dutch Turkish and Japanese.

The present paper proposes to very briefly analyse the representation of India in select novels of Divakaruni's. The novels—chosen for limited reviewing—are *Mistress of Spices, Sister of my Heart, The Palace of Illusions, Oleander Girl, The Forest of Enchantments*, and *The Last Queen*. Generally, the principal plots of her novels are either strongly connected to or are set in India, and they present the traditional and conventional conceptions of Indians. As a novelist, Divakaruni has attempted to change the perception of the Indian and international readers about how the Indian women, including those settled in the West, have revolutionised the societal set-up in the twenty-first century. She is a perfect interpreter of a cultural multiplicity of India. Since she is Bengali by birth, most of her works are 'firmly rooted in Bengal' (qtd. in *Culture and Tradition*). Her novels reflect Indian—especially Bengali - traditional customs and culture of India. Moreover, they depict the love of Indian people for their country even after leaving and moving abroad somewhere. The Indians who go to settle abroad try to preserve their culture and the way of thinking as were in India.

In Divakaruni's fictional-prose-narratives, India is presented as a land of strong beliefs in traditional culture, and as a preserver of the prestige of its cultural heritage. Many other expatriate Indian writers have depicted the Indian culture and traditional beliefs in their works too, but Divakaruni exceptionalises herself through her dexterous and appreciable employment of indigenous myths and legends. Divakaruni is one of those writers who know the efficient usage of myths, dreams, fantasy, culture and magic in her novels, and these—other than giving the international readers an idea of the Indian history, tradition, and beliefs—also, as a sort of 'strategic essentialism'—exoticise India to them.

Divakaruni's *Arranged Marriage* is her first collection-of-short-stories (and her first major publication) to be released in 1995, and it spent five weeks on the *San Francisco Chronicle Bestseller List*. It is a collection of 11 short-stories that deal with the life of Bengali women based in Kolkata and different American cities. In the stories, Divakaruni succeeds in creating a beautiful ambience that blends sights, smells, and memories from the villages and cities of Bengal—especially the umpteen corners of Kolkata. All the stories revolve around women who are caught in difficult circumstances. Divakaruni's women are caged between their Indian upbringing and their (often unpalatable) experiences with the culture of the U.S.A. Each woman's story is different from the next, and these narratives capture the orthodox concepts and old-fashioned notions of the Indians back home. Divakaruni—almost objectively—offers a glimpse of cruel India by focussing on the 'crucial beliefs' of Indian patriarchs regarding exploitation of the women through domestic violence, orthodox beliefs, gender discrimination, and conservative thinking. Divakaruni's India ensures that though the women of her short-stories are from well-off families, they have to go through the sufferings and hardships immediately after their marriages.

Marriage is the crux of any culture, and, in Divakaruni's writings, it becomes the central metaphor through the *lens* of which a not-so-endearing patriarchal image of India emerges. The issue of marriage predominates all the eleven stories of the 1995-publication too. As the title suggests, all the stories highlight the flawed and faulty concept of arranged marriages, and readers come to know that since ages, the Indian people have moulded and shaped this concept through their own traditional, patriarchal thoughts. Each protagonist in her story is different, and yet they all are similar in their fighting against multiple issues and challenges that result from their arranged marriages which seem to have been designed to break their inner spirit and to mute their voices. The introspection of these women is dramatically altered, and they are forced to acquire different (symbolic) *lenses* to look at themselves. The stories and sufferings of these women 'present' a different image of India in which women are forced to live on the boundaries. Even today, in the 21st century, many inconsiderate traditional rituals and orthodox thoughts and culture are ardently followed by the Indian society. Rebellious in her nature, the novelist, in all her stories, has not only highlighter but also (symbolically) opposed such imposition of subaltern status on the married Indian women, including those settled in the West.

Divakaruni's *The Mistress of Spices*, since its publication in 1997, has steadily remained one of the more popularly-read specimens of novels by the expatriate Indian writers. *The Mistress of Spices* narrates the story of a girl Tilottama, a mysterious 'priestess' who has been trained in the art of dispensing spices for therapeutic usage, while she also personally has magical powers. The novel is an evocative classic and a magical-mystical tale of a girl who sells spices that can soothe individuals' soul. The girl in question—perceptively—is from India, and has her spice-selling-shop in San Francisco. She is the 'mistress of spices' of that shop, which means she has been placed in that shop to help people with her 'magic', but only through spices. She is supposed to help people, but, in Divakaruni's description, she too has to inhabit the societal margins. There are some rules for her—especially those against relationships and sexualities—and the story is about how she becomes the 'mistress of spices', how and why she breaks all her 'rules', and the 'consequences' that follow.

In *The Mistress of Spices*, India is aptly named the 'land of spices', with its rich spice heritage and production dominance. This concurs with the real-life statistics: India was, and, even in the 21st century, is the leading producer and exporter of spices in the world. The novel, moreover, is filled with magic realism. The fifteen chapters are entitled as 'Tilo', 'Turmeric', 'Cinnamon', 'Fenugreek', 'Asafoetida', 'Fennel', 'Ginger', 'Peppercorn', 'Kalo jire', 'Neem', 'Red chilli', 'Makaradwaj', 'Lotus Root', 'Sesame', and 'Maya'. All these spices are produced in India to a great extent. Chilli, cumin, coriander, turmeric and ginger constitute 75 percent of the whole spices produced in India. Divakaruni's way of narrating story and describing every minute detail regarding the Indian and Indianised ways of life in the novel is commendable. Her description of all the magic and all the spices and what can be prepared from all those spices leave readers' stomach churning for food.

Sister of My Heart, published two years after *The Mistress of Spices*, is the story of two Indian girls, Anju and Sudha. This is an intensely rich and complex novel with its virtual tapestry of plots. As for its representation of India and the Indian ways of life in both India and the West, it shows the usual patriarchal dominance, cultural conflicts, and traditionalism of the Indian society. The girls narrate their stories in alternating chapters. Anju and Sudha, the two cousins, were born twelve hours apart in the same house. The novel depicts the inseparable relationship of two women who share everything they need from their life—friendship, love, respect, council and support. The novel is complex in its plot and reveals the underlying tension between the two generations. The mothers of these girls embrace the traditional concepts and Indian culture but the girls are captivated by the western mindset and way of life. The feminist bonding of the duo is put to a crucial test when they are physically separated by their arranged marriages and encounter challenges in their personal lives.

As already mentioned, the highly traditional and conventional marriage rituals of India are presented in *Sister of My Heart*. Divakaruni's reflections on the preparations of Indian wedding are meticulous. In addition, she has wonderfully interspersed her narrative with the vivid particularity of detail on the exotic Indian cuisine to show the variety and rich culture of India in a unique and magnificent way. The female protagonists are shown in the novel turn to each other once again for support, sustenance, solidarity and friendship, despite the distance between them. In fact, women in Divakaruni's novels, feel trapped in cages because of the limitations put on them by the Indian society, and they are always subordinated by/to men. In her 1999-novel, the novelist—other than dealing with the usual concerns of Indian English diasporic novels, including *in-between-ness*, cultural confusion, identity-crises, hybridity/mimicry, and rootlessness—has also presented two different images of India, On the one hand, she has portrayed the typical and traditional Indian concepts: the dowry system, toxic in-laws and abusive husbands; and, the other hand, she lays stress on the consciousness-raising of the female protagonist.

Seemingly a step away from the familiar diasporic writings, *The Palace of Illusions* is an exquisite retelling of world-famous Indian epic, the *Mahabharata*. Divakaruni shows that the Indian myths are not mere fables, and that they, *in fact*, contain moral instructions to lead life in a 'good way'. Jaya Prasad, in *Myth and the Indian English Novel*, considers 'myth' as:

> "[...] [a] way of living, loving and learning. It is a way of life. It tries to channelise human energy, focus human attention, govern human relationship and coordinate human interaction, that is, guide human life in general. Myth, in reality, is actually a part of culture and cultural ethos" (14).

The saga is written from the Pandava's wife Draupadi's perspective—Draupadi being also known as 'Panchali'. The narration gives the readers a new, feminist interpretation of life and its ways from the outlook of Draupadi, and it also brings in certain historical perspectives. The novel, in fact, traces the life of princess Panchali, beginning from her childhood to an adolescent girl who has her own perspectives and outlooks. She has the spirit to ask questions against patriarchal concepts, and she is shown to be on a quest to reclaim her birthright. The novel, while attempting to portray the traditional ways of life in India, also, as a kind of exception, depicts her struggles to balance in her married life with her five husbands. Panchali, in Divakaruni's description, is a fiery female who knows to manage life even in the worst conditions—for example, during the period when she, with her five husbands, go through the years of exile and face the civil war and its consequences. Divakaruni has taken one of the fundamental pieces of Indian literature—she focuses on the story of Panchali and links it to the life of Indian females.

The novel *Oleander Girls* depicts India through the eyes of 'Korobi Roy', the young and vivacious protagonist. The story revolves around the young girl from a distinguished and conventional Bengali heritage who falls in love with a rich businessman in Kolkata. The novel is set in 2002, in the fraught world of post-9/11-U.S.A., and during the February-March 2002-*Godhra Riots* in Gujarat. In an interview published in *The Wall Street Journal* (which is presently available on https://www.wsj.com/articles/BL-IRTB-18217), Divakaruni remarked that '*Oleander Girls* was one of the most difficult novels as she was trying to write', and that it is 'the story of an individual—Korobi—in a way that mirrors a particular juncture in the life of a country, India'. The novel, as already stated, deals with the story of Korobi, an orphan girl who has had been parented by her grandparents. Her world shatters when, on the day of her engagement, she gets to know about her real father. By leaving everything she starts her journey to the West in search of her father and her quest of real identity. In between, Divakaruni presents various scenes from Indian life, and explores the issues of Indianness and indigenousness.

The Forest of Enchantments—published in 2019—is the retelling of the great Indian epic, the *Ramayana*. The novel has been written in Sita's perspective, and is, actually, Sita's feminist version of the epic. As an Indian woman, the novelist is highly inspired by the Indian mythological stories, particularly Indian epics, the *Ramayana* and the *Mahabharata*. She explores the rich but patriarchal socio-cultural heritage of India and its history in the novel, which especially focuses on the self-awakening and self-identity of Sita. Relieving-ly, the contemporary Indian writers, including Divakaruni, have changed the traditional portrayal of women, and are increasingly presenting them as self-reliant and courageous women. This is altering the picture of India, gradually. In Divakaruni's novel, though Sita is the narrator of the story, and, yet, other mythologically-important women have been also given the space to share their sufferings and hardships—the voices belong to Urmila, Ahalya, Mandodari and Surpankha.

Divakaruni's latest novel *The Last Queen*, published in 2021, deals with the story of Rani Jind Kaur's life. In this novel, Divakaruni has delved deep into Indian history to unearth the story of a forgotten heroine, Rani Jind Kaur (1817-63), the youngest and most favourite queen of Maharaja Ranjit Singh

(1780–1839). Maharaja Ranjit Singh was a leader of the Sikh Empire, and is considered by numerous socio-historians to be one of the braver and more efficient rulers of the 19th century India (Kirpal). Divakaruni's narrative, while portraying snippets from the 19th-century Indian life, forefronts Rani Jind Kaur's predicaments, her rule, her English-supervised-imprisonment, and her exile. In Divakaruni's novel, after numerous betrayals and deceit, Jind Kaur's five-year-old son Duleep Singh (1838-93) inherits his father's throne. The story is about an unbreakable bond between a mother and her child. The book is written in four parts—'Girl', 'Bride', 'Queen', and 'Rebel'—and each chapter is named after the central themes of the biography-based novel.

Divakaruni, in several of her novels, show how long years fume in anger, conspire, and grieve in vivid detail. In addition, one could observe that many of her characters are grounded in the South-Asian America diaspora. Their identities and interpersonal relationships as friends, lovers, companions, family members and citizens have universal ramifications and pivotal significance. They together serve to present different pictures of the late-20th and early-21st-century India.

A celebrated woman novelist of the India diaspora like Chitra Banerjee Divakarani deftly, in her novels, deploys a wide gamut of survival strategies as she comes forward to resist being crushed down by the powerful forces of alienation. She has wonderfully recreated the system that will assist her in sustaining and surfacing amidst the pressures extended by the hostland and dominant culture. Her reinventions of icons of her own religion, belief, myths therefore serve as sorts of 'defence mechanisms' in her life (Vijayshree 135). They also complete her picture of the 21st-century India.

Focussing on Divakaruni's concern with the diasporic existence, Indian life and its *Indianness*, and her own feminism, Vijayasree succinctly writes in *Survival as an Ethic: South Asian Immigrant Women's Writing*:

"Migration and relocation may be better conceptualised as cases of rupture and disjuncture crisis. [In Divakaruni's novels] [,] [t]his rupture and crisis acquire an extra edge of urgency and pungency in the case of gentle immigrants because for them diasporic living entails double distancing/double exile. [...] It is this sense of perpetual *elsewhere-ness* that steadily reinforces the woman's need for survival and self-preservation" (131).

Women writers of the Indian diaspora have steadily emerged on the literary scene with their lived experiences. Divakaruni adds her own perspectives on Indian life to these 'lived experiences'. It is time for reader and critics alike to realise that theories of diaspora are moving slowly away from abstractions to concretised empirical evidences (including snippets of life in the host nations and back in home countries), with a specific focus on gender and class. Divakaruni's poignantly-brilliant poem, "Yuba City School" (first published in *Indivisible: An Anthology of Contemporary South Asian American Poetry*, 1993, pp. 54-56), is worth mentioning here. Habituated with the welcoming reception back at homeland—which Divakaruni routinely describes in her novels—the speaker of the poem, a working-class-immigrant is really hurt to sense the discrimination being meted out to her son at school, and she resolves to meet the teacher: "Tomorrow in my blue shirt I / Will go / To see the teacher, my tongue / Stiff and swollen / In my unwilling mouth, my few / English phrases".

In diasporic novels by the Indian writers in English, the so-called 'Longing for Homeland'—as present, perceptively, in the indignant mother of Divakaruni's poem— usually stems out of a sense of dislocation of people who migrate to a foreign land, where it is quite natural to undergo the experience of a *lack of belonging*. Needless to say, Divakaruni had similar first-hand experiences as an immigrant woman and mother in the hostland. Her consequent 'longing' probably leads her to depict India and *Indianness* in such vivid details in her various novels. This also acts as a kind of 'defence mechanism'.

Works cited:

"*Culture and Tradition*: Rudiments of Chitra Banerjee Divakaruni's Novels". *Edubirdie* 18 March 2022. Accessed on 20 October 2022 <https://edubirdie.com/examples/culture-and-tradition-rudiments-of-chitra-banerjee-divakarunis-novels/>

Divakaruni, Chitra Banerjee. *Arranged Marriage: Stories*. New York: Anchor Books, 1995.

---. *The Mistress of Spices*. New York: Anchor Books, 1998.

---. *Queen of Dreams*. New York: Anchor Books, 2005.

---. *The Palace of Illusions*. New York: Doubleday Broadway Publishing Group, 2008.

---.*Oleander Girls*. London: Penguin Books, 2013.

---. *The Forest of Enchantments*. New York: HarperCollins Publishers, 2019.

---. *The Last Queen*. New York: Harper Collins, 2021.

Kirpal, Neha. "Interview: 'Current Generation can be inspired by Rani Jindan Kaur's qualities', says Author Chitra Banerjee Divakaruni". *The New Indian Express* 21 February 2021. Accessed on 20 October 2022 <https://www.newindianexpress.com/lifestyle/books/2021/feb/21/interview-current-generation-can-be-inspired-by-rani-jindan-kaurs-qualities-says-authorchitra-baner-2266081.html>

Prasad, Jaya. *Myth and the Indian English Novel: A Critical Study*. New Delhi: Prestige Books, 2017.

Shekar, Sujata. "Chitra Banerjee Divakaruni: Sisters and Spices". Guernica 3 August 2015. Accessed on 20 October 2022 <https://www.guernicamag.com/sisters-and-spices/>

Vijayasree, C. "*Survival as an Ethic*: South Asian Immigrant Women's Writings". In Diaspora: Theories, Histories, and Texts. Ed. Makarand Paranjape. New Delhi: IndiaLog Publications, 2003. 130-40.

'The Forgotten Voices'
Indian Indentured Women in Select Diasporic Novels

— Amrit Sen

The abolition of slavery and the continued rise of a vibrant sugar industry in the British colonies introduced the experience of indenture to hundreds of thousands of Indian labourers. Popularly known as 'coolies', these displaced migrant labourers have subsequently formed a sizable proportion of the Indian diaspora. The demand for a community of indentured labourers spurred the colonial administration to encourage the migration of women across categories of caste and class. This paper looks at archival and fictional representations of Indian women indentured labourers to ask a series of questions. Why did they migrate? Did the migration offer them any agency, or did it merely replicate the structures of power? How were these women viewed within the discourse of Indian nationalism? In probing these questions, I shall use archival documents, fictional biographies and novels including Amitav Ghosh's *Ibis Trilogy*, Abhimanyu Unuth's *Lal Pasina* (2010) and Peggy Mohan's *Jahajin* (2008).

The demand for sugar had increased by leaps and bounds with the proliferation of colonialism. In the ten-year period between 1825 and 1835, the demand increased almost three times from GBP 217,397 to GBP 648,548 (Teelock 71). The surge of sugar prices, fuelled by this unprecedented rise in demand, provoked the colonial government to generate more production. With the increase of heavy machinery to crush the sugarcane plant, cheap human labour was in great demand and the abolition of slavery added to the crisis. The tropical sugar producing countries had hostile conditions and labour mortality rates were extremely high. As Teelock points out:

> "The extent to which sugar is cultivated in the different sugar colonies is generally speaking a more accurate index of the mortality among the slaves. In the colonies where the soil is more prolific and where sugar is grown more abundantly, it is proved by the returns of the slave population that the death far exceeds the births and the number of slaves is consequently in a course of rapid diminution." (48).

The colonial government thus urgently needed a way to recruit more hands and the system of indenture came into being. The labourer entered into a contract of bond with the government agreeing to work for a minimum time period (generally five years), extendable by mutual consent for specific wages. In most cases, harsh penal codes were imposed for breach of contract, thereby favouring the plantation owner. This notion of agreement generated the word 'girmitiya' (a distorted version of agreement) to refer to these labourers. The labourer was required to carry his ticket issued by the colonial government on his person at all times. While the wages were higher than their Indian counterparts, the labourers found that higher living costs meant that they were consigned to misery. This meant that they virtually became slaves by another name, ruthlessly exploited by the plantation owners. Thus, Marina Carter points out that indentured labourers "occupied a narrow space between the white plantation and black peasant societies belonging to neither but relational to both" (Carter5). Most of the people who travelled were illiterate and poor and had little access to the *Office of the Protector of Immigrants*. The process started in 1834 with the arrival of 36 'coolies' but the numbers rose phenomenally. Government statistics reveal that British Guyana received 239, 000 migrants, Mauritius 450,000, Natal 150,000and Trinidad 240,000labourers. The other islands where they travelled included the French Caribbean, Fiji, and Jamaica, among others (*Indenture from Prejudice to Pride* 27).

The coolies travelled from all across India. Close to 40 percent of the entire group was from Bihar, 31 percent from the

Madras Presidency and only 9 percent were from the Bombay Presidency. The remaining 20 percent travelled from Uttar Pradesh and Bengal. They frequently travelled across the Ganges to Kolkata, from where they boarded indenture ships. Of the total migrants, a fourth was women. Most of these people were fleeing from poverty and were from the belonged to the lower castes; most of them were also illiterate. While some men did manage to record their experiences the voices of the doubly marginalized women have been largely absent. Ramabai Espinet comments on the 'phenomenon of invisibility' of Indian women in diasporic fiction "because no novelist had been able to regard her existence [...] and give voice to the peculiarities and perceptions of that particular existence" (Espinet 2008).

The reasons for such rapid migration varied. The rise of indigo an opium trade by the East India Company had already wreaked havoc on the peasants, generating a massive internal migration. Women were doubly oppressed with poverty and harsh social customs like 'sati'. In Amitav Ghosh's *Sea of Poppies*, the protagonist Deeti becomes the subject of predatory advances by her brother-in-law, Chandan Singh, once she is widowed. Chandan plans to burn her as a 'sati' to usurp her land and she is rescued from the pyre by the lower caste Kalua whom she accepts as her husband. Fleeing from society Deeti and Kalua join the 'girmitiyas' and are transformed to Aditi and Maddow Colver in their new identities in Mauritius. Ironically before this event Deeti had speculated about the trauma that a *girmitiya* would undergo in leaving the homeland:

> "How was it possible that the marchers could stay on their feet? She tried to imagine what it would be like to be in their place, to know that you were forever an outcaste; to know that you would never again enter your father's house; that you would never again enter your father's house; that you would never again your father's house; that you would never again throw your arms around your mother; never eat a meal with you brothers and sisters; never feel the cleansing touch of the Ganga. And to know that for the rest of your days you would else out a living on some wild, demon-plagued island?" (*Sea* 80).

Often widowed women preferred to be a 'girmitiya' rather to withstand the harsh realities of widowhood as Parbotia Rai in the novel (240). Women constrained by unhappy marriages also joined the 'girmitiya' parties as the figure of Heeru who runs away from her abusive husband arguing "Had he perhaps intended to abandon her all along, seizing any opportunity that arose? Certainly he had berated and beaten her often enough in the past: what would he do if she returned to him now?" (243). Peggy Mohan's *Jahajin* (2008) tells the story of Deeda who left her village in Basti with her four old son, Kalloo, to escape the famine which had hit her village. She travels to Faizabad where she meets the *arkatti* who promises her a year's contract in Chinidad (Trinidad) at inflated wages.

However, a major section of the 'coolies' were also duped by the middlemen or 'arkattis', who tricked them by false promises that they would be taken for pilgrimage to mythological lands like *Mareechdesh* or *Ramdesh*. In numerous cases, relatives abandoned these women or sold them to the 'arkattis' and human trafficking became rampant. As Marina Carter notes:

> "A widow trying to find her way back to her parents' village after a quarrel with her mother-in-law met a recruiter on the road. All her jewellery was bundled in her scarf and she had a son with her. The recruiter stole the jewellery and put her on the coolie depot. Phuljharee a high caste widow lost her son. The recruiter promised to help but instead took her to the depot" (Carter 15).

In few cases, women also went to the colonies in case they had relatives already working there. The case of Duffadari Banoo is interesting—having being tricked by an 'arkatti', she herself became one and recruited more women. Amitav Ghosh narrates the multiple motivations in *The Sea of Poppies*:

> "Ratna and Champa, sisters, married to a pair of brothers whose lands were contracted to the opium factory and could not support them; rather starve they had decided to indenture themselves—whatever happened in future, they would at least have the consolation of a shared fate. Doolharee was another married woman travelling with her husband: having long

endured the oppressions of a violently abusive mother-in-law, she considered it fortunate that her husband had joined her in escape" (241).

For the colonial government, the presence of such migrants was crucial. The restless plantation workers had to be settled and communities had to be established with social structures of the mainland being replicated. In 1842, women were only 12 percent of the total migrant population, but by 1859, the number had increased to 50 percent, of which 15 percent were widows. However, most of these widows were either middle aged or young, since the 'arkattis' preferred women who could work. Although the planters initially resisted the influx of women as unproductive labour, they soon realised the value that they brought for settling the men and soon all the plantations had colonies of migrants representing a mini-India.

Interestingly, the other substantial category of women who migrated comprised of prostitutes. With the *Contagious Diseases Act*, prostitutes were often criminalised for passing on sexually transmitted diseases. They saw the opportunity of migration to erase their past and forge a new identity for them. However, this meant that a bulk of women migrants were often branded as prostitutes as substantiated by the protector of the Madras Depot:

> "As to the so-called single woman, many of them are prostitutes, others are kept women, and the remainder after entering the depot in almost every case attach themselves to some man they meet there. No female of good character emigrates, except with her husband, father or some very near relation" (qtd. in Carter 27).

The women who travelled were doing so under extreme conditions of vulnerability. On the ship, they were often raped by the male 'coolies' and the crew. When they arrived at the depot, they could be randomly assigned to men who had applied for wives. One such application by a male coolie is illustrative:

> "Being in want of a wife and having led to believe that there are many Indian women lately arrived without husbands, I beg that you will be good enough [...] to facilitate me in getting one as I find the impossibility of

getting any breakfast cooked in the morning [...] and to take care of my orphan children" (*ibid*. 64).

Jahajin narrates the back-breaking nature of the work and the angry outburst of the overseer, "Go back to work! Don't skylark! Strip cane. Make bundles. Move on" (Mohan 24). Epidemics like malaria and dengue often swept the barracks. Single women were often accosted on the field by European plantation owners and ruthlessly exploited. Not only were they subject to harsh physical labour, the condition of gendered oppression of the women was replicated in the indentured *bustees*.

While the vulnerabilities existed, indenture was also often liberating. Most of these women had faced severe oppression and patriarchal violence in the mainland; some even had flirted with death. Indenture offered then alternative identities and the possibility of a new birth along with new relationships and allegiances. Once they were on the ship, they were casting aside all earlier identities and they were merely 'jahaji bhais' and 'jahajibehns'. The first of the cultural units in which social relations were resisted and renegotiated—the ship and the passage becomes chronotopic—it produced a site where earlier priorities where largely lost and a new socialization was created. Social interactions during these lengthy sea voyages began a process that led to remarking of cultural and ethnic identities, to a critical self reflexivity of the kind missing from the stratified and less mobile institutions of the homeland. *Jahajin* narrates the traumatic journey by ship and the singing of popular songs by Bhojpuri women that "floated off like we used to at night on the boat with the words [...] lapping like tiny waves against the barrack walls" (Mohan 67).

Yet, by the end of the journey many of these women saw this journey as liberating. As Deeti thrillingly realises, the voyage offered her and her compatriots a rare degree of freedom from the sufferings of their earlier life:

> "From now on and forever afterwards we will all be ship-siblings jahazbhai's and jahazbehans to each other, there will be no difference

between us ... not in a lifetime of thinking Deeti knew would she have stumbled upon an answer so complete, so satisfactory and so thrilling in its possibilities. In the glow of the moments, she did something she would never have done otherwise: she reached out to take the stranger's hand in her own. Instantly, in emulation of her gesture, every other woman reached out too, to share in this communion of touch [...]. It was now that Deeti understood why the image of the vessel had been revealed to her that day when she stood inversed in the Ganga: it was because of her new self, her new life had been gestating all this while in the belly of this creature, this vessel that was the Mother-Father of her new family, a great wooden Mai-bap, an adoptive ancestor and parent of dynasties yet to come: here she was, the Ibis" (112).

Deeda too has a similar epiphany in Jahajin: "At that moment it suddenly came to me, as clear as the sky, that I was never going back, that I would live and die across the kala-pani". (Mohan 7). It is also interesting to note how Mohan handles the elements of folklore in *Jahajin*. The stories of Sada Brij and Saranga with the fantastic elements of the 'urankhatola' (flying-carpet) underline the flight of the migrant and the nostalgia for homeland and the people left behind. A sense of folklore often helped the migrants cope with the trauma of displacement by linkage to traditional journeys of exile.

The women could often choose new partners in the immigration depots, the ships and the plantations and this offered them a power that was erstwhile denied to them. In *Sea of Poppies*, Heeru a young girl accepts a partner arguing that "Bhauji they say in Mareech, a woman on her own will be torn apart [...] devoured [...] so many men and so few women [...] can you think Bhauji what it would be like, to be alone there [...] Yes I'm ready" (Ghosh, *Sea* 440). As Deeti speculates "Had they been at home, the match would have been inconceivable- but over here, on the island what would it matter [...]. Surely all the old ties were immaterial now that the sea had washed away their past" (*ibid*. 431). Even at the time of disembarking or at the plantation they could change partners thereby increasing the potential of choice. Critics have debated whether this choice entailed a greater agency for indentured women. Peter Emmer has argued for this case feeling that India women "could emancipate themselves from illiberal, inhibiting and very hierarchical social system in India" (Emmer 195), and his idea is supported by Rhonda Reddock when she argues "women could now on their own accord leave one husband for another or have a parallel relationship with another man" (Reddock 83).

While this is true to a certain extent, there were restrictive structures to such behaviour. The replication of Indian community laws within the *bustee* meant that such behaviour was restricted; besides the threat of rape loomed large over women in general. Women also faced the same problem of domestic abuse from their partners. However, women with their wages certainly wrested economic freedom, also added to their income from growing vegetables (Poynting 135). Niranjana, thus, concluded that indentureship, within the structures of hard labour enabled a different sort of accession to the modern for the subaltern diaspora than what was consolidated in India during the late-nineteenth and early-twentieth centuries (64). Women also played an important role in preserving the cultural ethos of India and the shrines of Shiva, Hanuman and Kali Mayi indicate how the Indian women maintained their allegiance to the mainland culture. The presence of the older nurses, who cared for the children while the women were working, meant that they had a degree of freedom from the normal chores of household work. Women also formed their own networks and support systems. Deeda in *Jahajin* reveals the formation of the networks of support among women who often took the young arrivals under their care and often acted as midwives during their pregnancy. The jahajibehn thus promoted a "poetics of resistance and agency but also a poetics of coalition [...] building with other women of colour" (Mahabir and Phirbhai 140).

The differing perspectives of women's prospects have been represented in two different fictions. In Amitav Ghosh's *Ibis Trilogy,* Deeti escapes to Mauritius to create a shrine where she etches the major in a rock in her own personal shrine. For Ghosh,

Mauritius offers Deeti the potential for a matriarchal society that is quite unlike her household in the mainland. Her arrival and subsequent consolidation of property in the mainland elides over the vigorous account of labour and hardship. The Hindi Mauritian novel, *Lal Pasina*, offers a largely different account. Tracing the lives of two generations of diaspora, it is a ruthless account of beatings, labour, rape, disease and sickness. Unnuth uses a Mauritian song to make his point; *"Ramji ki tune chus li meethiyan/ Humre khatir chod gayi seethiyan ho Rama"* (You have sucked the sugarcane dry of its sweetness/ And left the dry waste for us) (85). The *Birha* (song) on which the story is based calls upon accounts of scarring by violence:

> "O Lord of the sugar estate! Why are you exhausting yourself now? Hold on to your whip. Stop it. My back is full of slashing marks. There is no place left on it for any print. What's the use of tiring yourself by slashing in vain?" (*Slices* 21).

The 'bitter sugar' generates plantations where women are oppressed alike by colonisers and their own countrymen, consigned to hard labour inside and outside the domestic space. Indian *bustee*s are seen largely as closed communities largely cut off from other diasporic communities like Chinese or Creoles. Women face unprecedented violence in these societies and the elderly widows often face destitution and suicide. Marina Carter points out that younger widows had the possibility to choose newer husbands, elderly women had high rates of suicide if they were widowed Pansah, a sixty year old woman threw herself in the Riviere Profonde. Tetaree, aged forty, drowned herself unable to watch her sickly husband. Mariam Chikory drowned herself because she was crippled (Carter 156). The colonial government often offered these destitute women free passage home, but very few survived. Illiterate women were also at the mercy of the Protector and his officials — they could often be cheated of their rights, inherences and wages at will. There are accounts of women who thrived on their single status, moving from one man to another. The ship surgeon on board The Nimrod noted the case of one such woman who amassed cash and jewellery and she moved about like the Queen of Sheeba (*ibid.* 52). The case of Daya Kisto, a rich widow is interesting. She built a temple after being widowed, pointing to the fact that through successive generations diasporic women had access to both wealth and land. With the arrival of Arya Samajis in the twentieth century, certain social structures of relief also emerged destitute Indian women.

The Indian indentured women interestingly became a focal point in the nationalist discourse. C.F. Andrews castigated the colonial administration arguing that Indian woman was totally disempowered in the sugar plantations "it has been proved that as far as Indian women are concerned, indenture is a form of legal prostitution" and that Indian women were like "rudderless vessel moving from one man to the other" and that coolie barracks were often like 'kasbighars' (qtd. in Lal 58). The case of Kunti, a widowed woman fired the nationalist imagination. In 1913, she was threatened with rape by a white planter and committed suicide to protect her honour. The nationalist outrage was summarised by Mohandas Karamchand Gandhi's associate Totaram Sanadhya, who categorised her as Sita and the compared the British to Ravana in their oppression of indentured women. Kunti was valorised by Bharat Mitra as the ideal of Indian womanhood: "we cannot refrain from admiring the patience, bravery and strength shown by Kunti. In spite of being of the cobbler caste she has surpassed many well to do ladies by her courage" (ibid. 65). A protesting Sarojini Naidu led a delegation of Indian women to Lord Chelmsford to brief him howas "women we have felt the misery and shame of our sisters of the colonies as if they were our own" (ibid. 66). With sustained pressure, the colonial government decided to cancel all 'coolie' contracts from 1919.

The trauma of departure, labour, settlement and the battle to win rights was an integral part of Indian indentured labourer. Women shared this trauma and were often victims of double oppression—from the process of indenture and by their own fellow male migrants. Their stories have largely remained unrepresented; yet within these parameters many of them used the structures indenture to escape from oppressive patriarchal norms, forged new identities to eke out a living and to search for new partnerships. As they gathered economic rights, it was often women who established a degree of control over their own destinies. It was through their efforts that Indian customs, family structures were preserved and it was in their songs that cultural values were preserved, leading to the hyphenated diasporic identities. The silent history of these women is gradually being rewritten by their descendants and fiction writers alike as they urge us to excavate their silent histories.

> "There are no headstones, epitaphs, dates
> ... They lie like texts
> Waiting to wither by children
> For whom they hacked and ploughed and saved
> To send to faraway schools" (Dabydeen 35).

Works cited:

Carter, Marina. *Lakshmi's Legacy: The Testimonies of Women in 19th Century Mauritius*. Mauritius: Editions De L'Ocean Indien, 1994.

Dabydeen, David. "Coolie Odyssey".*They Came in Ships: An Anthology of Indo-Guyanese Prose and Poetry*. London: Peepal Press, 1998.

Emmer, Paul. "The Importation of British Indians into Surinam 1873 - 1916". *International Labour Migration: Historical Perspectives*. Ed. S. Marks and M. Richardson. London: South Temple, 1984.

Espinet, Ramabai. "The Invisible Women in West Indian Fiction". *World Literature Witten in English*. 29.2, 1989. pp. 116-126.

Ghosh, Amitav. *The Sea of Poppies*. New Delhi: Penguin, 2008.

---. *The River of Smoke*. New Delhi: Penguin, 2011.

---. *The Flood of Fire*. New Delhi: Hamish Hamilton, 2015.

Indenture: from Prejudice to Pride. Souvnir Magazine. 180th Anniversary of the Arrival of Indentured Laboureres in Marituus. Mauritius: ApravasiGaht Trust Fund, 2014.

Lal, Brij. V. "Kunti's Cry: Indentured Women on Fiji Plantations".*Indian Economic and Social History Review* 22 (March, 1985): 55-71.

Mahabir, Joy and Mariam Phirbhai. *Critical Perspectives on Indo-Caribbean Literature*. New York: Routledge, 2013.

Mohan, Peggy. *Jahajin*. New Delhi: Harper Collins India, 2008.

Poynting, Jeremy. "East Indian Women in the Caribbean: Experience, Image and Voice". *Journal of South Asian Literature* 21.1 (Winter and Spring, 1986): 133-80.

Niranjana, Tejaswini. *Mobilizing India: Women, Music, and Migration between India and Trinidad*. Durham: Duke University Press, 2006.

Reddock, Rhoda. *Women, Labour and Politics in Trinidad and Tobago*. London: Zed Books, 1994.

Teelock, Vijaya. *Bitter Sugar: Sugar and Slavery in 19th Century Mauritius.* Mauritius: Mahatma Gandhi Institute, 1998.

Unnuth, Abhimanyu. *Lal Pasina.* New Delhi: Rajkamal Publications, 2010.

---. *Slices from a Life: Memoirs of a Great Author from Mauritius.* New Delhi: Diamond Pocket Books, 2018.

Curry Nation/Carry Nation
Indian Diasporic Cuisine

—Indrajit Chattopadhyay

"If Britain once colonised India, India has now returned the favour by watching spellbound as its food completely colonised Britain".
—Jaffrey (6)

Derived from the Greek words *dia* ('through') and *speirein* ('scatter'), the term 'diaspora' was originally used to refer to the shared experiences of exile and displacement of the Jewish communities who maintained their unique sense of identity while relocating themselves at different parts of the world (ref. to Brah 178). With time, the term has acquired wider significance and has been adapted to describe the dislocation and relocation of various races / communities across the globe. A remarkable feature shared by the Diasporic communities is a nostalgic sense of belonging to the homeland from which they have immigrated. This shared sense of belonging is being celebrated by the diasporic group through different cultural practices. Culinary culture—cooking and food habits—is one of the most prominent areas of establishing such Diasporic identity in the settled land. Food is a potent signifier that works, in a plurality of ways, to form the identities of the self, the sect and the nation. But at the same time, an equally interesting tendency to acculturate to the new culture and eating habits of the adapted country is also being marked. Since food is a seminal marker of cultural identity, food studies have undergone a sea change and have emerged from 'scholarship lite' to an integral part of cultural studies. As the present article intends to focus on Indian Diasporic cuisine and food culture, the foremost thing that should be kept in mind is that, like India herself, the Indian diasporic community encapsulates cultural, ethnic and religious pluralities. As India is not merely, as the title of Chetan Bhagat's 2009-bestseller goes, 'Two States' but many more which have their unique foodways which are, in turn, readjusted according to the socio-cultural situation of the settled community and the availability of ingredients there, any effort of understanding Indian Diasporic cuisine in homogenous terms may lead us to a 'boiling cauldron' of disputes.

If we try to understand the complexity of the Indian diaspora in chronological terms, this demographic dislocation could be categorised, according to Sudesh Mishra, in two phases: the old 'sugar' diaspora of forced migration to plantation colonies like Fiji, Mauritius, Trinidad, Guyana and South Africa between 1830 and 1917, and the new 'masala' diaspora of voluntary exile in thriving metropolitan centres of Europe, Australia, United States of America, and Canada after the Second World War (276). But Diasporic dislocation could be more complicated than this simple categorisation. For example, the writer of the culinary-memoire *The Settler's Cookbook: A Memoir of Love, Migration and Food*, Yasmin Alibhai-Brown is a Ugandan Asian Muslim whose parents decided to migrate from pre-independent India to the then East Africa where she was born. After a few decades of peaceful life, the tyranny of Idi Amin practically compelled her family to migrate to Britain where she has settled now. There are innumerable Indian Hindu Bengalis who, or their parents, had been forced to leave their home at East Pakistan, which later became Bangladesh, and take refuge and settle in India. Many such Indians are now settled abroad. Even now, the aged among them, grow nostalgic about their childhood days spent at 'home', in Bangladesh.

The dislocation, travel and relocation of the diasporic community run parallel to a similar translocation of food which is closely related to memory, nostalgia and a sense of identity. The images of cooking, serving and consuming food are instantly being called to mind as the migrant yearns for the home left behind. Therefore, along with the literary texts which are replete with references to cooking and consuming, such as Githa Hariharan's *The Remains of the Feast* (1993), Anita Desai's *Fasting, Feasting* (1999), or Kamila Shamsie's *Salt and Saffron* (2000), the cookbooks, like Madhur Jaffrey's *An Invitation to Indian Cooking* (1973), *Curry Nation: Britain's 100 Favourite Recipes* (2012) and culinary memoirs like Shoba Narayan's *Monsoon Diary: A Memoir with Recipes* (2003), also become prime foci of food studies. And at the same time, "[M]igrant or mobile food [...] carries multiple significations of home [....]. In representing or remembering a particular Indian food or meal being prepared, the pull of nostalgia is strong; yet the [culinary] texts [...] problematise the notion of a static, authentic dish/memory that can be recreated whole. Nostalgia makes way for adaptation and an acknowledgement that food is provisional, always on the move and that recipes are not perfect" (Bryden 24). In fact, back in 1994, Homi Bhabha rejected the ideas of 'original' identity and 'originary' home in his *The Location of Culture*. He argued in favour of a "terrain for elaborating strategies of selfhood ... that initiate new signs of identity, and innovative sites of collaboration, and contestation" (Bhabha 2). He insisted on seeing identity as a process of negotiation and articulation. And in the cases of voluntary exile the feeling of nostalgia is mixed with the desire of not practically returning to that homeland which exists only in imagination. As Salman Rushdie narrates in *Imaginary Homelands*, the experience of his actual visit to his old, emigrated house in Bombay (now Mumbai), he expresses such a mixed feeling: "It may be that writers in my position, exiles or emigrants or expatriates, are haunted by some sense of loss, some urge to reclaim. [...] But if we do look back, we must also do so in the knowledge [...] that our physical alienation from India almost inevitably means that we will not be capable of reclaiming precisely the thing that was lost; that we will [...] create fictions, not actual cities or villages, but [...] imaginary homelands, Indias of the mind" (10). In the cases of forced exile, the nostalgia remains, without the hope of return to the lost paradise. The Hindu diasporic community that has been forced to relocate from East Pakistan (now Bangladesh) to India, mostly to West Bengal, since the partition of India in 1947, consists of such people to whom I would like to return later.

For those writers of the Indian cookbooks who have willingly settled abroad, a similar 'imaginary homeland' factor could be detected. The New York-settled actress-and-food-writer, Madhur

Jaffrey (b. 1933), for example, writes in the 'Introduction' of her autobiographically designed recipe book *An Invitation to Indian Cooking*: "It was when I was twenty and went to England as a student that I started to learn how to cook. I was extremely homesick, and this homesickness took the form of a longing for Indian food" (6). Thus Indian food mediates between the author and her home 'back there'; a homesickness and nostalgia that could only be felt when one leaves the country, arrives on an alien shore that one gradually starts calling 'home' and then rues for the home 'back there'. Jaffrey's endeavours to cook and serve 'authentic Indian food' in a country where 'authentic Indian ingredients' are either unavailable or not preferred, construct that 'imaginary homeland' where she not willing to return. Study of diasporic cuisine helps us to understand the formation of this kind of identity which is plural, negotiable and complicated. Parallel to the discussion on diaspora in terms of nostalgia and homesickness, a fascinating aspect of the diasporic existence is the settler's *looking around* in the new homeland, instead of *looking back* to the lost homeland with rueful rumination (Sarkar 9). It is curious to note here that this cultural adaptation may go to such an extent that the diasporic culture could even 'eat' the host culture. The popularity of *Chicken Tikka Masala* in England, for example, is worth pondering over in this context: the item is an unauthentic Indian recipe which had never existed in India and was crafted in Britain to satiate the palate of the white Britons. It was first prepared by a Bangladeshi chef in an Indian restaurant, and the anecdote that is being circulated regarding its genesis, goes like this—as an Englishman was being served *Chicken Tikka*, a traditionally dry, spicy preparation of meat, the angry diner demanded to know where the gravy was in the dish ordered by him. To pacify the customer sahib, the intelligent cook readily whipped up a sauce made of tomato-soup, cream, and some spices. Thus *Chicken Tikka Masala*, popularly referred to as the *C.T.M.*, was born and by now it has already made history in terms of demand and supply. The English consumer market has legitimised the *C.T.M.* as an 'English' dish, and in 2001, the-then English foreign secretary, Robin Cook, claimed the *C.T.M.* to be

'England's national dish' (Mannur 3-4). While Robin Cook's assertion of the *Chicken Tikka Masala* as 'England's national food' is an effort of glorifying the English national character "for its ability and willingness to 'absorb' from and adapt the culinary histories of its immigrants and formerly colonized subjects", Anita Mannur explains in *Culinary Fictions: Food in South Asian Diasporic Culture*, how it tactfully avoids mentioning "the very conditions of colonialism that brought Indians to Britain, and the conditions of race and class [,] [...] which made it necessary for [...] [the] immigrants to [...] [make] Indianness palatable to Western tastes" (*ibid.* 4).

Archaeological evidence dates the history of Indian cuisine back to the days of Indus valley civilization as preserved vegetables and cereals which were used 5,000 years ago are now being found (Rogobete 30). Through the long process of evolution variety has always been a characteristic feature Indian cuisine which incorporates not only geographically determined North Indian, South Indian or North-Eastern cuisines, but also culturally rooted Mughal, Chinese, Goan, Chettinad, Bengali, and many more which are often lumped together blandly as 'Indian'. Therefore, it is really "difficult to define an authentic and unique *Indian cuisine*", where 'bread' itself comes in such a variety as 'roti', 'paratha', 'loochi', 'nan', 'kulcha', 'bhatura', 'chapati' and many more (*ibid.* 30-31). Dean Mohamed's *Hindostanee Coffee-House* was the first Indian—in fact, South Asian—restaurant in England that catered mainly to the white Anglo-Indians during 1810-12. Via its menu and décor, the restaurant presented a fantasised, exotic, and oriental image of India and addressed to the English imperial culture. Following the same motto, established in 1927 by Edward Palmer, an Englishman with Anglo-Indian lineage, *Veeraswamy's* remains one of England's older existing restaurants. Simultaneously, a more rustic food culture emerged as result of increased migration from the subcontinent. By virtue of the royal charter the East India Company monopolised commercial exploitation of India's wealth and capital. For this business the English shipping industry employed innumerable seamen from British India, to be precise from Sylhet. These Sylhetti seamen were traditionally known as 'lascars'. Gradually Company's responsibility and commitment to these lascars dwindled roughly around the *Sepoy Mutiny* of 1857 and they were compelled to take shelter in the lodging houses established by former lascars and other migrants. Popular Indian restaurants in England started emerging; they provided not only cheap food but accommodation and served as places of social gathering and camaraderie among the migrants undergoing hard times (Highmore 7-13). In the twentieth century, the number of Indian migrants, coming mainly for study, from diverse geo-cultural locations, steadily increased and the influx multiplied after the Second World War. Indian eating houses were slowly but surely becoming popular among the English who were not related to the *British Raj* and were feeling attracted to the concoction served in the Indian restaurants. Although the growth of Indian restaurants was initially restricted to certain areas of Britain yet some key features could be marked in these establishments which have by now undoubtedly proved themselves to be the markers of socio-cultural change. Owned exclusively by men, managed by underpaid staff that had to do overtime duties at no extra payment, in unhygienic conditions, these restaurants served at cheap rate only those Indian items (like *Chicken Tikka Masala* and *Balti Chicken*) which had become part of the English food-culture. Significantly enough, such establishments also played the role of community certres for socio-cultural as well as ethnic groups. The role of Bangladeshi restaurants during the *Bangladesh Liberation War* of 1971 could be mentioned in this context. London's Southhall became the ghetto of the people from India's Punjab who started selling *Paratha* (fried flatbread), *Aloo Gobi* (a traditional potato and cauliflower preparation) and *lassi* (Punjabi yoghurt drink). 1960s' and the 1970s' saw the arrival of a clan of Indian immigrants (a considerable section of them Gujarati businessmen with their families) from Africa compelled to relocate due to rise of violent nationalism and leaders like Idi Amin. While the journey of these eateries started with the imperial nomenclature of 'Indian' restaurants, the non-entity of *an authentic Indian cuisine* was gradually felt by the host culture, and by the

1980s *Good Food Guide* started categorising Indian food in terms of 'Tamil', 'Gujarati',' Bengali' and such regional cuisines (ibid. 20).

While these restaurants were exclusively male owned, Indian diasporic cuisine was also undergoing sea-change at the household of the Indian settlers whose kitchen was a territory of the women of the family. Their memoirs and recipe books re-visit the regional authenticity of Indian dishes. Since the targets of these cookbooks are considerably different from the Sylehtti-lascars, one could easily notice a keen interest in authenticity, culinary nostalgia and a gastronomic re-creation of the 'imaginary homeland'. The famous (female) Indian chef-and-cookbook-author Balbir Singh's *Indian Cookery*, published in 1961 by *Mills and Boon*, was the ground-breaking work that started the long tradition of Indian cookbooks written for the English and the Indians living in England. The recipe books of Madhur Jaffrey's furthered this tradition, in the West, of focusing on the exclusivity of regional Indian food with the publication of her *An Invitation to Indian* Cooking (1973, in the U.S.A.) and in 1982, her establishment of *Bombay Brasserie* (at London) that started dishing out authentic regional Indian food to the English commoners satisfactorily. In the 'Introduction' to *Madhur Jaffrey's Curry Nation*, she tells us about her journey from a student who was compelled, for certain reasons, to cook Indian food at home, to a *food diva* who is now credited with introducing the West to Indian food. She begins by defending her efforts of serving, through the cookbook, the 'authentic' and yet distinctly regional flavours of Indian food which, she regrets, are unavailable to the Americans: "I begin to feel a familiar upsurge of guilt and patriotic responsibility [...] someone had to let Americans know what authentic Indian food was like and that I couldn't heartlessly ignore their curiosity and interest" (*Invitation* 4). This "upsurge of guilt and patriotic responsibility" could also be read in the light of what Partha Chatterjee has so appropriately reminded us in the context of India's nationalist struggle for freedom. While men were busy reconstructing the outer, political world, "[t]he home was the principal site for expressing the spiritual quality of the national culture, and women must take the main responsibility of protecting and nurturing this quality. No matter what the changes in the external conditions of life for women, they must not lose their essentially spiritual (i.e. feminine) virtues; they must not [...] become *essentially* Westernised" (Chatterjee 243). The patriarchy-determined 'patriotic' responsibility of conserving and furthering 'the spiritual quality of the national culture' thus goes to the women who must preserve the sanctity of the said culture through their engagement in culinary and such other domestic tradition. During his survey among a cross-section of Diasporic Indians, the 'West-Bengali Americans', to understand the interrelatedness of 'Meals, Migration, and Modernity', Krishnendu Ray found out that for most of respondents, "it is implied that to be a good Bengali, a woman must cook at least one hot ethnic meal every day" (196). But in spite of being a patriarchy imposed role, cooking creates a bond among women (not only diasporic, but women in general) and they emerge as makers of culture through their recipes in an interesting way. Etymologically speaking, the Latin root of the word 'recipe', *recipere*, connotes an act of exchange. Recipes thus, create a culture that is construed out of an act of exchange—verbal or textual. It is in this context that food becomes, as Jon Holtzman has observed, "particularly feminine forms of memory" (370). The process of sharing recipes happens usually between the generations of women in a family or a network of women belonging to the same socio-cultural and ethnic group. Writers of culinary memoires, like Madhur Jaffery's *An Invitation to Indian Cooking*, therefore, not only become the sites of the author's exchange of her own memories with the readers, they also ignite the readers' similar memories that they can exchange with others. Madhur's childhood days at Delhi, visit to her mother's house, the elaborate meals there, her memories of making pickle—all have unmistakable reverberations that many of her readers share with not only the author but other friends and relatives. Thus recipes are often encoded with and surrounded by shared stories that define a particular culture.

But Diasporic cuisine is not only about looking back; it is also about looking around and more significantly perhaps, looking forward. It is marked by a desire to adapt and assimilate in the settled land. Both the ingredients and the method undergo sea-changes—the use of canned tomatoes instead of the fresh variety and the use of gas burner instead of coal fire are two such examples about which Madhur Jaffrey talks in the 'Introduction' of her *An Invitation to Indian Cooking* (6). While cooking 'Chana Masala', a regular Indian dish of spiced chick-peas, the Indian communities living in the European countries, Australia, or the United States of America, generally use tinned chick-peas, instead of the raw variety that they used to soak overnight and cook slowly at home before frying it with onion and a mixture of spices. Among these spices the *desi* 'Garam Masala' is often substituted by all spice powder. Sometimes such gastronomic adjustments take the form of more individualised form of experimentation, as was done during the advent of the *Chicken Tikka Masala*. In a way, that signalized a trend in the diasporic communities—fusion cuisine which has elaborated itself over the decades and is now a distinct phenomenon of Diasporic cuisine. Literary works of the Indian diaspora, dipped in culinary flavours also replicate this hybridity. In Bharati Mukherjee's *Jasmine*, for example, such experimentation with food becomes the protagonist's way of connecting herself with the Americans and their culinary culture: "I am subverting the taste buds of the Elsa Country. I put some of last night's *matar panir* in the microwave. It goes well with pork, believe me" (Mukherjee 19).

Another nostalgic culinary appropriation opens Jhumpa Lahiri's *The Namesake* as Ashima Ganguly stands in her kitchen "combining Rice Krispies and Planters peanuts and chopped red onion in a bowl. She adds salt, lemon juice, thin slices of green chili pepper, wishing there were mustard oil to pour into the mix …. [which was] a humble approximation of the snack sold for pennies on Calcutta sidewalks" (Lahiri, *Namesake* 1). Ashima's yearning for *Jhal Muri* has been instrumental in this 'approximation', as it was impossible for her to acquire all the necessary ingredients of the original recipe; it at once reminds her of her home and pushes her to adapt to her present situation.

This crossover across culinary cultures has been explained by Yasmin Alibhai-Brown in her memoir in a philosophic way: "Our food bears testimony to this dynamic existence—creative, sometimes impertinent and playful blends ... forever in flux ....[O]ur food is constantly updated, adapted , altered, recast" (Alibhai-Brown 16). The cultural blockades and the resultant crises faced by the immigrant, forms the core of Lahiri's story "Mrs. Sen's", belonging to her Pulitzer-winning collection of short stories, *Interpreter of Maladies*. The story could be read in terms of how food and eating habits constitute the ideas of racial identity, belonging and alienation in a foreign culture. The eponymous Mrs. Sen is uprooted from her culture, family and friends through her marriage with a university teacher who teaches at New England. To fight out her loneliness, she starts babysitting eleven-year old Eliot, a White American boy. During the long hours of the day she spends with Eliot, we get a scope to understand, through Eliot's eyes, the "semiotics of diaspora. The behaviour and activities that signify what is perfectly homely and desirable in India, turn awkward and asocial in the States. The signified changes with the change of culture and place though the signifier remains unchanged" (Chattopadhyay 160-61). Hence, Mrs. Sen's offering snacks to Eliot's mother who comes to pick him up every evening creates embarrassment for the latter, although the former does not find anything unusual in it. Mrs. Sen's obsession with buying, cooking and consuming fish appears to weird Eliot as is her way of handling the Bengali kitchen-knife:

> "He especially enjoyed watching Mrs. Sen as she chopped things, seated on newspapers on the living room floor. Instead of a knife she used a blade that curved like the prow of a Viking ship, sailing to battle in distant seas. The blade was hinged at one end to a narrow wooden base. The steel, more black than silver, lacked a uniform polish, and had a serrated crest, she told Eliot, for grating. [...] While she worked she kept an eye on the television and an eye on Eliot, but she never seemed to keep an eye on the blade" (Lahiri, *Interpreter* 114).

Mrs. Sen's efforts of acculturation starts with Eliot but unfortunately, soon comes to a jolting halt as Mrs. Sen, a novice in driving, hits a pole with Eliot in tow. No one is hurt but the bond between the two worlds is snipped. Eliot's mother takes him out of Mrs. Sen's custody and she has to go back to her exiled entity that reminds one of John Keats's portrayal of the plight of the Biblical Ruth in "Ode to A Nightingale": 'the sad heart of Ruth, when sick for home, / She stood in tears amid the alien corn' (Keats 212). "Mrs. Sen's" tells the story of those immigrant Indian women who stay indoors and are burdened with maintaining traditions of 'home' back there. Later, in an interview with the *Newsweek International,* Lahiri revealed that the protagonist of this story was created in the shade of her mother who came to the United States in the 1960s' under more or less similar circumstances: "one character is based on my mother who babysat in our home. I saw her one way but imagined that an American child may see her differently, reacting with curiosity, fascination, or fear to the things I took for granted" (Patel 60).

While talking about Indian Diasporic cuisine in terms of variety and cross-cultural reciprocation of cooking and food habits, it should be kept in mind that India itself has such a huge range of geographical and cultural diversity, and an amazing history of co-existence of such numerous "imagined communities", to use Benedict Anderson's oft-quoted (Anderson 6) term, that there are a number of diasporic cuisines *in India*. The Syrian Christians and the Parsi Zoroastrians are the two diasporic communities settled in India who have maintained their distinct culinary identities. Back in A.D. 52, Christianity was introduced in Kerala (and in India) by St. Thomas, one of the twelve disciples of Jesus Christ. St Thomas' followers are known as *Thomasine Christians* or *Syrian Christians* whose cuisine shows a unique combination of strong Western influence along with local spices and cooking methods. Along with roast and stew, their menu also includes items like *Molee, Mappas* and *Appam*. During the Christmas, special fish-delicacies like *Meen Molee*, *Meen Vevichathu*, and *Karimeen Mollechathu* are prepared by using fresh fish, coconut, tamarind, and red chili, which are essential ingredients of this cuisine[1]. On the other hand, the migration of the Parsis was the result of the Islamic victory over the Zoroastrian Sasanian dynasty approximately 1,200 years ago. A group of expatriates came to coastal areas of Gujarat, seeking refuge. They were named 'Parsi' as they were people from 'Paras', an ancient name of Persia. Interestingly, the story of their settlement (known as 'Quissa-e-Sanjaan'), being allowed by the local ruler Jadi Rana, is linked with gastronomic metaphor. Rana sent a tumbler full of milk in response to the appeal of seeking refuge, implying that the settlement was full with local people and hence there was no space for outsiders. The chief of the migrants dropped some sugar into the milk which absorbed it quickly. The message was clear. The Parsis settled, flourished and scattered through India through their skill and dedication. Parsi delicacies like *Dhansak* (mutton with a mixture of lentils and vegetables, served with caramelized rice), *Patra ni Machchi* (fish fillets wrapped in banana leaves) or *Lagan nu Custard* (custard with the flavor of nutmeg) have now been known widely through India and non-Parsis are also taking delicious interest in them[2]. The Hindu diasporic community forced to relocate itself from East Pakistan (now Bangladesh) to India, mostly to West Bengal, since the partition of India in 1947, is another such community whom I have mentioned earlier. Although the once-emigrated Hindu Bengali settled in West Bengal and the domiciled Hindu Bengali of West Bengal broadly share the same Bengali cuisine, they have sharp reservations regarding each others' culinary habits. Coming from erstwhile East Pakistan, referred commonly as 'East Bengal', the immigrants got the pejorative identity marker—'Bangal'— from the hosts of West Bengal whom they greeted with the *return-gift*: 'Ghoti'. 'Bangal' and 'Ghoti' cuisines, their culinary preferences and taste buds, are so distinctly different that they even the same fish—*Ilish* (that is, *Tenualosa ilisha*)—is being prepared by them in radically different ways while the cooks of each clan keep claiming that theirs' is the authentic recipe.

I started with the diasporic journey of Indian cuisine and the sea-change it underwent. This circumnavigation should come to an end from where it began. Indian cuisine has continued its journey overseas through the decades and the tradition of setting up restaurants, writing cookbooks has its visible effects in the heart and guts of the West. Indian celebrity chef and judge like Vikas Khanna and Maneet Chauhan have continued to win accolades; regular participation of Indians in different culinary competitions has continued to unravel to the West, the charm and delicacy of Indian cuisine in a diasporic context. In the United States blogger and cookbook writers like Kankana Saxena (*Taste of Eastern India*), Nandita Iyer (*The Everyday Healthy Vegetarian*), Richa Hingle (*Indian Kitchen*), Mallika Basu (*Miss Masala: Real Indian Cooking for Busy Living*), Sandipa Mukherjee Dutta (*Bong Mom's Cookbook*) have carried forward the legacy of Mrs. Balbir Singh's *Indian Cookery*. As Vikas Khanna, restaurateur, food writer, the winner of *Michelin Star* and the host of the television-show *MasterChef India*, informs us, "In 2003, there were as many as 10,000 restaurants serving Indian cuisine in England and Wales alone. According to England's *Food Standards Agency*, the Indian food-industry in the United Kingdom is worth 3.2 billion pounds" [3]. Like Indian diasporic food, food-studies has also come across a long way from a trespasser in the field of literary studies to a core area of cultural studies where the syntagmatic study of the 'aroma of spices' meets the paradigmatic study of 'eating culture'.

Notes:

1. "The Mouth-watering Dishes of Syrian Christians in Kerala that everyone wants to taste". *Experience Kerala* 3 November 2019. Accessed on 4 July 2022 <*https://experiencekerala.in/kerala-tourism-blog/the-syrian-christian-cuisine-of-kerala/*>
2. "How Parsis, with Persian roots, flowered in Indian soil". *The Hindu – Businessline* 12 January 2018. Accessed on 4 July 2022 <*https://www.thehindubusinessline.com/news/variety/how-parsis-with-persian-roots-flowered-in-indian-soil/article9730657.ece*>
3. Khanna, Vikas. "Cuisine and Diplomacy". *Government of India (Ministry of External Affairs) – Public Diplomacy* 18 August 2014. Accessed on 4 July 2022 <*https://mea.gov.in/in-focus-article.htm?23938/Cuisine+and+Diplomacy*>

Works cited:

Anderson, Benedict. *Imagined Communities: Reflections on the Origins and Spread of Nationalism*. Rev. edn. London: Verso, 2006.

Alibhai-Brown, Yasmin. *The Settler's Cookbook: A Memoir of Love, Migration and Food*. London: Portobello Books, 2009.

Bhagat, Chetan. *Two States: The Story of My Marriage*. New Delhi: Rupa, 2014.

Bhabha, Homi K. *The Location of Culture*. London and New York: Routledge, 2004.

Brah, Avtar. *Cartographies of Diaspora: Contesting Identities*. New York and London: Routledge, 1996.

Bryden, Inga. "An Aroma of Spices [...] Magnified the Sense of What It Meant to Live in England: Travel, 'Real' Food and 'Misshapen' Identity". *Mapping Appetite: Essays on Food, Fiction and Culture*. Eds. Jopi Nymn and Pere Gallardo. Newcastle-upon-Tyne: Cambridge Scholars Publishing, 2007. 8-27.

Chatterjee, Partha. "The Nationalist Resolution of the Women's Question". *Recasting Women: Essays in Colonial History*. Eds. Kumkum Sangari and Sudesh Vaid. New Delhi: Kali for Women, 1999. 233-53.

Chattopadhyay, Indrajit. "Interpreter of Womanhood: Jhumpa Lahiri's Stories of Bengal and Beyond". *The Postcolonial Woman Question*. Eds. Girindra Narayan Ray and Jaydip Sarkar. Kolkata: Books Way, 2011. 156-63.

Highmore, Ben. "*The Taj Mahal in the High Street*: The Indian Restaurant as Diasporic Popular Culture in Britain". *Food, Culture and Society* 12.2 (2009): 1-31.

Holtzman, Jon. "Food and Memory". *Annual Review of Anthropology* 35 (2006): 361-78.

Jaffrey, Madhur. *An Invitation to Indian Cooking*. New York: Vintage Books, 1973.

---. *Curry Nation: Britain's 100 Favourite Recipes*. London: Ebury Press, 2012.

Keats, John. *Selected Poems*. Harmondsworth: Penguin, 1992.

Lahiri, Jhumpa. *The Namesake*. New York: Houghton Mifflin, 2004.

---. *Interpreter of Maladies*. 6th impression. New Delhi: Harper Collins, 2001.

Mannur, Anita. *Culinary Fictions: Food in South Asian Diasporic Culture*. Philadelphia: Temple University Press, 2010.

Mishra, Sudesh. *"From Sugar to Masala*: Writings by the Indian Diaspora". *An Illustrated History of Indian Literature in English.* Ed. A. K. Mehrotra. 2nd edn. New Delhi: Permanent Black, 2008. 279-94.

Mukherjee, Bharati. *Jasmine.* New York: Grove, 1989.

Patel, Vibuthi. "The Maladies of Belonging". *Newsweek* (Pacific edn.) 20 September 1999: 60.

Ray, Krishnendu. "Meals, Migration, and Modernity". *Food: Critical Concepts in the Social Sciences.* Eds. David Inglis, Debra Gimlin, and Chris Thorpe. Vol. V. New York and London: Routledge, 2008. 170-204.

Rogobete, Daniela. "Sweet Taste of India: Food Metaphors in Contemporary Indian Fiction in English". *Mapping Appetite: Essays on Food, Fiction and Culture.* Eds. Jopi Nymn and Pere Gallardo. Newcastle: Cambridge Scholars Publishing, 2007. 28-51.

Rushdie, Salman. *Imaginary Homelands.* London: Granta Books, 1991.

Sarkar, Sucharita. "Culinary Memoirs of the Indian Diaspora". *Muse India* 65, January-February 2016. n.pag. 28 January 2016 <*www.museindia. com/featurecontent.asp?issid=62&id=5935*>

A Historical Understanding of the National Mores
The Autobiography of an Unknown Indian

—Saptarshi Mallick

Introduction:

In spite of a beautiful blend of subjective and objective elements the literary creations of Nirad C. Chaudhuri (1897-1999) have often rendered him to be an anti-Indian, pro-British individual and a writer as atavistic as was India during the nineteenth century when literary London often considered the writers from the colonies as 'exotic outsiders, solitary figures and objects of curiosity' (Ranasinha 68). He was not a historian but a scholar who was attracted to history through the dynamism of his creativity. These authors were considered to be able to communicate the intricacies of their native culture, embody newness, and possess the entelechy to describe the colonies as well as the British from an exotic perspective. However, different writers from the colonies interrogated this preconceived dominant cultural assumption in their own manner to facilitate the process of an aesthetic translation. Nirad C. Chaudhuri published his memoir, *The Autobiography of an Unknown Indian* (1951) with Macmillan while he was working as a commentator of All India Radio in New Delhi. Through this work he 'discovers himself through India and India through himself' (Rao 64) – a creative reworking of his experiences. It was not accepted as an autobiography but as a piece of work delineating 'contemporary history' through the 'story of the struggle of a civilisation with a hostile environment, in which the destiny of British rule in India became necessarily involved' – a study of 'the conditions of in which an Indian grew to manhood in the early decades of this century' (*The Autobiography* Preface). Though critics have critiqued him for several justifiable disturbing elements in his work, there are certain tendencies like his evoking the sense of place, his humour, his independence of judgement in the teeth of opposition and his phenomenal ability to keep working, which—taken together—are commendable. As one of his better-known books, *The Autobiography of an Unknown Indian*, embodies an impassioned detail description of 'the conditions in which an Indian grew to manhood in the early decades of the 20th century' (*The Autobiography* Preface). Since the expression 'the conditions' entails several overlapping influences—social, cultural and political—Chaudhuri's memoir emerges to be more of national history over personal story where the 'personal is merged into the national', as the author viewed 'in his own microcosm the macrocosm of the whole Hindu ethos' (Karnani). Eunice de Souza is of the opinion that Chaudhuri's *The Autobiography* is 'more of an exercise in descriptive ethnology than an autobiography' ("Nirad C. Chaudhuri" 209). Chaudhuri details the four environments which had an important impact upon his life: Kishorganj, his birthplace and where he lived till he was twelve, Bangram, his ancestral village, Kalikutch, his mother's village and the England of his imagination. There are also references to Kolkata, the Indian Renaissance, the beginning of the nationalist movement, the author's experience of the colonial English arrogance in India which are all presented in contrast to the idyllic constructions of civilisation as 'the greatest civilisation on earth' ("Interview" 7). The author's opinion regarding history, politics and culture that binds a civilisation are all based on certain thematic constructions which seem to pervade his work. In this context we have to remember that Chaudhuri had not visited Britain till he was 57, when he came with the sponsorship of the B.B.C. He moved to the United Kingdom at the age of 73, and settled in Oxford for the rest of his life with his wife. Besides *The Autobiography of an Unknown Indian*, the second volume of his autobiography, *Thy Hand, Great Anarch! India: 1921-57* (1987) is a historical document of his life as a student in Calcutta and as a secretary to the Congress leader, Sarat Chandra Bose. Writing an autobiography is a literary endeavour whose national significance bears witness to contemporary history. As such, Babur's *Autobiography*, Jahangir's *Tuzuk-i-Jahangiri*, Mahatma Gandhi's *My Experiments with Truth*, Jawaharlal Nehru's *An Autobiography*, Rabindranath Tagore's *My Boyhood Days* and

Rathindranath Tagore's *On the Edges of Time* to name a few works whose 'retrospective prose [facilitated towards] the development of [author's] personality' (Lejeune 202).

Nirad C. Chaudhuri's personal history and experiences have also been documented in his books on Indian culture and national history, worth mentioning in this context, as they are a witness to and account of the decline of Bengal, which he considered 'as matched by the failure of British imperialists to bequeath a lasting cultural legacy in India' (Ranasinha 71).

This has enabled him to assert his autonomy and disinterest from his milieu, as autobiography is associated with the idea of the potency of self-identity and separate selfhood (McClintock 313), and it further facilitates the possibility of self-creation, masking the agency of cultural institutions at work in the life history that determines our stories and our selves (*On Autobiography* 192).

An Autobiographical Narration of History:
'The creative clash of two civilisations' (Walsh 52), *The Autobiography of an Unknown Indian* tells the story of the early period of Nirad C. Chaudhuri's life and documents the condition 'in which an Indian grew into manhood in the early decades of this century' (*The Autobiography* Preface). Though Chaudhuri's presentation and interpretation of the history of India establishes his critical insight in association with his subjective approach to the problems of Indian history, society, politics and culture, yet his self-Westernization remained static and lifeless throughout his long career. It is due to his self-Westernization that his sharp and merciless views of post-Independent India in *The Autobiography of an Unknown Indian*, and his hallowing of the 'Timeless England' in *A Passage to England* were received with favour in Britain, however in due time by associating to the 'obsolete notions of 'Englishness' and subscribing to largely discredited imperial ideas' (Ranasinha 72), Chaudhuri progressively subscribed to a system of prolepsis. *The Autobiography of an Unknown Indian* is an Indian's self portrait, mirroring the tortured assertiveness of a scholarly spirit who embraced in his life a uniquely extreme dislocation. *The Autobiography* embodies the perspectives of the author along with

the truth to the text, facilitating a direct access to a clearly visible self—'an intention to honour the signature' (Lejeune 202) by being true to his experiences and their respective honest documentation in his *The Autobiography*.

Verdict: The British/the Indians:
The Autobiography of an Unknown Indian presents us coherent and imaginative portrayal of India's history since all the chapters focus on social and cultural perspectives. Chaudhuri believes that it is the 'unity in diversity' of India that has urged the British to consider the Indians with an attitude of esteem and honour. Indian civilisation is a history of past achievements along with a single community in spite of being 'endowed with multi-racial and multi-lingual culture' as the author puts it, '...the same species as the Homo sapiens historicas of Europe' (*The Autobiography* 442). Chaudhuri's real purpose is to document history through the autobiographical exercise solely as an avenue to get the history inaugurated. Since his early college days he was fascinated with history (Iyengar 591). *The Autobiography of an Unknown Indian* has defied all the vignettes of biography, only to be 'the story of one's life written by one's self' (Mulgan 27). Chaudhuri's aim is neither to depict an autobiographical document, nor to reveal on the surface the various facets of his own self. The book is the author's verdict on the British Raj as well as a virulent attack of the Indians practising poor mimicry of the notion of Western materialistic culture whom Bhabha has described as 'mimic men' and established by Naipaul in his novels. Historical in motive, Chaudhuri points, 'My intention is thus historical […] the book may be considered as a contribution to contemporary history' (*The Autobiography* Preface). Clash between the cultures of the natives and the foreigners took place at mundane levels of existence. Chaudhuri brings in the reference to the incident of 1916, stating how the boys of the matriculation class bowed down to the locomotives as if they were Gods. His interaction with the West was chiefly concerned with the spiritual realm of existence, 'My westernization is of the older pattern, concerned more with the mind than the material things' (Swain 80). In spite of the impact of

the West upon him, the occidental influences upon his psyche were expressed through his consciousness and were manifested through 'culture'. Chaudhuri is of the opinion that the British Empire conferred subjecthood (*The Autobiography* 171) on us at the same time it withheld citizenship (Fanon 38), and the cultural contact was psychologically and imaginatively experienced by him. In Chapter IV of Book I, the author with a perceptive eye has presented the spirit of England as a place agitating the birth of a space out of the mytho-geography from books read and pictures seen and circulated. In his accounts England has been conjured up as one of the shaping forces of his life (Sharma 1066). Chaudhuri states, 'the chiaroscuro of our knowledge of England was extremely sensational' (*The Autobiography* 101), as he aimed to revisit history and the autobiographical overtones become the means to have the matter started, as Iyengar comments,

> "The places that held an influence on Nirad's boyhood, the family antecedents, the cultural milieu, the nationalist Bengal, the cold war between the ruling and the subject races, the city and the University of Calcutta, the coming of Gandhi and the eruption of the new politics of the twenties these many environmental layers receive as much attention as the quirks and quiddities of Nirad's own temperament or the vicissitudes of his childhood, boyhood and youth" (*Indian Writing In English* 591).

'Dependence Complex':
Chaudhuri's voluntary affiliation to English culture and history, especially his passionate support of the British Raj, and his affirmation of India's need for English rule, recalls Octavio D. Mannoni's theory of 'dependence complex' (*The Intellectual* 26). Mannoni states that some races feel the cognitive urge to be dependent and be under imperial rule and this is due to their endurance of an unanswered dependence complex as colonization was 'expected—even desired by the future subject peoples' (Mannoni 86). Chaudhuri's reading of Indian history is biased and it manifests itself in these terms. He emphasizes that India can only progress through British rule. After the Indian independence when the British left India it resulted to a repudiation of their duty towards the Indians they had ruled before the official declaration of the Indian independence (*Thy Hand* 26). Chaudhuri's

observations can be re-viewed from Fanon's criticism of Mannoni's theory and theorization of hostility. Mannoni claims colonial xenophobia to be the result of paltry officials, small traders and colonial ineffectual people, not European civilisation and its foremost agents. Three possibilities have been observed for natives as a ramification of colonisation. The first is assimilation, which also consequences the natives to be unable to connect with their own roots. Secondly, a native can encounter a half-way assimilation where psychological antagonism take place usually concluding in malice directed at Europeans. Finally, no assimilation can take place (Mannoni 24). Fanon emphasizes that if there is any evidence of this complex, then it is the 'pathology of the colonized representing the effect and not the cause' (Ranasinha 80). Fanon states that the colonized subject lives in a society that allows his 'inferiority complex' to evolve and paves the way towards firmness from the bolstering of this complex: 'it is the racist who creates his inferior' (*Black Skin* 84, 85, 93). Chaudhuri ironically vindicates the detraction of imperialism and as Naipaul states with regards to Chaudhuri's *The Autobiography*, 'no better account of the penetration of the Indian mind by the West—and by extension, of one culture by another—will be or can now be written' (*The Overcrowded* 59).

Chaudhuri divides the entire span of Indian civilisation into Indo-Aryan, Indo-Islamic and Indo-European periods and establishes the fact that Indian civilisation in all the three periods has been strongly influenced by foreign civilisation stating that,

> "[...] three of the greatest historical movements have forced their way into India in successive ages and created three different types of civilisation; [...] the civilisations have remained essentially foreign even at the highest point of their development within India and have ceased to be living as soon as they have been cut off from the source, [...] neither political order nor civilisation has come into being in India when a powerful external force has not been in possession of the country" (*The Autobiography* 513).

Due to his zeal for a foreign culture's influence on Indian civilisation, Chaudhuri goes on to say that he expects, 'either the United States singly or a combination of the United States and the British Commonwealth to re-establish and rejuvenate the foreign domination of India' (*The Autobiography* 519). However, Chaudhuri's quest was not for a search of his own identity, as he never lost it or had any doubts regarding it (*Thy Hand* xxviii). His was an assimilation of Western traditions within a Bengali heart to emerge as Bengali humanist. His humanism is evident in his praise for the people and their adherence to equality of existence, where he states,

> "Within the body of citizens there was a remarkable feeling of equality. Being Hindu or Muslim, high caste or low caste, Brahmin or non-Brahmin, made no difference. Being rich or comparatively poor made some, but not much as could make the poorer man feel individiously treated. It was somewhat of a surprise to see a society given entirely over to the business of making money showing such good taste in respects of differences on wealth…we were not snobbish to inferiors either, not even to the sweepers and menials. There was nothing which was looked upon and judged with greater disapproval than the parading of wealth and the expectation of flattery or obsequiousness from men of lower position" (*The Autobiography* 40, 41).

Chaudhuri also refers to the different communities showing respect to each other and their respective sentiments, when he states,

> "If we, who were Kayasths asked Brahmins to dinner (which we did) we had to get the cooking and waiting done by Brahmins; if, on the other hand we asked Muslims (as also we did) we had to engage Muslim cooks and waiters for a Muslim of position too would no more eat at the hands of a Hindu than a Hindu would do at his. But this was a matter which concerned religion, which no body expected to be mixed up with the manners and customs of social life" (*The Autobiography* 41).

The Modernising Tradition:
Chaudhuri refers to William Shakespeare, John Webster, Charles Lamb and even Jane Austen and establishes their work as lucid, inviting a comparative study. His obvious parallelism is noted in his statements regarding *The Iliad* and *The Ramayana*. However, it must be considered that Chaudhuri's lucid prose at times degenerates into hyperboles parading his insular sentiments as, 'if any whole hearted Bonapartist were to be found anywhere in the world at the end of the 19th century and the beginning of the 20th century they were to be found in Bengal' (*The Autobiography* 105). Though there is an attitude of love for the Bengali intellectuals and

literary calibres, yet the author bears a curious mixture of the feelings of love and hatred towards the English people. On the one hand he admires Raja Ram Mohan Roy, who argues for English education in India from 1823 and Bankim Chandra Chattopadhyay and Swami Vivekananda due to their objective criticism of the conservative Hindu culture. On the other hand his account of European history is an epitome for man's struggle for freedom, '[...] fertilising freedom had been enlarged in ever widening circles in the course of modern history' (*The Autobiography* 111). It is therefore important to locate him in the context of modernising tradition within India, and not just as an eccentric Anglophile (Ranasinha 79). Chaudhuri sees himself as an object in a landscape or an impulse in a more inclusive and controlling rhythm and his whole presentation of the self is impressively tranquil and objective ("The Meeting of Language" 115); an intellectual's self that was shaped by the classical ideal of Greece and Rome. As a historian, Chaudhuri was of the opinion that he was an impartial judge of men and events. He is a man who speaking to men about ideas on religion and politics. As objectivity is a significant breakthrough towards a fundamental idea from the historical perspective which is the fountain of the idea of change, Chaudhuri establishes the loss of the distinguished past of India by stating that 'we shall never again achieve anything like the greatness and individuality of the Hindu civilisation [as] that civilisation is dead forever, and cannot be resuscitated (*The Autobiography* 521). He then goes on to praise the British Raj stating, 'None of the poems gave my brother and me greater amusement than those in the dialects including two in the Dorset dialect' (*The Autobiography* 199). This fortifies that Chaudhuri was a different individual by then, someone who had a psychic change through an internalizing of orientalist images by extolling India's past along with the ideas of India's present decay, and consequently the positive force of an imperial civilising mission (Ranasinha 79).

The Synthesis between West and East:
Chaudhuri's admiration and love for England and English literature makes him call Shakespeare 'the epitome, test and symbol

of literary culture' (*The Autobiography* 197). His idea of England was that of 'a country of great beauty [...] which possessed beautiful spots' (*ibid*. 113) which is an effect of a self-conscious detachment from his own culture, time and space, as the early twentieth-century European modernist writers. *The Autobiography of an Unknown Indian* is dedicated to 'The Memory of the British Empire in India' that describes all that was noble and ideal within as moulded and transformed by the Raj in India. Chaudhuri's argument is established 'from the personal standard point, the historical thesis has emancipated him from the malaise that has haunted me [him] throughout the life' (*ibid*. 526). In his view, India has remained static in its appearance in spite of mimicking all that is 'Western'. Chaudhuri demeans that Indian endeavour and this he does vehemently in his text in order to carve out a new culture of the stereotyped East which may be an answer to the binaries that the West constructs and thereby bring in a cultural synthesis. In this context he brings in the reference to the literary creations of Michael Madhusudan Dutta, Raja Rammohan Roy and Bankim Chandra who all contributed to bringing up an East-West cultural assimilation. Chaudhuri's attitude towards the decline of Bengal springs from 'an anxiety of an entrenched but now somewhat beleaguered literati about the effects of democratisation'. This decline of Bengal has been critiqued as one that

> "easily lends itself to a social conservatism that justifies class privilege by dressing it up as a meritocracy and a celebration of the nineteenth-century 'synthesis' of West and East'" (Chatterjee vii),

and Chaudhuri becomes an extreme proponent of this view. Chaudhuri critiques the English for their hostile outlook in comparison to the orthodox Hindus who are believers of bigotry and false practices. In 1951, Mortimer, in the *Sunday Times*, commented:

> "If Mr. Chaudhuri sees nothing good in his country do not imagine that he is indulgent to the English. He speaks with loathing of our superciliousness, cruelty and despotism in the days of the Raj; he is equally severe upon those English who now — always from the lowest motive — express sympathy with India" ("The Square Peg" 3).

John Squire, in addition, wrote,

> "Chaudhuri, a realist, is certainly no indiscriminate belauder of British rule; he has some damning things to say about the attitude of the British communities [...] towards the native inhabitants of India" ("A Bridge Between" 706).

M. K. Naik and R. Parvathy are of the opinion that Chaudhuri cannot be considered as 'anti-Indian' because he has entertained no ambition of hobnobbing with the English in India. Chaudhuri has condemned Indian society when he states that:

> "[...] the Hindu civilisation was created by a people who were actively conscious of their fair complexion in contrast to the dark skin of the autochthons and their greatest preoccupation was how to maintain the pristine purity of the blood-stream which carried this colour. The Hindu regards himself as heir to the oldest conscious tradition of superior colour and the carrier of the purest and most exclusive stream of blood which created that colour. When with this consciousness and pride he encounters a despised [...] [Mlechchha], an unclean foreigner, with a complexion fairer than his, his whole being is outraged. The creature tries to console himself with the illusion that if in this world there is a foreigner fairer than him, it is only because that foreigner is a leper" (*The Autobiography* 129, 130).

William Walsh attempts to refute the charges put against Nirad C. Chaudhuri's Anglophilia by referring to his stringent attacks upon the colonial impertinence of the local British Raj ("The Meeting of Language" 119). Though Chaudhuri had a special fascination for the beauty which is associated with English life — an unmistakable Romantic impression on his mind (Agarwal 29-39) — he could never think of England as he had perceived of Bengal and of India. We remember Chaudhuri's humorous presentation of the Indianisation of the text books that are in English for an easy comprehension for the Indian masses. He sarcastically adds that the British falls from its glory due to 'the bankruptcy of European civilisation, its spiritual poverty and its moral in its inequity.' C. D. Narasimhaiah dismisses him: 'he seeks [...] to placate his western readers' (*Moving Frontiers* 24). A reader for Macmillan observed,

> "It would seem to us difficult to doubt the nationalist feeling of the author of the *Autobiography*, but he has been criticised in India for being too partial to the West, and too critical of his own countrymen" (Watson).

As a result we can deduce that Chaudhuri's criticism arises from a 'desperate concern, rather than from professed and perceived detachment' (Ranasinha 91).

Conclusion:

Through an objective method of history [long disapproved], as advocated by Acton, over Collingwood and Croce,[1] Chaudhuri's presentation of India as a moribund culture which has become stagnant due to the lack of dynamism makes him debunk the Hindu culture. For him, it is 'dead forever and cannot be resuscitated and to hope to create a second civilisation of the same order is for us today a superannuated piece of folly' (*The Autobiography* 521). His is a fiercely independent spirit whose reproval against India and Bengal were not always consciously framed in the context of a colonial perspective, for a colonial Big Other (Almond 170). Chaudhuri believed that all Indian endeavours in imitating the West have been a failure and what one sees is nothing but an immense expense of an Europeanization which has been debased in nature along with the Hindu and Muslim traits for which we are still not in a position to assume ourselves as modern in terms of spirit and temper. Chaudhuri's thesis in *The Autobiography of an Unknown Indian* epitomizes Indian history as consisting of three cycles during each of which 'a strong and creative foreign influence provided by a primary motive force, viz., the mid-European Aryan, the Muslim and the British respectively […] appears very much like an intellectual extension of the wish-fulfilment of self-confessed Anglophile alienated from his own culture' (Naik 265). Therefore, Chaudhuri eulogizes the British love for the actual which he found lacking in Indian civilisation. Through his intransigent severance from his countrymen, Chaudhuri entreats his 'location as an intellectual outside the dominant group' facilitating him 'to be free from ideological constraints or allegiance to any particular national constituency' (Ranasinha 88). Therefore, as a colonial one needs to dissociate one's own self from the amicable and concentrate upon the personal achievement before undertaking the authority for others, which involves endeavouring towards an honest dialogue with her/his own 'undeveloped' society (Rowe-Evans 27). In spite of all the allegations regarding the various biased arguments of the author, it cannot be denied that *The Autobiography of an Unknown Indian* has several merits which outweigh the faults in terms of logic, eloquent style, intellectual overturns and outspoken arguments which make the text a canon in Indian Writings in English. William Walsh considers *The Autobiography of an Unknown Indian* as:

> "one of the finest examples of this genre to appear in English in this century and the most significant, single discursive work to be written by the love and hate of Indian-British relationship" (*Indian Literature in English* 45).

In an interview for the *Times of London*, Nirad C. Chaudhuri is reported to have said, 'People are about half and half, against me and for. Previously all were against me. I know I am extreme. It is like a tug-of-war. I cannot stand up straight or the other side will pull me down. But I *know* my exaggerations' (Iyengar 601). Chaudhuri has reiterated the path of his estrangement and 'intellectual isolation' from the nationalistic overtones championed by his 'countrymen and contemporaries' that, according to him, emerged to be growingly 'impenetrable' (*The Autobiography* 414). Vindicating his alienation, Chaudhuri refers to Max Muller's observations that all Aryans in India are relocated and deranged as colonial Englishmen, because they were themselves immigrants to India (Ranasinha 83). This argument has been further developed by the author in his *The Continent of Circe* where he describes the atrophy of the Aryans in India. The 'Aryan heritage' is indicative of the imperialist communication of the elite, and it forges a parallel way of establishing the associations between the British and the Indians (Ranasinha 83, 84). Nirad C. Chaudhuri's writing is cathartic and his presentation of his alienation is liberating for him as evident when he states, 'my intellect has indeed at last emancipated itself from my country', which has facilitated the dawn of autonomy in him without dislocating or uprooting himself 'from the native soil by sojourn in a foreign country or schooling' (*The Autobiography* 607).

Note:

1. Chaudhuri fails to realise the 'cult of facts' propagated by Collingwood and Croce and the 'objectivity in history' of the type which Acton wanted, is an impossibility because the historian can only view the past through the eyes of the present (Sinha 64).

Works cited:

Agarwal, Nilanshu Kumar. "Burial of the Motherland: A Critical Appreciation of Nirad C. Chaudhuri's *The Autobiography of an Unknown Indian.*" *Pegasus – A Journal of Literary and Critical Studies* III (2004): 29-39.

Almond, Ian. *The Thought of Nirad C. Chaudhuri: Islam, Empire and Loss.* Cambridge: Cambridge University Press, 2015.

Chatterjee, Partha. *The Present History of West Bengal: Essays in Political Criticism.* New Delhi: Oxford University Press, 1997.

Chaudhuri, Nirad C. *The Intellectual in India.* New Delhi: Associated Publishing House, 1967. Print.

---. "Interview." *Everyman.* 26 June 1983. 1-30.

---. *Thy Hand, Great Anarch! India, 1921 – 52.* London: Hogarth Press, 1987.

---. *The Continent of Circe.* Mumbai: Jaico Publishing House, 1996.

---. *The Autobiography of an Unknown Indian.* Mumbai: Jaico Publishing House, 1997.

Dasgupta, Swapan, ed. Nirad C. Chaudhuri: *The First Hundred Years A Celebration.* Noida: Harper Collins, 1997.

de Souza, Eunice. "Nirad C. Chaudhuri." *An Illustrated History of Indian Literature in English.* Ed. A. K. Mehrotra. New Delhi: Permanent Black, 2003. 209-18.

Fanon, Frantz. *Black Skin, White Masks.* Trans. Charles Lam Markmann. London: Pluto Press, 1986.

Iyengar, K. R. S. *Indian Writing in English.* New Delhi: Sterling Publishers, 1985.

Karnani, Chetan. "Nirad C. Chaudhuri and the Continent of Circe." Quest 57 (April-June, 1968): *https://gfgc.kar.nic.in/bilikere/FileHandler /82-a564d2ce-e210-440b-a7ad-46f8da782e6a*

Lejeune, Phillepe. "The Autobiographical Contract." *French Literary Theory Today: A Reader.* Ed. Tzvetan Todorov. Cambridge: Cambridge University Press, 1982. 192-222.

---. *On Autobiography*. Trans. Katherine Leary. Minneapolis: University of Minnesota Press, 1989.

Mallick, Saptarshi. "History, Self-Alienation and A Study of Cultures: Studying Nirad C. Chaudhuri's *The Autobiography of an Unknown Indian*." *Journal of the Department of English, Vidyasagar University* 13.1 (2020): 134-44.

Mannoni, O. D. *Prospero and Caliban: The Psychology of Colonialism*. Trans. Pamela Powesland. New York: Praeger, 1964.

McClintock, Anne. *Imperial Leather: Race, Gender and Sexuality in the Colonial Context*. London: Routledge, 1995.

Mortimer, Raymond. "The Square Peg." *The Sunday Times* 9 September 1951, 3.

Mulgan, John. *The Concise Oxford Dictionary of English Literature*. Oxford: Clarendon Press, 1942.

Naik, M. K. *A History of Indian English Literature*. New Delhi: Sahitya Akademi, 1982.

Naipaul, V. S. *The Mimic Men*. London: Penguin, 1967.

---. *The Overcrowded Barracoon and other Articles*. London: Andre Deutsch, 1972.

Narasimhaiah, C. D. *Moving Frontiers of English Studies in India*. New Delhi: S. Chand and Co. Ltd., 1977.

Ranasinha, Ruvani. *South Asian Writers in Twentieth-Century Britain: Culture in Translation*. Oxford: Oxford University Press, 2007.

Rao, M.V. Chakrapani. "Autobiography as Discovery." *The Two-Fold Voice: Essays on Indian Writings in English*. Ed. D.V.C. Raghavacharyulu, Guntur: Navodaya Publishers, 1971.

Rowe-Evans, Adrian. "V.S. Naipaul: A Transition Interview 1971." *Conversations with V. S. Naipaul*. Ed. Feroza Jussawalla. Jackson: University Press of Mississipi, 1997. 24-36.

Sharma, Meenakshi. "Postcolonial Responses to England: A Passage to England and Delinquent Chacha." *Economic and Political Weekly* 40. 11 (2005): 1063-68.

Sinha, Tara. *Nirad C. Chaudhuri: A Sociological and Stylistic Study of his Writings During the Period 1951 – 72*. Patna: Janaki Prakashan, 1981.

Squire, J. C. "A Bridge Between England and India." *Illustrated London News* 3 November 1951, 706.

Swain, S. P. "*The Autobiography of an Unknown Indian*: A Critique." *Nirad C. Chaudhuri The Scholar Extraordinary*. Ed. R. K. Dhawan. London: Sangam Books, 2000. 79- 89.

Walsh, William. "The Meeting of Language and Literature and the Indian Example." *Writers in the East—West Encounter.* Ed. Guy Amirthanayagam. Basingstoke: Macmillan, 1982. 100-37.

---. *Indian Literature in English.* New York: Longman, 1990.

Watson, Francis. *First Reader's Report on Circe* 28 June 1961.

Home and Memory in the Cross-Border-Musings of Indian Diaspora
A Poetic Survey

—Neha Arora

> "Dislocations can be of diverse kinds: physical, psychological, emotional, political marginalisation, it can be alienation or self-alienation, or social ostracism, or a removal from familiar environments of family, kinship and cultural, it can come through political upheavals, mass migration or natural disaster. It can be individual or collective. But no dislocation is ever complete, terminal or permanent in itself. There is always a looking back in some way or the other. This may be through memory, recollection, history, parallels or differences. Cultural memories have a tendency to surface again and again and establish a connection with the future; they do not allow the individual to snap ties with the past. History governs power relations and intervenes with the construction of the present" (Jain XII).

The above-stated lines form a prologue to the contents of the present paper. The main argument of the author is to bring forth the ceaseless connection and perennial presence of 'Home' in the very existence of a diaspora. Crossing the national borders does in no way cut the umbilical cord; memory is the repertoire of everything left behind, everything desired earnestly. Amongst various variables associated with diaspora, the present paper would engage primarily with the idea of 'home' and 'memory' in the select diaspora Indian poets.

Becoming Diaspora:
It should be accepted without doubts that both, the old and the new diaspora, left the homelands in search of better prospects, and both 'still hanker for their homeland, feel nostalgic and also suffer the pangs of alienation more or less the same way' (Rai 138). While the so-called *first wave* (mid-19th century) of diasporic migration/immigration was due to imperialism—especially, to provide cheap labour to the newly acquired lands, the *second wave* (later half of the 20th century) was a by-product of capitalism and individuals' choice. (*ibid*. 138).

The diasporic immigrants—as it can be perceived—are perpetually (and symbolically) swinging between two spaces: locational as well as cultural; acceptance by the host land and the nostalgia for the homeland. The inherent constant relationship with the homeland creates the metaphor of *trishanku* for the modern diaspora in the third space, with a ceaseless conflict of 'pulls' (of the country of origin) and 'pressures' (of the country of adoption). The construction of cultural identities of diasporas, as Lata Mishra puts it, thus involves a dialogue between "there" and "here", past and future, between heritage and politics (35). In addition, Feroz Jussawalla word-paints a beautiful picture of the diaspora: "We are like 'Chiffon saris'—a sort of cross-breed attempting to adjust to the pressures of a new world; while actually being from another older one" (583).

Understanding 'Home':

> "Homes are not about inclusions and wide open arms as much as they are about places carved out of closed doors, closed borders and screening apparatuses" (George 19).

'Home' has always been the 'centre' in diaspora discourse. In plain terms, 'Home' means emotional attachment to a place, and thus, loss of homeland keeps haunting the minds. Borrowing from Gaston Bachelard's "topophilia" (8), the idea of 'home' can be expanded to refer to the sense of place that is closely connected to one's identity. 'Home' is always present, both, in the literal and in the metaphorical sense, and is directly connected with the idea of 'belongingness'. Referring to Peter van der Veer's argument on "longing" and "belonging", Aparna Dharwadker explains 'Home' as a 'rooted, secure, and established unity, while departure is the disruptive choice that makes change and movement possible' (73). Manpreet Kaur and Sanjaleen Prasad draw on the cultural theories propounded by such U.S.A.-based academicians as Aamir Mufti and Ella Shohat, and argue that 'Home' is often constructed as a place of protection, belonging and comfort; it is where one originates or where one is raised (149). However, to understand 'home' as merely an anchorage, the land of residence/ origin, would be too simple a thing. In fact, the notion of 'home', as Tsagarousianou elaborates, 'is much more complex than approaches to diaspora premised on the power of nostalgia would us believe. It is intrinsically linked with the way in which the processes of inclusion or exclusion operate and are subjectively experienced under given circumstances. It relates to the complex political and personal struggles over the social regulation of 'belonging" (52). Kaur and Prasad list down the myriad interpretations of 'Home', referring to Appadurai problematising the 'dangers of restricting the definition of 'home' only as a secure, unified space of belonging' (148), while Theano Terkenli defines 'home' as 'a physical and psychically shielding domestic residence' (149). In addition, to take up Avtar Brah's perspective, 'the *referent* of *home* [...] [is] qualitatively different [...] [;] *home* in the form of a simultaneously floating and rooted signifier. It is an invocation of narratives of *the nation*. In racialised or nationalist discourses this signifier can become the basis of claims [...] that a group settled *in* a place is not necessarily *of* it' (3).

Losing Home:
Reviewing the issue of presentation of the sense of 'home' in diasporic literature, Friedman emphatically writes, "Home comes into being most powerfully when it is gone, lost, left behind, desired and imagined" (202). The sense of 'Home' permeates every aspect of the diasporic individuals. Very relevantly, Friedman draws on the orthographic homonym by sociologists Roger Friedland and Deirdre Boden to describe the shift in the meaning of 'Home' from 'now here' to 'no where' (*ibid*. 192). She furthers her argument on 'Home' by quoting Janet Zandy that '*home* is an idea, an inner geography where the ache to belong finally quits, where there is no sense of *otherness*, where there is, at last, a community". (1)

Homi Bhabha, in *The World and the Home*, introduced the concept 'unhomely' (141) to express the pain of the diaspora who relocates to a new land but fails to connect with the place and constantly feels nostalgic and alienated. Madhuri Prabhakar begins discussing the pain of the homeless diaspora with poignant lines from Umebinyou and Rupi Kaur:

> "So,
> here you are
> too foreign for home
> too foreign for here.
> never enough for both" (Ijeoma Umebinyuo in "Diaspora Blues"),

and,

> "They have no idea what it is like to lose home at the risk of never finding home again
> have your entire life split between two lands and become the bridge between two countries" (Rupi Kaur, "First Generation Immigrant")

Remembering Home:

'Remembering Home' forms the very bedrock of any diaspora discourse. The notion of 'remembering home' accentuates the yearning for home, as Roger Kennedy rightly points out, '[H]aving a home implies both having a physical entity, the physical structure of the dwelling, the house, but also something that goes beyond the building blocks into the area of the interior of the soul [...] [.] If exiled, we may be able to carry the sense of home with us, yet there is often a poignant yearning for the original home' (12). This urge for 'home' is a means for the diaspora to trace their roots, as Chandrima Karmakar writes, 'Engagement with the idea of 'home' is not merely an intellectual quest for the diasporic Indians. It is an engagement that helps them resolve their existential and identity issues' (80).

Writing Home:

Talking about the consequences of crossing the geographical and cultural borders on the diaspora, Susan Friedman refers to Meena Alexander's "Alphabets of Flesh" (1996) to explain the impossibility of intimacy of the immigrants with the host land: 'assimilation translated into doing well, very well, not just making do. But the streets lined with gold are hard to walk and what happens with the heart can give one pause' (190).

The acute sense of loss of a familiar place, of belongingness, results in the abundance of 'Home' motif in diaspora writings. Friedman believes 'Memory' to be 'the first rewriting of home, an act of re-presentation of what was as the precondition for writing home in the medium of text—the page, the book as the corpus of memory' (*ibid*. 206). However, literature for diaspora writers does not remain a mere imaginary/ creative exercise, a piece of fiction/ art, it in fact is the repository, the store-house of native culture that the immigrants take with them. To speak in native language, to relish the native cuisine, to preserve the native recipes and also the native rituals—literature becomes a complete archive in the hands of the writers. Azade Seyhan rightly writes, "In so far as culture is memory, it is embedded in the past and will have to be retrieved in symbolic action. Memory marks a loss. It is always a re-presentation, making present that which once was and no longer is" (4). So when Jhumpa Lahiri's Mrs. Sen craves for 'local fish', it does not just remain a mere food-item but her roots, her past. By penning down their experiences, the writers attempt to give vent to their pain, thus, as Feuerverger says, 'Writing becomes (is) a means of reclaiming territory' ("My Yiddish Voice", 19) Similar thoughts are echoed by Carole Boyce Davies: "Migration creates the desire for home, which in turn produces the rewriting of home. Homesickness or homelessness, this rejection of home or the longing for home become motivating factors in this rewriting" (113).

Departure from the native culture, the geographical shift from the native place, the pain of loss of home, the prick of isolation, etc affects the individual's consciousness, resulting in some kind of psychological crisis. These form the main thematic concerns of diaspora literature. The present study is an attempt to include some diasporic voices from different generations to discuss the various themes explored in their works, and how each has an underlying echo of 'home'.

The women writers of Indian diaspora have an added variable in their corpus, besides identity crisis in the new land due to dislocation. The heavy content on gender discourse provides an alternative perspective to diaspora literature, by taking the readers into the female world. Some worth-mentioning writers are Suniti Namjoshi (b. 1941), Meena Alexander (1951-2018), Bashabi Fraser (b. 1954), Sujata Bhatt (b. 1956), Chitra Banerjee Divakaruni (b. 1956), Rishma Dunlop (b. 1956), Bhanu Kapil (b. 1968), and Mona Arshi (b. 1970), to name a few. In their respective poetry-collections/ poems, 'home' acquires a different dimension—it becomes family, food, clothes—everything that defines 'comfort zone' to them. For example, in different poetry-collections published by Fraser (presently working as the *Professor Emerita of English and Creative Writing* at Edinburgh Napier University, and as the Director, *Scottish Centre of Tagore Studies*) like *Rainbow Worlds* (2003), *Tartan and Turban* (2004), *From the Ganga to the Tay* (2009), *Ragas and Reels* (2012), and *Letters to my Mother and Other Mothers* (2015)—the sense of 'home' is omnipresent: it is her memories from her 'home' and 'homeland' which comfort the poet when she tries to comprehend the ways of life and the surroundings in the West—in her case, the northern portion of Britain. Carla Rodriguez Gonzalez has particularly appreciated Fraser for her 'attempts to build a literary bridge between Indian and Scotland' (Gamez-Fernandez and Dwivedi 42) through her poems—between the 'host-land' and 'home'. Alan Riach also traces a commendable employment of history in Fraser's poems (Goertschacher and Malcolm 400)—which, obviously, is not immune to her reminiscences of 'home'.

However, to homogenise the writings of these diasporic Indian poets would, again, be a fallacy. So if we have Jhumpa Lahiri's Ashima (*The Namesake*) yearning for the homeland, we also have Bharti Mukherjee's female immigrants who represent what she calls 'cultural mongerlisation' (qtd. in Jha 43). Her women bring the host (U.S.A.) and home (India) together, without compromising with either. Likewise, Rupinder Kaur also discusses the different approach of Chitra Banerjee Divakaruni's and Rishma Dunlop's, towards their host land. She writes about the subtle differences as reflected in their respective poetry, "While Divakaruni objectively assesses her host country and indulges in memories of the homeland, utilising her new experience to assess and weigh up the situation back home, Dunlop accepts and adapts to the life of the host country" (34).

While Divakaruni was already an adult when she left for the U.S.A., Dunlop was just four years old when she went to the new land with her family. She recalls:

> "A curious mix, my cultural education. I am not raised on Indian dance or music... We did not attend a Gurudwara, a Sikh temple, on a regular basis—only if there was a wedding or special occasion. My father did not believe in organized religion but, he was a spiritual man who lived his life according to humanist principles" (*Memoirs of a Sirdar's Daughter*, 127/130).

Chitra Banerjee Divakaruni's women are mostly immigrant due to marriage and therefore they find it all the more difficult to adjust in the new environment which is quite contrary to what they have seen back home. The new world is open, liberating but these women carry the cultural baggage of native traditions and are expected to preserve them and also pass them down to the new generation. Her first collection of poetry, *Black Candle* (1991) is about the women from India, Pakistan and Bangladesh. The collection reads into the condition of women who are forced into an exiled life in the new land. There are many poems such as "The Room", "Gouri Mashima", "Bengal Night", and the likes that evoke the sub-continent's women very vividly. To talk about the fears, apprehensions and insecurity of women who cross the thresholds of the homeland to be with their husbands in the new, strange land, Divakaruni's poems like "The Brides Come to Yuba City", "Yuba City School", and "Restroom" can be referred. Poems such as "The Brides Come to Yuba City" and "Leaving Yuba City" expose the culture of marrying off young brides to unknown older men, who are settled abroad, and it is only after a long wait (may be years together) that the bride eventually gets to see her husband, a stranger, in a strange environment.

Rishma Dunlop's approach is different from that of Divakaruni's. She comes before the readers as someone who has accepted her new life, new world. The collections in the volume *The Body of My Garden* (2002) exemplify the feeling of compromise and acceptance. Her women strive hard to survive; they do not merely crave for the homeland, instead try to get accustomed to the hostland. "Reading like a Girl", the title-poem of the 2004-collection of the same name, gives us a picture of liberated women:

> And when I grew up I became them Nancy and Cherry
> I cut off my long black braids styled my hair into a bob,
> I became the girl detective, the nurse, capable of building
> Nations and soothing the hearts of men for a while.

Dunlop's women are liberated as Bharti Mukherjee's *Jasmine*, whose Americanisation is in no way to be read as anti-homeland. Mukherjee presents acculturation as the idea. Similarly, Dunlop also acknowledges and celebrates the hostland. She writes in *"Memoirs of a Sirdar's Daughter in Canada*: Hybridity and Writing Home" (2018), presently available on *https://www.degruyter.com/document/doi/10.3138/9781442673878-008/pdf*, that "Canada has allowed me an existence of hybridity, shaped by my individual experience and the factors of class, gender, education and circumstance in my life".

Meena Alexander is a case of multi-layered diaspora. Born in India, brought up in Africa, Europe and America, her poetry chiefly portrays the inner mind of Indian women. She writes in her 1993-autobiography, *Fault Lines:*

> "Others had suffered its brutality and were silent. In my years of growing up, from time to time, I was filled with the image of what women might suffer—whether through mutilation or through shame—suffering caused purely by being female. And I felt in a dim, unspoken way that there was a connection between how I came to language and what it meant to be cast out unhoused" (111).

Her experience in the U.S.A. was not comfortable—she faced alienation and fractured identity. As she writes in *The Shock of Arrival: Reflections on Postcolonial Experience* (1993):

> Everything that comes to me is
> Hyphenated. A woman poet,
> a woman poet of colour, a south

> Indian woman poet who makes up
> lines in English, a post-colonial
> language... (193).

Yearning for home and nostalgia can well be sensed in her poems, "Grand Mother's Mirror", "House of Thousand Doors", "Her Garden", and so on. Her diasporic sensibility could be well read in the following lines from her memoir:

> "After all,
> for such as we are the
> territories are not free.
> The world is not open,
> that endless space the emptiness
> of the American sublime to worse
> than a lie" (43).

Talking about nostalgia in Meena Alexander, G. Yamini writes:

> "The acute sense of loss and nostalgia is reflected in the creative output of Alexander. Her desperate feeling of being rootless and the search of anchorage, a mooring compel her to belong somewhere and she finds that anchorage in poetry and calls poetry as place. The creation and migration are closely connected because the migration imposes anonymity, loss of identity on the immigrant. Therefore, the immigrant uses the medium of creation to escape from the situation of oblivion of anonymity to ensure the performance in a changing world. The agony of migration made poet to write survive" (32).

Hessa A. Alghadeer, in "*Exploring Third Space*: Place and Memory in Meena Alexander's Memoir and Poems", thus writes about Alexander:

> "Straddling between cultures and countries, from India, through Sudan, England and America, is a poignant experience initiating multiplicity and dislocation in Alexander's past and present, and consequently reframing both her life and writing career. Against a backdrop of dissimilar geographical territories, Alexander depicts several migratory experiments to convey numerous literary languages expressions of the hybrid languages expressions of the hybrid condition" (86).

Born in 1944 in Amritsar, the Indo-Canadian poet Surjeet Kalsey's poetry is a reflection of women issues, especially who are far away from their comfort zones. Her poem, "I Want My Chaos Back" (1983) brings out the pain caused by the distance:

> "This is a real loneliness
> This is a real barrenness
> ....
> Today I am three thousand miles away
> from throbbing bubbling figurines of
> my flesh.....
> how much I miss their presence....
> how much...the very thought of not being
> with them makes my heart droop" (57).

In her famous poem "Migratory Birds", Kalsey uses the analogy of birds who fly off to different regions in different seasons, but always have 'home' on their minds, to return to:

> "We
> the migratory birds
> are here this season
> thinking
> we will fly
> back to our home
> for sure.
> But
> no one knows
> which invisible cage imprisons us?
> and the flight begins to die slowly
> in our wings" (40).

The hopeless, the desperate urge to come back, the loneliness in the new land is clearly visible in the lines:

> "No sun, no earth/ where to look at, what to look for?....
> How shall we reach the threshold / of our home with crumbling self?" (15-18).

Lakshmi Gill (b. 1943) takes the desolation of Canada a step further and adds a different colour to the understanding of Canada. She is of Indian origin, born in Manila, and settled in Canada—but, to her, Canada is no haven. In her poem "Letter to a Prospective Immigrant", collected in *Returning the Empties: Selected Poems, 1960s-1990s* (1999), she dissuades the prospective immigrant from coming to Canada:

"Don't come naked
In ten years your proud figure will bend like natives hunched under coats.
....
Joy? There is no joy, just a long dull ache
Ice hot (not event pain) of want
They need an orgy, communion, sacrifice, expiation
If you can bring blessings, come then
(don't expect blessings in return);
hell does not give
But takes" (45)

Besides gender and nostalgia, Gill also touches upon the issue of racial discrimination in her poem, "Legacy", also collected in the 1999-publication:

"'She's not white',
complained the Asian Student
to my department head
'Why is she teaching English?'
Unable to teach anything else,
I may have to stop teaching
Unable to speak anything else
I may have to stop speaking
Student's got my tongue" (19).

Himani Bannerji (b. 1942), the octogenarian sociologist from Kolkata (presently settled in Canada) lays bare the issue of racial discrimination in Canada. Her approach to Canada is expressed in her essay *Geography Lessons*:

"'Canada' then cannot be taken as a given. It is obviously a construction, a set of representations, embodying certain types of political and cultural communities and their operations. These communities were themselves constructed in agreement with certain ideas regarding skin colour, history, language (English/ French) and other cultural signifiers — all of which may be subsumed under the ideological category 'White'. A 'Canada' constructed on this basis contains certain notions of nation, state, formation, and economy. Europeanness as 'whiteness' thus translates into 'Canada' and provides it with its 'imagined community'" (qtd. in *The Dark Side of the Nation* 64).

Her poem "Apart-Hate", collected in *Doing Time: Poems* (1986), pronounces loudly the camouflaged 'apart-hate' (playing on the word 'apartheid') practised in Canada:

> "In this whiteland
> Chinese coolies, black slaves, Indian indentures
> Immigration, head tax, virginity tests
> Apart-hate
> ....
> In this whiteland
> Skin is fingered like pelt
> Skin is sold and the ivory of her eyes
> The category human has no meaning
> When spoken in white
> Apart-hate" (46-47).

Alvarez reads Bannerji's Marxist, feminist, and anti-racist perspective in her research paper to validate that "all her [that is, Bannerji's] critical studies are a consequence of what she calls "how I was received in Canada" as a non-white woman" (11). Bannerji does not glorify the image of Canada as a developed nation; on the contrary she illustrates the 'colonial-like' approach of Canada towards the "visible minorities"[1] (12). Studying the immigrants further, Bannerji brings in the gender construct as well. She believes: "Women are thus advised or presumed to be contended with their status of 'non-autonomous, non-bourgeoisie, non-secular personhood'" (*Of Property and Propriety* 56). Alverez explores the usage of "visible minorities" by Bannerji in her poems to delineate the marginalisation and subordination of women; they are defined as "a raced individual manipulated and silenced by the patriarchal community and nation". (15) Bannerji's poem, "Doing Time" summarises her perspective perfectly well:

> "If we who are not white, and also women, have not yet seen that here we live in a prison, that we are doing time, then we are fools, playing unenjoyable games with ourselves" (*Doing Time* 9).

Rupi Kaur (b. 1992) is a young voice from India and settled in Ontario, Canada. Her first poetry-collection *Milk and Honey* (2014) created waves in the literary world. Also noteworthy is her style: there is no usage of upper case, and no punctuation marks. Also, keeping pace with her age, Kaur is publishing her poetry on *Tumblr* and *Instagram*. She captures the pain of the first generation migrants in the image of her mother:

"leaving her soil earth and roots
was not easy for my mother
i still catch her searching for them
in foreign films and
the international food aisle" (Kaur 2014).

The struggle of the immigrant to feel comfortable in the new land cannot be overlooked. But being a second generation writer herself, Kaur also is very pragmatic in giving her readers a picture of the acclimatized/ acculturation:

"my voice is the offspring
of two countries colliding
what is there to be ashamed of
if english and my mother tongue
made love
my voice is her father's words
and mother's accent
what is the matter if
my mouth carries two worlds" (Kaur, "Accent", 2016).

If the women writers in/of diaspora included the gender aspect in their works, the male writers were mostly preoccupied with the various issues of the immigrants. G.S. Sharat Chandra (1935-2000), a poet of Indian diaspora, born in Mysore (and settled, until his death, at the Kansas City, Missouri, U.S.A.), focuses on home, homeland, family, and so on. The titles of his poetry-collection speak of his themes: *April in Nanjangud* (1971), *Heirloom* (1978), *Immigrants of Loss* (1993), and *Family of Mirrors* (1993). He writes about his native place, his country of origin, and also about the pain of leaving the homeland. Basavaraj Naikar writes, "While in India he prepares himself to go to America and while in America, he nostalgically remembers India and corresponds with his father and other relatives" (66). The poems in *Heirloom* vividly bring forth the South Indian life. In "Poems for My Father", the last moments of his father are recounted:

"In the kitchen my father
squats as usual,
the family gathers around
to discuss his last illness,
my father looks well,

> he scoops up the rice and curry
> eats it calmly,
> he too is talking of his illness" (qtd. in Naikar 66).

In another poem titled "Return", G.S. Sharat Chandra describes the experience of a diaspora when he/she returns to his/her homeland and feels the contrast in the weather, the entire environment:

> "At the airport
> The family Fiat
> crackles in the heat,
> the doors are hot
> as the underside
> of an electric iron.
> ....
> The roads to home
> are scant bound as ever
> collies move along the potholes
> with gravel pans on their head
> bullock carts trundle
> in and out the car's wheel-span" (qtd. in Naikar 67-68).

Another very significant poem to be discussed here is "My Thirty-Fifth Birthday" that presents a complete contrasting image of India and America, of his past and present:

> "Inside a touring talkies
> Gandhi himself pointed
> his fingers at me from a slide
> which read
> 'Be worthy of your mother country.'
> .....
> All this
> just because
> until late in the night
> in this American town
> I drank sotch
> and cursed in English" (qtd. in Naikar 70-71).

Agha Shahid Ali (1949-2001) (the famous gay Indian poet who passed away in Amherst, Massachusetts) mourns the loss of the beauty of Kashmir in the conflict-ridden times of the 20th century. The paradise on earth, Kashmir now is just about tensed atmosphere, military presence, curfew, and exodus of Kashmiri Pandits. In "Snow on Desert", Ali's pain becomes quite apparent: "and I had lost, of all/ that I would lose, /of all that I was losing". The changed political topography of Kashmir, the lurking fear is captured in his "Some Vision of the World Cashmere" where he recalls the outhouse his grandmother used to live in, but is now occupied by the army "dust everywhere, on old phones, on damp files, on broken desks" (Ali 188). In Ali's poetry, readers can find the aching heart over the loss of home, but he expands the meaning of 'home' to include the migration of the Kashmiri Pandits from the valley. The wounds caused by such migration are in no way less painful than those caused by leaving the national borders for the Western countries. In "I See Kashmir from New Delhi at Midnight", he talks about this displacement: "By that dazzling light/ we see men removing statues from temples./We beg them, 'Who will protect us if you leave?'/ They don't answer, they just disappear/ on the road to the plains, clutching the gods" (175).

The longing for home can be very intensely read in the poem "Homeless" by Vikram Seth (b. 1952), a trained economist and a bi-sexual Indian poet who divides his time between the U.K. and India. The poem also raises the questions of belongingness, stability and security, when one has no firm roots in either of the lands he/she occupies:

> "I envy those
> Who have a house of their own
> Who can say their feet
> Rest on what is theirs alone,
> Who do not live on sufferance
> In stranger's shells,
> As my family has all our life,
> And as I probably will" (*The Collected Poems* 112).

Daljit Nagra (b. 1966), a second-generation Indian Sikh poet based in London, explores the idea of home in his innovative style of writing in *Punglish* (a mix of Punjabi and English). His debut book of collection of poetry, *Look We Have Come to Dover!*, was released in 2004. This collection 'connects to the experiences of British-born

Indians caught up in the 'double-ness' of their lives' (Prabhakar 1). He blatantly comments upon the racial discrimination against the Asians in the U.K.:

> "Swarms of us, grafting in the black within shot of the moon's spotlight, banking on the miracle of the sun— span its rainbow, passport us to life. Only then can it be human to hoick ourselves, bare-faced for the clear.
>
> Imagine my love and I, our sundry others, Blair'd in the cash of our beeswax'd cars, our crash clothes, free, we raise our charged glasses over unparasol'd tables East, babbling our lingoes, flecked by the chalk of Britannia!" (Nagra 32).

Himself a second generation immigrant, Nagra is well aware of another significant problem that troubles this generation—feeling ashamed/ uncomfortable of their parents' incompetency on English language and English lifestyle. He discusses this tension in the poem "In a White Town":

> "She never looked like other boys' mums.
> No one ever looked without looking again
> at the pink kameez and balloon'd bottoms,
> mustard oiled trail of hair, brocaded pink
> sandals and the smell of curry. That's why
> I'd bin the letters about Parents' Evenings,
> why I'd police the noise of her holy songs,
> check the net curtains were hugging the edges,
> lavender spray the hallway when someone knocked,
> pluck all the gold top milk from its crate
> in case the mickey-takers would later disclose it,
> never confessing my parents' weird names
> or the code of our address when I was licked
> by Skin-heads (by a toilet seat)
> desperate to flush out the enemy within.
> I would have felt more at home had she hidden
> that illiterate body, bumping noisily into women
> at the market, bulging into its drama'd gossip,
> for homework—in the public library with my mates,
> she'd call, scratching on the windows. Scratching again
> until later, her red face would be in my red face,
> two of us alone, I'd strain on my poor Punjabi,
> she'd laugh and say I was a gora, I'd only be freed
> by a bride from India who would double as her saathi.
> Nowadays, when I visit, when she hovers upward,
> hobbling towards me to kiss my forehead
> as she once used to, I wish I could fall forward" (Nagra 2007).

Reconstructing Home:

The above discussion attempted to read the various facets of "Indiannes" that exists in the disapora of every generation—the meaning and yearning may vary, but its presence cannot be denied, as Amba Pande rightly describes Diasporas as "the transnational communities wedded to host lands and profoundly connected to homelands" (59). The porous borders and hypermobility of the present times bring about cultural interaction and not just cultural schizophrenia, and through the select voices in the paper, the researcher has attempted to explore the various dimensions of 'home' and 'memory'. Though the idea of 'home', as the "most common formulations of the concept of geographical place associate it (home) with stasis and nostalgia, and with an enclosed security" (Massey 167), it is equally important to have a wider understanding of 'home' in the changing times. The inclusion of the new generation voices in the paper is deliberate to establish the fact that "[...] the diasporic South Asians are not merely assimilating to their host cultures but they are also actively *reshaping* them through their own, new voices bringing new definitions of identity" (Kuortti 6).

Note:

1. Referring to the 'non-whites'—in the 30th page of Himani Bannerji's *The Dark Side of the Nation*.

Works cited:

Alexander, Meena. "Alphabets of Flesh." *Talking Visions: Multicultural Feminism in a Transnational Age*. Ed. Ella Shohat. Cambridge: M.I.T. Press, 1998. 149.

---. *Fault Lines*. Toronto: Penguin Random House Canada, 1993.

Alghadeer, Heesa A. "*Exploring Third Space*: Place and Memory in Meena Alexander's Memoir and Poems". *International Journal of Humanities and Social Science* 3. 20 (December 2013): 86.

Ali, Agha Shahid. *The Veiled Suite*. New York: W. W. Norton, 2009.

Alvarez, Maria Laura Arce. "*Too Visible*: Race, Gender and Resistance in the Construction of a Canadian Identity in the Poetry of Himani Bannerji". *Miscelanea: A Journal of English and American Studies* 36 (2007): 11-23.

Appadurai, Arjun. "*Global Ethnoscapes*: Notes and Queries for a Transnational Anthropology." *Recapturing Anthropology: Writing in the Present.* Ed. Richard Gabriel Fox. Santa Fe: School of American Research Press, 1991. 191-210.

Bachelard, Gaston. *The Poetics of Space.* Boston: Beacon Press, 1964.

Bannerji, Himani. *The Dark Side of the Nation: Essays on Multiculturalism, Nationalism and Gender.* Toronto: Canadian's Scholars Press, 2000.

---. *Of Property and Propriety: The Role of Gender and Class in Imperialism and Nationalism.* Toronto: Toronto University Press, 2001.

---. *Doing Time.* Toronto: Sister Vision, 1986.

Bhabha, Homi K. "The World and the Home." *Signs: Journal of Women in Culture and Society* 32. 32 (1992): 141-53.

Brah, Avtar. *Cartographies of Diaspora: Contesting Identities.* New York and London: Routledge, 1996.

Davies, Carol Boyce. *Black Women, Writing and Identity: Migrations of the Subject.* New York and London: Routledge, 1994.

Dharwadker, Aparna. "Diaspora, Nation, and the Failure of Home: Two Contemporary Indian Plays". *Theatre Journal* 50.1 (March 1998): 71-94. *JSTOR* <https://www.jstor.org/stable/25068484>. Accessed on 3 June 2022.

Divakaruni, Chitra Banerjee. *Black Candle.* Corvallis: Calyx Books, 1996.

Dunlop, Rishma. "Memoirs of a Sirdar's Daughter in Canada: Hybridity and Writing Home". *Diaspora, Memory, and Identity: A Search for Home.* Ed. Vijay Agnew. Toronto: University of Toronto Press, 2005.

---. *Reading like a Girl.* Windsor-Ontario: Black Moss Press. 2004.

Feuerverger, Grace. "My Yiddish Voice." *Journal of Curriculum Theorising* 16. 4 (2000): 19.

Friedman, Susan Stanford. "*Bodies on the Move*: A Poetics of Home and Diaspora". *Tulsa Studies in Women's Literature* 23. 2 (Autumn 2004): 189-212. *JSTOR* <http://www.jstor.com/stable/20455187>. Accessed on 3 June 2022.

Gamez-Fernandez, Cristina, and Veena Dwivedi (eds.). *Shaping Indian Diaspora: Literary Representations and Bollywood Consumption away from the Desi.* Lanham: Lexington Books, 2015.

George, Rosemary Marangoly. *The Politics of Home: Postcolonial Relations & Twentieth-century Fiction*. Cambridge: Cambridge University Press, 1996.

Goertschacher, Wolfgang, and David Malcolm (eds.). *A Companion to Contemporary British and Irish Poetry, 1960-2015*. Hoboken: Wiley-Blackwell, 2021.

Jain, Jasbir. "Introduction". *Dislocations and Multiculturalism*. Ed. Jasbir Jain. Jaipur: Rawat Publications, 2004.

Jha, Gauri Shankar. *Indian Diaspora: Women English Writers*. Jaipur: Yking Books, 2013.

Jussawala, Feroz. "*Chiffon Sari*: The Plight of Asian Immigrants in the New World". *Massachusetts Review* 29. 4 (1988): 583-95.

Kalsey, Surjeet. "Migratory Birds." *Canadian Voices*. Eds. Shirin Kudchedkar and Jameela Begum. New Delhi: Pencraft International, 1996.

Karmakar, Chandrima. "The Conundrum of 'Home' in the Literature of the Indian Diaspora: An Interpretive Analysis". *Sociological Bulletin* 64. 1 (January-April 2015): 77-90. JSTOR <https://www.jstor.org/stable/26290721>. Accessed on 3 June 2022.

Kaur, Manpreet and Sanjaleen Prasad. "*Home, Migration, and a New Identity*: Some Reflections". *Fijian Studies* 15. 1 (August 2018): 145-58. *ResearchGate* <https://www.researchgate.net/publication/327172828>. Accessed on 3 June 2022.

Kaur, Rupi. "I'm Taking My Body Back." *YouTube* (uploaded by *TEDx Talks*), 3 September 2016 <https://www.youtube.com/watch?v=RlToQQfSlLA>

--- Instagram <https://www.instagram.com/rupikaur_/?hl=en>

Kaur, Rupinder. "Poetic Echoes from the Indian Diaspora in North America". *Literature of Indian Diaspora*. Ed. T. S. Anand. New Delhi: Creative Books, 2010, pp 34-45.

Kennedy, Roger. *The Psychic Home: Psychoanalysis, Consciousness and the Human Soul*. New York and London: Routledge, 2014.

Kuortti, Joel. *Writing Imagined Diasporas South Asian Women Reshaping North American Identity*. Newcastle-upon-Tyne: Cambridge Scholars Publishing, 2007.

Massey, Doreen. *Introduction to Chapter Three, Space, Place, and Gender*. Minneapolis: University of Minneapolis Press, 1993.

Mishra, Lata. "The Politics of Sharing and Survival in Stephen Gill's *Immigrant*." *Diasporic Writings: India and Abroad*. Eds. V. S. Patel and M. F. Patel. Bengaluru: Sunrise Publishers and Distributors, 2010. 27-36.

Mufti, Amir, and Ella Shohat. *Introduction in Dangerous Liaisons*. Minneapolis: University of Minnesota Press, 1997.

Nagra, Daljit. *Look we have come to Dover!*. London: Faber and Faber, 2010.

Naikar, Basavaraj. "The Diasporic Poetry of G.S. Sharat Chandra." *Diasporic Writings: India and Abroad*. Eds. V. S. Patel and M. F. Patel. Jaipur: Sunrise Publishers, 2010. 65-78.

Pande, Amba. "*Conceptualising Indian Diaspora*: Diversities within a Common Identity." *Economic and Political Weekly* 48.49 (7 December 2013): 59-65.

Prabhakar, Madhuri. "Poetry as Resistance: Hybridity and the 'Third Space' of Indian Diaspora." *Noise Summer School* (2016). Available in October 2022 on <https://gcids2017.org/wp-content/uploads/2017/09/Madhuri-Prabhakar-Full-Paper.pdf>

Rai, Awanish. "Indian Diaspora: Old and New". *Facets of Indian Diasporic Writings*. Eds. Ram Prakash Pradhan and Supriya Shukla. New Delhi: Atlantic Publishers and Distributors, 2016. 135-44.

Seth, Vikram. *The Collected Poems*. New Delhi: Penguin India, 1995.

Seyhan, Azade. *Writing Outside the Nation*. Princeton: Princeton University Press, 2001.

Terkenli, Theano. "Home as Region." *Geographical Review* 85.3 (1995): 324-34.

Tsagarousianou, Roza. "*Rethinking the concept of Diaspora*: Mobility, Connectivity and communication in a Globalised World". *Westminster Papers in Communication and Culture* 1.1 (2004): 52-65.

Vertovec, Steven. "Three Meanings of Diaspora, exemplified among South Asian Religions". *Diaspora* 6.3 (Winter 1997): 277-99.

Yamini. G. "Dislocation and Diasporic Consciousness in the Poetry of Meena Alexander". *Asia Pacific Journal of Research* 1. 25 (2015): 150-53.

Zandy, Janet. *Calling Home: Working-Class Women's Writings*. New Brunswick: Rutgers University Press, 1990.

Poetics of Denial
Negotiating the Performative in Contemporary English Poetry by Diasporic Indian Women Poets

—Rupayan Mukherjee & Jaydip Sarkar

> "Did I know when I turned away, denying everything, denying the necessity, denying the event, denying the prediction, denying the error and the truth, denying the cruelty, denying the innocence, denying the patient, the hopeful words, denying each and every fault, denying the facts, the features, the eyes, the mouth the tongue the hands the nose, did I know I was denying who I was denying?" (Cixous 5).

In her affluent introduction to *The Second Sex*, a milestone work on feminist criticism, Simone de Beauvoir defines the woman as a relative being, one who is defined, governed, appropriated and systematised, as the double of man. She is that what the man is not, thereby infringed in a domain of denial by the systematic/ poetics and hermeneutics of phallogocentricism, "Determined and differentiated in relation to man" (Beauvoir 27). In the extensive research that follows, Beauvoir identifies the woman as a socio-cultural category whose ontological essence is formulated around an aura of the incomplete, where a phenomenology of absence defines and determines her presence. Luce Irigaray describes 'woman' as a lot who are communed on their consciousness of lack. What is more, Irigaray argues that this lack is not merely biological, which is anatomically validated by the absence of a penis but is rather characterised by the lack of a phallus. Within the framework of Irigaray's understanding (which is in turn influenced by Lacan), the phallus acquires a different connotation from the biological penis; it is "the signifier of desire" (Irigaray 61). Jacques Lacan defines the phallus as a "signifier whose function, in the intra-subjective economy of analysis, may lift the veil from the function it served in the mysteries. For it is the signifier that is destined to designate meaning effects as a whole, insofar as the signifier conditions them by its presence as a signifier" (579). He points out the ambiguity that the phallus exists as a symbolic truth in its simultaneous evocations of a "subject reality in this signifier" (*ibid.* 582), and in its rendering "unreal the relations to be signified" (*ibid.* 582). The signifier of phallus, in Lacan's opinion, is the subject of desire for the woman and the feminine disposition, and yet it is primordially founded on a principle of denial, a forbidden fruit which lies beyond the purview of the autonomy of the feminine. The signifier of desire for the woman within the phillic order is the phallic, a dispossession of which makes her turn towards the subject who has it. In doing so the woman perceptively rejects "an essential part of her femininity" (Irigaray 62). In her words,

> "It is for that which she is not-that is, the love of phallus-that she asks to be desired and simultaneously to be loved. But she finds the signifier of her own desire in the body of the one- who is supposed to have it- to whom she addresses her demand for love" (*ibid.* 62).

It is for what she is not, that the woman finds her being within the economy of love and desire. Her desire is thus disenfranchised, evolving around a poetics of denial, which is in turn strictly regulated by the patriarchal economy/ law of the Father. The phallic sustains as the logos in patriarchy; it is the law that locates the woman in a perpetual wait and in a liminality of desire, a satiation of which is promised but is never arrived at.

Diasporas are disenfranchised communities; in the global arena of displacement, as Vijay Mishra opines, all diasporas "are unhappy in their own way" (1). Of the many definitions of diasporas that William Safran explores in his celebrated seminal essay "*Diasporas in Modern Societies*: Myths of Homeland and Return", one sustains as "(they) retain a collective memory, vision, or myth about their original homeland-its physical location, history, and achievements" (83). The homeland and the ideal of home is that fertile signifier through which the diaspora defines itself; it is the spectre that lingers in the ontological fissures of the displaced subject. The diasporas are not defined so much by what they are but rather by what they are not, it is in their distinctiveness from the host citizens and communities that they are identified as differences. Their difference is characteristic of an incompleteness or lack, much of which is nurtured and subjectivised through a performative of loss. The logos of home and homeland form that founding fulcrum around which diasporas enchant a culture of absence; home is the signifying desire which the diaspora is deprived of. Yet, it is in their dispossession of the signifier and a denial of it, that diasporas locate themselves within the economy of desire. Resembling the woman who is a denied subject in a patriarchal discursive domain regulated by the law of the Father, diasporas are denied selves within the dictum of the law of the land, consolidating and affirming their selves on what could be called the 'poetics of denial'.

Diasporic consciousness is haunted by a loss and the diasporic subject is in a state of incessant mourning. Mourning, as Derrida argues, is not just about the continuous subjection of the self to the realisation of absence, rather it is also about the stability of the suffering self which is carefully poised with the certainty of loss. Derrida argues that ignorance and doubt are not faithful compatriots to mourning and thus "Nothing could be worse, for the work of mourning, than confusion or doubt" (9). It is in the absence of the truth/ logos of mourning that Diasporas are imbibed in a culture of absence and their essence of loss is often idealised within the performative of mourning. Vijay Mishra observes, "True mourning cannot be delinked from trope, from metaphoricity" (8), and thus, within the metaphor of representation and the performed ideologues of mourning, the homeland and its absence linger for the diasporic.

The generic trend of diasporic poetry has been to interrogate into the fictions of home and homeland against the starching reality of displacement; it has been a febrile genre that is vibrant with the contraries of multiculturalism and ethnicity, identity and being, remembrance and amnesia. Radhakrishnan observes that "the diasporic location is the space of the hyphen that tries to coordinate, within an evolving relationship, the identity politics of one's place of origin with that of one's present home" (xiii) and much of diasporic poetry seeks to evolve within the interstitial space of now and then, the 'here' and the 'there'. Radhakrishnan further stresses that diasporas are engaged in a perpetual tension between the ethnic and national, which is structuralised, validated and aestheticised by the medium of representation.

Hence, loss becomes the routine, homologized essence of the diasporic imaginary and mourning is the performative that the diasporic sensibility indulges in expression, affirmation and validation of the agency. What is more, the diasporic is often stereotyped by the host Nation on their idealised conjectures of absence. The paper will at this point take into consideration a few selected poems by Indo-English diasporic women poets and will seek to understand their locationality within the standardised techtonics and poetics of diasporic poetry. The paper will further explore the politics of assimilation and departure of these women poets from the greater milieu of diasporic writing. Consequently, the paper will argue that owing to their double marginality, these women poets have nurtured a critical eye for any appropriative measures that the collective engages in, for the nominalisation of identities. Thus, home and homeland are not always the idealised and cherished truth of absence for them. Even when it is, these poets, owing to their feminine sensibility, are ambiguously aware of the element of performative and impersonation, which are foundational in the evocation of the lost homeland and the attempted valorisation of the ritual of mourning. They are ruthlessly self-critical in their 'techne', not just writing their self but also questioning the claims of authenticity of the self that is constructed through writing and is per-formed in process. Does formation of the self demand an adherence with the systematic of identity that is desired of the diaspora?

In her review of Mona Dash's collection of poems *A Certain Way*, Reshma Ruia comments that they are manifestations of a "heightened sensibility that straddles the East and the West" (185). In reference to Dash's title poem in the collection, Ruia comments that the poem "reflects (this) paradox of *in-between-ness* and adjustment that defines the diaspora" (*ibid.* 185). No denying, for Dash's poem in particular and the collection in general poeticises her liminality. However, what is more intriguing is probably Dash's awareness of the liminal and interstitial as not just a particular experience but rather as something that is pre-conditioned and appropriated within the performative that tends to stereotype the lived and the particular 'real'. The poem begins with the salient observation: "As an immigrant, / I am expected to behave in a way / A certain way" (Dash 4).

The modalities of behaviour appear pre-registered, it is a reality that has been nominalised in culture and has been endowed to the diasporic subject as a predicament. In other words, the experience of displacement is an anticipated, universal truth to which the diasporic subject must adhere to. The 'certain way' that has been predicted for the displaced subject is founded on a pre-existing baggage of categorical imperatives turned performatives and Dash describes them at length: "Colour the walls with turmeric / Fill my soul with lament / ……. / …… / Dream the stars of the eastern skies / In this land, the land I call my own, / but never to be my own" (*ibid.* 4).

The lived experience of the subject does not match with the desired ideal of diasporic subject; the writing self refutes to be in coherence/ resonance with the generic ethos of diasporic poetic sensibility. While the diasporic self mourns for the homeland and is essentialised within the sacrosanct economy of mourning and loss, the poetic self confesses: "Instead, my mind / Soothed by the nourishing cool green / Of the land I live in, / energised by the glowing orange sun / of the land I come from, / decorates ice cubes with spice" (*ibid.* 4).

The poem engages with "parallel truths", where the diasporic self in its alien culture and habitus, doesn't necessarily mourn and pine for the loss of the familiar that it ought to, within the essentialist milieu of stereotype. 'The certain way' of living that is expected of the diasporic isn't endorsed by the poetic self. Instead, her experience of the diasporic condition appears distinct, it involves a wilful and easy engagement with the cultures of foreign land, promoting an authentic culture of hybridity. Going beyond the contours of 'fixity', which in the words of Bhabha, is characterised by "rigidity and an unchanging order" (Bhabha 94), the poet locates the diasporic consciousness in the interstices of intersubjectivity, which is founded on the equilibrium of "a little of this, a little of that" (Dash 4).

This interstitial self that is different from the stereotyped persona of the diasporic subject is conditioned to an exclusion and liminality which is beyond the recognised orientations and experiences of marginality. It is an alien experience that is outside the registered performatives of the outsider; she is an outsider whom not even the host can recognise. In other words, the generic systematics and performatives which the host expects from the alien/ stranger is denied by the hyphenated subject. The hyphen for this subject does not essentially split the ethnic and the national, it extends further to signify a breach between the performatives of the host and counter-performatives of the diaspora. The hyphen carries the connotative significance of a subjectivity which is bare, divorced from the collective of both the host and the diasporic. Her's is an *in-between-ness* that Radhakrishnan defines as a "two-way street" (206), only with the sole exception that she stands with each of her limbs rooted in either, refusing to traverse any one of them singularly.

This creates the tension between denial and acceptance as the diasporic self neither belongs here (in the alienness of the host) nor there (the sacrosanct climate of home). Dash's poem explores the void of belonging that her unperformed self has been subjected to as she reflects in her poem "Belonging": "Corporate men, pinstripe suits / in deep discussion, in accents / lilting French, baritone German, twangy American. / Among them an Indian, worse, a woman, Indian. / When I speak in tone, walk with the step / eyebrows raise, they lean forward to hear better, / talk louder when addressing me, as if I am deaf / telling me silently: / You shouldn't be here" (Dash 5).

The implications are clear. The alien foreign politicos called the host Nation is at unease with a diasporic identity who is trying to belong with them; like them; in them. Her gendered ethnic identity convinces them of her incapacity and inefficiency and her denial to perform her lack, only complicates the hermeneutics of generalisation and essentialism through which the host is habituated in appropriation of the diasporic 'other'. The other that does not fit into the categorical performatives and imperatives of the 'other' discontents the dominant self of the host Nation. Thus at public gatherings and private night lives, at work and leisure, the non-conformed diasporic subject listens to silent calls of exclusion, "You shouldn't be here" (Dash 5).

The 'here' is not just a territorial or geographical signifier in the poem, rather it is a referent of belongingness. The 'here' is a ploy that locates the subject into a question of validity and validation, provoking the legitimacy of the discursive field in which the subject is contextualised. The subject and her unperformed sense of being in continuum are restrained and the diasporic consciousness now shifts to the contrasted locale of being; the cultural reality of the ethnic: "Welcoming smiles, women in sarees, / Grinding masalas, rolling chapattis, / television is the world, content / in the four walls, within set boundaries" (*ibid*. 5).

These are performed imaginings and occurrences that remind the poet of her hometown, of her roots; which are "so far from my branches" (*ibid*. 5). They are unfamiliar to the poetic consciousness, sounding distant and surviving merely as remembrances from past. While the perceptions of memory and the remembered do not deny her the belonging and do not question her legitimacy within the spatial paradigm of home, the poet realises: ""Ill at ease I sit / listening to my own voice / telling me silently: / You shouldn't be here" (*ibid*. 5).

This is an epiphanic moment of reconciliation where the subject realises that the cultural authenticities called home and roots; in other words, the lineage with which diasporas are usually identified and nominalised, do not stand validated for her. She is far too removed in her displaced reality to identify with the constructs and imaginings of home and homeland. The counter-performative fails to accommodate her as miserably as her realities are denied in the performatives of belonging as one with/of the hosts.

This denied sense of being and ontology haunts the poet consistently, her materiality is constituted in a denial, as she writes in her poem "Rejection": "The land I come from / Says sorry, we want to be more than what we are. / We can't have you, as you remind us of us / You stink of the familiar. // The land I live in / Says sorry you are not smelling enough of / The land you come from, you remind us of us. / You need to be more different" (*ibid.* 10).

The performatives and the counter-performatives of belonging are both denied by the lived real of the poet, her materiality lingers as a surplus, which fails to be accommodated within the hermeneutics of identity. Usha Kishore, another diasporic female Indian poet, explores this surplus of being and its polymorphous manifestation of identity as she writes: "for I am half swallow, half chakora. / I am not one, but two" (Kishore 13).

This ambivalence of being for Kishore is a moment of estrangement, as she realises that her doubleness has stripped her from the collective of 'flock' and its categorical imperatives which include music and culture. In her doubleness, Kishore claims to be the only estranged voice of hybridity, denied a heredity and ancestry: "I sing with my forked tongue / Of strange new worlds and / stranger ways" (*ibid.* 13). She is, in her own words, "A child, holding the hand of Postcoloniality" (*ibid.* 10), and for her the postcolonial condition is not merely an experience of the self, it is the possibility of engaging with the threshold of a newness, where "a new horizon opens" (*ibid.* 10).

However, Kishore problematises the essence of novelty that the postcolonial self is promised and seeks to register her lived reality as not merely a de-historicised state of being that is spontaneous and valid in a beyond of the registered modalities of living. Instead, she soon balances the paradigm of a "new horizon" (*ibid.* 10) with the metaphor of "borrowed robes" (*ibid.* 10). She writes: "A new horizon opens, and I / dressed in borrowed robes, / journey into a foreign tongue" (*ibid.* 10).

The displaced subject steps into the arena of newness in 'borrowed robes'; she is already conditioned to a being that has been predicted by the hermeneutics of history. The ideal of an unrehearsed and unpredicted essence of subjectivity, which appeared to be discontinuous and sporadic, is in actual a part of the historical burdened binary conflict between the coloniser and colonised, the oppressor and oppressed. In her "Postcolonial Poem", Kishore discovers the striations of history in her elementary sense of being: "You are the enterprising seafarer / in search of adventure. // I am the wild orient, waiting / to be discovered...// ...You teach me your language. / I curse in your language... //...Your guns thunder down. / I die. But I rise again... // I engage in non-violence. I desire truth. / I non co-operate. I fast unto death..." (*ibid.* 11)

The subject experiences herself as the persona of history; her materiality isn't just restrained to the temporal and spatial reality of displacement. Instead, she is Walter Benjamin's "angel of history" (Benjamin IX) — located in the liminal between the historical and the actual, the occurred and the occurring. The unprecedented becomes a component in the greater schema of the elegiac as the poet observes: "My swelling masses flood you out. / Your sun is set. You saw me in two... / ...we pretend to ignore each other. / But we need each other" (Kishore 12).

With this salient observation, the poet depicts her consciousness of a mediated and meditated condition of being, which is rehearsed in the operas of history. The displaced subject and her experience is annotated by interpretation, which turns experience into performance and which is designed and regulated by pre-existent models of existence turned performatives. Judith Butler describes the performative as a "foundational premise that guarantees a presocial ontology" (4), and the presocial ontology for the diasporic subject becomes an inevitability; hers is a helpless surrender to the fatalities determined by history.

The redemption from history and the urge to surpass the persona of an actor engaged in the performative of an identity that has been historically determined necessitates the diasporic self into an ideal of quest for the possibilities/ traces of an elemental sense of being. Bashabi Fraser's *Letters to My Mother and Other Mothers* can be read as the displaced subject's search for a residual self that is not just pre-social but is also beyond the foundational logos of performatives. While homes and homelands are geopolitically appropriated spaces striated by the rubric of history where the diasporic self is conditioned into an ideal of a fabricated identity, the memory of the maternal becomes a sacrosanct trope of mourning for the displaced agency. It is through the evoked cult of the mother that the displaced poetic persona revokes the performative of mourning and engages in true mourning. The memory of the maternal becomes the confluence of intimate and lived histories for the displaced subject and it is through an elegiac remonstration of the mother that Fraser seeks to incorporate the authenticated memories of loss that are beyond the stalk performatives of mourning which the diasporic sensibility is often conditioned to engage in. The personal and the intimate enfolds within itself the greater imaginary called homeland and through the elegiac address to the cult of the mother, that "fantasy of a lost continent" (Kristeva and Goldhammer 133), Fraser intersperses the ideal of homeland as a surplus within the eulogised elegy to her mother. The fragments of memory of the lost homeland come fleeting to the poet through the mediated remembrance of her mother and as such they are annotated mnemonics, which carry an interpretive potential that is deeply personal. The historicised homeland and the ritual of mourning that is an already appropriated and stereotyped predicament for the diasporic, owing to the materiality of her displacement, is surpassed by Fraser in her attempted infusion of the historicised space of the homeland with the intimate memory of the Mother: "You could tend the mango tree to tender sweetness / You could urge guavas and lemons to abundance / You could fill the lonely evenings with Iman ragas" (Fraser 18).

The memories nurtured through the remembrance of the mother are personal, which have interpretive implications to the contemplating self alone. Obliquely however, the visions of a tropical homeland creep in and through the mnemonic of the mother, greater memories of home and homeland sieve through in spontaneity. The Mother evolves as a necessary instantaneous in the continuum of the displaced consciousness which is otherwise incomplete. Fraser's poetic conjectures of her Mother is emblematic of an openness and it is within the rituals of the discontinuous and spontaneous that the reminiscences of the mother and the implied ideologues of home evolves. Hence, it is within the spectrum of the evolving daily that the daughter perceives the impressions of the Mother and reflects: "Whenever I see a door open / To a beggar, and watch a woman / Pour grain and money, offer a sari / I see you once again. / Soon following it up with / ...Whenever there is a thirst to quench / I see your spirit revealed" (*ibid.* 19)

This 'thirst' is symptomatic of a lack and the Mother evolves as a response to the lack that has been discussed before. The consciousness of displacement convolutes into a 'thirst'; a perpetual incompleteness that is founded on the poetics of loss. The personalised memory of Mother becomes the mnemonic to a greater dynamic of loss and it is in this spontaneous, unrehearsed and unmeditated arrival that the mnemonic of the Mother enables the displaced subject to transcend the performatives of memory and the consequent validation of identity on stalk reminiscences of the spatial trope of home and homeland. Instead, home is evoked in the intimate remembrances of the personalised, remembered cult of the Mother. The Mother becomes inextricably attached to the home of "marmalade, toast and Darjeeling Tea" (*ibid.* 20), the "cane mora" (*ibid.* 23) and such other perceived delicacies, which become the signifiers and fragments of a remembered home. What is more, this remembered home continuously slips into the present and thus the chronicle of loss that the diasporic sensibility is often subjected to, evolves not as an absence but as a manifestation of the absent in the existent present. The consciousness of the absence lingers in the paradigm of presence as a spectral truth and not merely as an idealised loss which can validate the mourning subject. The absence does not merely haunt; it also hybridises the temporal locale in contingence with the lived which 'was' and no longer 'is'. The diasporic consciousness of Fraser is thus a deviation from the standardised ethos of loss, instead it is conceived as a validation of return. In other words, loss and return in Fraser is complementary, the performative of loss do not necessarily valorise the ethos of a lack;

instead it is a relentless speculation of the absent in the present. Fraser denies the materiality of home as an absence, and in doing so, she engages in a denial of the usual performative of loss that is pivotal to a diasporic consciousness.

Denial is thus central to the poetic sensibility of these contemporary women diasporic poets. All three of them are deeply critical of the performative of loss and tend to deny the appropriation of diasporas as figments of loss. The experience of loss are instead sublimated and reconciled with through the stratagems of objectivity, ambiguity and a rumination of return respectively.

Works cited:

Beauvoir, Simone de. *The Second Sex*. Trans. Constance Borde, and Sheila Malovany-Chevallier. New York: Vintage Books, 2011.

Benjamin, Walter. "Theses on the Philosophy of History". Trans. Dennis Redmond. *Marxists.org*. Accessed on 12 June 2022 <*https://www.marxists.org/reference/archive/benjamin/1940/history.html*>

Bhabha, Homi K. *The Location of Culture*. New York and London: Routledge, 1994.

Butler, Judith. *Gender Trouble: Feminism and the Subversion of Identity*. New York and London: Routledge, 1990.

Cixous, Hélène. *The Day I wasn't there*. Trans. Beverley B. Brahic. Evanston: Northwestern University Press, 2006.

Dash, Mona. *A Certain Way*. Morden: Skylark Publications, 2017.

Derrida, Jacques. *The Spectres of Marx: The State of the Debt, the Work of Mourning and the New International*. Trans. Peggy Kamuf. New York and London: Routledge, 1994.

Fraser, Bashabi. *Letters to My Mother and Other Mothers*, Edinburgh: Luath Press Limited, 2015.

Irigaray, Luce. *This Sex which is not One*. Trans. Catherine Porter, and Carolyn Burke. New York: Cornell University Press, 1985.

Kishore, Usha. *Immigrant*, London: Eyewear Publishing Ltd., 2018.

Kristeva, Julia, and Arthur Goldhammer. "Stabat Mater." *Poetics Today* 6. 1-2 (1985): 133-52.

Lacan, Jacques. *Ecrits*. Trans. Bruce Fink. New York: W.W. Norton and Company, 2007.

Mishra, Vijay. *The Literature of the Indian Diaspora: Theorising the Diasporic Imaginary*, New York and London: Routledge, 2007. S

Radhakrishnan, R. *Diasporic Mediations: Between Home and Location*, Minneapolis: University of Minnesota Press, 1996.

Ruia, Reshma. "Book Review: *A Certain Way* by Mona Dash." *Episteme* 6.1 (June 2017): 185-86.

Safran, William. "Diasporas in Modern Societies: Myths of Homeland and Return". *Diaspora: A Journal of Transnational Studies* 1.1 (Spring 1991): 83-99.

Raising The Curtain of Indian Diasporic Theatre
An Insightful Overview

—Tanima Dutta

Raising the Curtain of Indian Diasporic Theatre:

> "Performance, be it in the Western world or the Eastern, has always been interdisciplinary. It has always negotiated with different kinds of concrete expressions in different media, it has always been cross-hatched with abstract or unseen forces which shape our lives. The language of theatre, its mode of expression, its area of operation vary from clime to clime, culture to culture, time to time, but the ingredients remain the same. [...] [.] The resultant theatrical flow of cultural energy opens up avenues of new discourse, new challenges for theatre research. [....] Unlike other forms of art, theatre survives through a direct contact with the audience during the time of the performance within a given space and this presence of a live audience is one of the fundamental factors behind the multiple modes of mediation that go into the making of theatre." (Gupta, "Introduction" to *Contemporary* 2)

It is no denying a fact that, in the poetics and aesthetics of performative arts of all kind, theatrical performance, with its "text-performance articulation" (Ubersfled 4), has been undergoing through a process of changes and improvisations by not only questioning the living condition within a society, but also interrogating and initiating the predominant literary arts of representation. "[A]s a unique and unrepeatable event unfolding in real time, in the physical co-presence of all participants" (Whitton ix), theatre directly gives vent to the pedagogic relationship between the playwright-reader-script writer-director-actor-spectator. Richard Schechner rightly sets a model of the performance of a play/drama thus:

> "The drama is the domain of the author, the composer, scenarist, shaman; the script is the domain of the teacher, guru, master; the theatre is the domain of the performers; the performance is the domain of the audience." (71)

The fluidity of the 'performative texts' of a drama, also called the 'emissaries of popular culture' (Chaubey and Devasundaram 1), makes audience perceive and think beyond the written words. Following the classical Western (Greco-Roman) tradition of theatre, it is "India among the other Asian countries [that] first stepped into the 'era of theatre'" (Thakur 278), as is clear from the dominant discourse of *Natyashastra*[1]. While talking about this Sanskrit text, Ravi Chaturvedi comments in his "Preface" to *Contemporary Indian Theatre: Theatricality and Artistic Crossovers* that:

> "The origin of theatre as described in the *Natyashastra* is not a mere entertaining story but points to a strongly built social concept of the expansion of knowledge of various arts and education of the society. This is the reason which motivated all involved to accept and include everything available that was useful and worthwhile in making the art of theatre" (xi).

Since its inception, theatre has actually been used as a very significant medium to voice for the underprivileged of the society. The inclusion of religion and different sacred rituals was meant for instilling moral values among people. The medieval period lacks in any such formal structure of theatre due to foreign invasion and exploitation. However, the European influences during the (post)colonial period bring in a rapid change and experimentation in the nature of modern Indian theatre, by rejuvenating the mythic and folk tradition of the country, in order to give voice to the national discourse. The interdisciplinary character of modern Indian theatre often successfully stages audio-visual semantics and semiotics of dance, opera, music and other modes of experimentations by comingling the local with the global. The theatrical performances, like films to some extent, are emotive, therapeutic and cathartic in nature. It is through the hands of the Indian playwrights/directors/actors like Habib Tanvir (1923-2009), Badal Sircar (1925-2011), Vijay Tendulkar (1928-2008), Girish Karnad (1938-2019), Poile Sengupta (b. 1948), Manjula Padmanabhan (b.1953), Mahesh Dattani (b.1958) and many more, that modern Indian English theatre has been evolved from its nascent stage, embracing either a "nationalist agenda" (Dharwadkar, "Diaspora, Nation" 73) or the diverse issues such as society, culture, religion, myth, politics, caste, feminism, gender, economy and so on. However, Indian play in the original English language is 'subordinate' to the plays written in indigenous languages such as Bengali, Kannada, Marathi, Bengali, and so on (*ibid.* 79). Only with the exceptions of few Indian playwrights, like Mahesh Dattani, who otherwise has naturalised English language so well that through this medium "he can best express what he wants to say" (Dattani 9), most of the playwrights prefer regional languages because, for the Indian actors or audience of a particular region, it is through indigenous language(s) that they can most naturally perform/watch the "lived experiences" on stage than in the colonial language like English, that may seem "imposed, limiting, alienating" (Dharwadker, "Diaspora, Nation" 80). So, although in printed texts the English as a language is comparatively accepted well in India (as is clear from the abundance of Indian English fiction, non-fiction and poetry), in case of any performative art like theatre in English, the response is not so much welcoming and effective.

Interestingly, the corpus of 'Indian diasporic theatre' too remains a less explored genre. Originating from the "Greek composite verb *diaspeírein—dia* ('through' or 'across') and *speirein* (to sow/ scatter)", the English noun derivative "diaspora" means "'to scatter through/across'- an act of dispersion or scattering" (Lahiri 7). In case of any nation-state or a country, the act of dispersion may happen within the states of a nation or within the countries of the globe. The movement from one smaller location to another within a country, however, should not be considered as 'internal diaspora'; rather it is better called 'internal migration'. The 'nation/nation-state' is the crux of any diaspora. As Lahiri elaborates:

> "Diaspora is a social formation *outside the nation of origin* [emphasis mine]. It is a phenomenon involving uprooting, forced or voluntary, of a mass of people from the 'homeland' and their 're-rooting' in the hostland(s). Diasporic subjects usually have a strong nostalgia for the land they have left behind and for its culture(s), but at the same time may, consciously

and/or unconsciously, tend to acculturate or assimilate to the dominant culture of the new space. More often than not, diasporic locations spawn hybrid cultures" (4)

Every diasporic experience varies from culture to culture, from nation to nation on the bases of diverse socio-cultural/ religious/ political/ economic/ ethno-communities. So, the present essay intends to focus on the performative texts or plays and theatre-productions by the expatriates of Indian origin, which comparatively lacks the critical attention it deserves unlike the Indian diasporic fiction, non-fiction and poetry. In fact, although Emmanuel S. Nelson catalogues fifty-eight Indian diasporic writers of almost all genres in his *Writers of the Indian Diaspora: A Bio-Bibliographical Critical Sourcebook* (1993), the authors of 'diasporic plays' are strikingly missing only with the exemptions of Farrukh Dhondy (b. 1944) and Hanif Kureishi (b. 1954), who, despite producing a number of plays, are not so popular for writing on diasporic experiences. Commenting on the same, Aparna Dharwadkar observes that "the marginality of theatre to diasporic experience suggests a complicated relation between genre, language, and location" ("Diaspora, Nation" 72). Whereas, the Indian playwrights prefer to stay in the country and write mostly in regional languages and sometimes in English, often embracing the 'nationalist agenda' by combining the 'textual and performative traditions' with 'modernity', the case for the emigrant authors is different as they prefer to maintain 'the privacy and relative self-sufficiency of print genres like fiction, non-fiction, and poetry over the complications of a collaborative, public, commercial, and performance-based medium like theatre'; to them the narration of a migrant experience, the dialectical discourse of 'longing' and 'belonging'are easier than performing the same (*ibid.* 73). In her another essay entitled "Diaspora and the Theatre of the Nation", Dharwadkar further explicates the situation thus:

> "Moreover, while novelists often employ diaspora as the enabling condition but not the subject of narrative, immigrant playwrights can create original theatre only when they distance themselves from their

cultures of origin and embrace the experience of residence in the host culture, with all its problems of acculturation and identity" (303).

Nevertheless, the increasing population of the South Asian communities in different host countries helps in a gradual development of South Asian Diasporic theatre in recent time. In "An Introduction to South Asian Diasporic Theatre", Neilesh Bose, while talking about seven nation states within South Asia—India, Pakistan, Bangladesh, Bhutan, Sri Lanka, Bhutan, and the Maldive Islands—also states that the South Asian Diasporic theatre with all these nation states deals with a 'diverse set of socio-political and aesthetic concerns' such as different structures of classics, 'realistic' presentation of 'drawing-room dramatics', experimentations with 'dramaturgy', the 'metropolitan theatre traditions' as well as the issues concerning the 'homeland' and the question of identity formation, thus setting up its own position in the diasporic literary tradition (*Beyond* 6). Most significantly, Indian diasporic theatre is comparatively more vibrant among the other six South Asian nation-states in the aesthetics of theatre-diaspora. This diasporic aesthetic, however, is more concerned with establishing the *sound, structures, forms and poetics of theatre of/from the homeland on the stages of the host countries* (emphasis mine).

Whether it is because of indentured labour, or some other professional grounds, or some historical/political situation such as the two World Wars and the 1947-Partition of the Indian subcontinent, Indian diasporic experiences in the host countries vary not only for diverse ethno-religio-socio-political-cultures, but also because many of the Western countries could not emancipate themselves from their mentality of the colonisers, even in the anti-colonial space and time. Indian diasporic theatre may be found with certain limitations in the host countries like Fiji, Malayasia, Singapore, Trinidad and Tobago, New Zealand, Australia; the present paper would, however, hone in on the comparatively more available and staged Indian diasporic plays in the U.K., Canada, the U.S.A., and South Africa.

The Indian Diasporic Theatre within India: Doongaji House:
Before giving an insightful overview of Indian Diasporic Theatre in the overseas, it would be unfair not to mention the issues of diaspora within the nation itself. In India, a multi-religious-lingual-cultural nation with Hindus being the majority, people face multiple displacements within the country itself; especially the diasporic religious minority groups such as Sikhs and Muslims are doubly displaced both in and outside the nation. By taking up two contemporary Indian plays with diasporic issues, such as Mahesh Elkunchwar's Marathi play *Wada Chirebandi* ("Old Stone Mansion", 1985), and Cyrus Mistry's English play *Doongaji House* (1978), Aparna Dharwadker focuses on 'the loss of home at home', the 'destruction of home', 'both as a material structure (a 'house'), and as an emotional space of ancestral memory, family attachments, and community bonds- [as] the unprivileged mirror stage of the nostalgia surrounding the figure of home in transnational diasporic consciousness' ("Diaspora, Nation" 75). Cyrus Mistry (b. 1956), belonging to the Parsi-Zoroastrian community of the writers of India, based at erstwhile-Bombay, and also the younger brother of the famous Indian diasporic author Rohinton Mistry (b. 1952), is well known for writing about the 'Bombay-Parsi' diasporic communities and their (post)colonial history. *Doongaji House*, Mistry's only full length English play for stage performance, other than *The Legacy of Rage* (1992), although faced some problems with its initial reception for being staged in the colonial language, is considered to be a seminal work in not only Indian English Theatre, but also in Indian English Diasporic Theatre. In the pre-colonial time (8th-10th century) Parsis migrated from Iran to India to protect their Zoroastrian religion from the Muslim invaders, and from that time onwards the glorious saga of Parsi community is a matter of political, historical, cultural and literary concerns. The issues, such as, ethnic identity, displacement, rootlessness, loss of home are the subjects of many of the Parsi literatures. Set in Bombay in the 1960s', Cyrus Mistry's *Doongaji House* tells the tale of the Pochkhanawalla-family, residing at a 'glorious' mansion named *Doongaji House* in the heart

of Bombay, which is now in a state of decay. In the backdrop of a family-drama, the play presents the house as a metaphor of Parsi community, which is also under the threat of extinction. The issues concerning Hindu-Parsi animosity, generation gap, repetitive nostalgia of a glorious past, the saddening transformation from 'elite Parsi' to 'Parsi *bawaji*' are painful for any Parsi man like Hormusji. The play ends with a tragic note when the old couple exit from their decaying house forever, and "[n]ow the Doongaji House too, is dead" (Mistry 181), thus hinting at the loss of a home, both as a place and space, and the extinction of a community as a whole. Dharwadkar sees these Parsi communities under a 'peculiar powerlessness', and their 'alienation from the [Hindu] majority community in India is so intense that they seem still to be in diaspora [...]' ("Diaspora, Nation" 90).

The Indian Diasporic Theatre in the United Kingdom:
While writing about the Indian diasporic theatre experience in any *host land* such as the United Kingdom, it is undoubtedly difficult for the present researcher residing at a faraway geographical place to accumulate all the Indian diasporic plays because very few such texts can be found in published format, and many such unpublished texts/scripts are made solely for theatrical performances. However, it is also a boon in bane for the researcher, based at an erstwhile English colony like India, to unleash the postcolonial experience while considering Indian diasporic plays in England or any such European nation. While tracing the history of the South Asian theatres in Britain, Neilesh Bose marks the mid-twentieth century as the beginning period of modern Indian/South-Asian theatre practices in England by some 'strolling players from Oudh' as 'hired by two English brothers, George and Edward Hanlon' (*Beyond* 250). It was later followed by some Indian students, leftists, and other anti-imperialist/colonialist-groups/ production houses in the twentieth century, till India achieved its independence in 1947. However, the historic human exodus during India-Pakistan partition followed by the independence of the two nations created

a topsy-turvy situation by unleashing the turpitude of mutual violence in the forms of communal riot, genocide, mutilation, abduction, rape, pillage, war, carnage, and violation. All these made the two new born nations suffer from 'fragile economies'; whereas "manpower exports were beneficial" to these nations, the English, just deposed from its colonial power, needed migrants from the former colonies for its 'own development' (Hussain 189). Hussain also informs that, mostly because of the cultural enrichment of the Indians and also for their economic contributions to both Britain and India, from 1950s' onwards, 'the Indian migrant group became the one of the most important non-European groups to settle in Britain' (189).

Albeit the economic migration of the Indians in Britain might seem economically advantageous in both ways, the racial discrimination began to surge even in the post-colonial phase. Theatre being the medium of protest once again got revolutionised through the hands of many diasporic playwrights cum actors/directors such as Jatinder Verma (b.1954), a 'twice migrant' (Bose 257) and others, who founded the *Tara Arts Theatre Company* in 1977 with the objective to stage plays mostly by Asian actors on the issues of racist attacks/murders, socio-cultural discriminations, the 'cultural contours of the migrants'[2], multicultural identities and other postcolonial factors. Tara Arts usually stage two types of plays: one being the plays of 'South Asian experiences in the British context' and other 'is that of British classic works with a South Asian spin on them' (Qari 31). Initially the group staged plays with no economic support from outside, but from 1986 onwards the Arts Council funding helped in staging new productions, such as Moliere's *Tartuffe* (1664), with the background of seventeenth-century Mughal India; it is also the first play directed by an Asian (Verma), in stylised Indian English language, to be performed at National Theatre. Neilesh Bose observes:

> "In this and subsequent productions, Tara Arts has established an aesthetic via its approach to language and dramaturgy, *Binglish*, in which the highly specific British South Asian experiences with language, culture, modernity and identity are fused in performance traditions that takes elements from

classical Indian inspirations, Western theatre practice, and postcolonial realities" (*Beyond* 251).

The (re)productions like *Macbeth, The Little Clay Cart, Le Bourgeoise Gentilhomme, Cyrano de Bergerac* and innumerable other Shakespearean and Brechtian plays not only touch on these specific diasporic aesthetics by juxtaposing Western and Eastern forms and techniques, but also manifest the paradox of 'centre' and the 'other' in the context of theatre in Britain in the last quarter of the twentieth century. To mention among the other few, Jatinder Verma's dramatic venture with *2001: A Ramayana Odyssey* reflects on several diasporic experiences such as migration, identity and gender issues, power-dynamics, and so on, by questioning classical Western classic like *Odyssey* in the web of Indian classical epic like *The Ramayana*. This 'inquiry', however, does not negate the Western classic from a postcolonial and 'subalternist' point of view, but rather 'questions', as Bose puts it, the existence of the 'West' and 'South Asia' in a diasporic context through the conversations between Odysseus and Rama by incorporating in the dramatic sequences the Indian aesthetics such as Vedic mantras, Indian classical dance forms of *Bharata Natyam*, Keralan martial arts, Indian music on *Rasa* aesthetics and so on (255-57). Verma's *Journey to the West: A Trilogy on Migration* (2002) explores the oral- diffusion- stories of three generations of East African Asians from India to East Africa and finally to Britain.

Other than Jatinder Verma, playwrights/actors like Sudha Bhuchar (b. 1961) (co-author of *Strictly Dandia*), Sanjeev Bhaskar (b. 1963) (*Goodness Gracious Me*), Hanif Kureishi (*Boderlines, Birds of Passage, Outskirts, The King and Me*), and Madhav Sharma (b. 1939) (*Actors Unlimited*) were some of the most promising talents associated with *Tara Arts* group. Among other theatre companies, mention must be made of Madhav Sharma's *Actors Unlimited* (that produced *Hedda in India*), *Tamasha* (a South Asian company founded by Sudha Bhuchar and Kristin London-Smith in 1889), *Kali Theatre Company* (formed by Rita Wolf and Rukhsana Ahmad in 1991), Rasa Theatre (founded by Rani Moorthy in 1998), which too speculate on diasporic issues through text performances, adaptations of the classics, novel dramaturgy and innovations. *Tamasha* productions like the dramatic adaptation of Mulk Raj Anand's novel *Untouchable* (1989), *House of the Sun* (1991), *Fourteen Songs, Two Weddings, and a Funeral* (1998), *A Tainted Dawn* (1997), *Strictly Dandia* (2002), *The Trouble with Asian Men* (2006- originally an adaptation of Rohinton Mistry's *A Fine Balance*) — all jointly authored by Sudha Bhuchar and Kristin London-Smith, *Child of the Divide* (2006) and *The House of Bilquis Bibi* (2010) by Sudha Bhuchar, *Made in India* (2017) by Satinder Chohan deal with diverse Indian diasporic themes such as partition, Indian regional dance forms like *Bhangra* and *Garba*, marriage, culture, or pan-Indian aesthetics. The artistic director cum founder of Rasa Theatre, Rani Moorthy has herself written and performed various plays with a variety of forms such as- *Dancing within Walls* (2003), *Too Close to Home* (2006), *Shades of Brown* (2007), *If Only Shahrukh Khan* (2013), *Looking for Cool* (2013), *States of Verbal Undress* (2014), *Whose Sari Now?* (2015), which too wonderfully capture the Indian aesthetics and culture, and also question the stereotypes and status quo. Another distinctive feature of Indian diasporic theatre in the United Kingdom can be traced in the productions of a considerable number of feminist plays written by women for women and society. The Kali Theatre productions are written mostly by budding female writers of South Asian descent, and they include such Indian diasporic plays like- *Behna* (2010) by Sonia Likhari, *Calcutta Kosher* (2012) by Shelley Silas, *Kabaddi Kabaddi Kabaddi* (2012) by Satinder Chohan, *Shared Memories* (2012) by Sayan Kent and Tuyen Do, *Tagore's Women: Endless Light* (2012) by Sayan Kent, *Tagore's Women: Purnjanam / Born Again* (2012), *My Daughter's Trial* (2013) by Gulshanah Choudhuri (Jabine Chaudri), *The Husbands* (2014) by Sharmila Chauhan and so on.

The diasporic authors do not always mark a distinct division between the homeland and host land; rather they attempt to create their own identity within the new home during the course of cultural shifting from one nation to another. In *Contemporary Black and Asian Women Playwrights in Britain*, Gabriele Griffin contends that:

"[...] whereas during the 1980s the plays were dominated by intergenerational conflicts as expressive of the difference between the adult subject who migrated and the child who, so to speak, was migrated, [...] by the 1990s plays tended to focus much more on how to live in Britain now, beyond the experience of the moment of migration" (25).

Daniela Salusso confirms Griffin's statement when she talks about these two stages of identity formation:

"[F]irst, through the confrontation with one's past and their different attitudes that the first and second generation migrants have towards Britain, dwelling on disappointed dreams, personal relationships and often relying on magic and myths; secondly, through the problematisation of race politics and a renovated interest in politically and socially committed theatre" (69).

Tanika Gupta (b. 1963), a British playwright of Indian descent belongs to the first group of diasporic writers and her plays such as *Skeleton* (1997), *The Waiting Room* (2000), *Inside Out* (2002), *Sanctuary* (2002), *Fragile Land* (2003) deal with many-folded issues like myths and magic, gender dynamics, cross-generational concerns, memory of immigrations, histories of violence, racism and interracial relationships. Griffin asserts that plays like *Sanctuary* make a "diasporic space in the graveyard and church ground which act as the site for multi-cultural encounter [...] suggesting that the displacements generated by political conflict create new and fragile micro-communities which remain haunted by their diverse pasts" (228). Although many of these diasporic playwrights often do not like the label of 'Asian-British playwrights', they successfully explore the diasporic space in a multicultural nation by redefining the concept of identity through their lived experiences.

The Indian Diasporic Theatre in the United States of America:
In his survey on Indian immigrations in the United States of America, Surendra K. Gupta shows that 'Indians are the third largest group, besides Chinese and Filipinos, among the Asians residing in the United States of America' (55). He further divides the Indian migrations to the U.S.A. into five periods, such as: i) 1904-23: Sikh migration from Canada to the West Coast of the

U.S.A.; ii) 1923-early 1930: illegal migration of around 3,000 Indians from Mexico; iii) 1930-46: No mentionable migration took place; iv) 1946-64: Quota period of limited migration; v) with the reformation of *American Immigration Act* in 1965, educated, technically skilled and professional migrations took place not only from India but other Asian countries as well (Gupta, *Indian* 57-58). The early Indian immigrants in the U.S.A. formed the 'Old Generation Diaspora', and the immigrants after 1965 formed the 'New Indian Diaspora'. The people born and brought up in the U.S.A. with Indian descent constitute the 'Second Generation Indians'. The U.S.A., being the land of opportunity and dream, has entertained the integration of different ethnic groups, often creating a 'cultural pluralism' with the '*melting pot syndrome*, one of complete assimilation and acculturation [...]' (Alam 67). What is interesting about Indian diaspora in the U.S.A. is that, India itself is a nation of diverse cultures, religions and languages with the pluralistic voice, and from almost every state of India with cultural and linguistic diversity the migration takes place.

In his fundamental write-up on the South Asian diasporic theatre in America in the recent times, Ashis Sengupta argues that Indian diaspora is comparatively a late phenomenon when compared with its other counterpart(s) as in the U.K. regarding the issue of literary and cultural practices in the U.S.A. (835). In support of his view, Sengupta, too, has cited Aparna Dharwadker's opinion on this, as is already mentioned at the introductory section of this present article, that an Indian author prefers other print genres like poetry, fiction or non-fiction over a 'collaborative', interactive, complicated, 'performance-based medium like theatre' for the former's nature of 'privacy' and 'self-sufficiency' ("Diaspora, Nation" 73). Sengupta then refers to the observations of two contemporary U.S.A.-based Indian diasporic playwrights, Sudipta Bhawmik (b. 1958) and Mrinalini Kamath (b. 1974), who think that factors like the 'lack' of 'funding', 'logistics', 'community support', 'collaboration' among the diasporic artists, 'training', and 'access to mainstream venues' are responsible for the slow development of such diasporic theatre (835-36). Since the reformation of the *1965 Immigration Act*, a nation like the U.S.A.

with multi-ethnic groups, has been witnessing the increase of the Indian immigrants or the descendants born in the U.S.A., now more formally educated, professionally skilled than the early immigrants. Their diasporic experiences are no more now restricted to the erstwhile nostalgia for the homeland or representation of the diasporic nation; rather this also includes how they are gradually internalising the pluralistic processes of acculturation and socialisation in the new home. The changing diasporic experiences thus give vent to the changing aesthetics of diasporic consciousness through different literary and cultural mediums, predominantly through theatre. Indian, or broadly speaking South Asian American diasporic theatre, 'dealing with the fractures of language, religion, and culture within its own demography, [...] is a double minority as part of the Asian American minority', as Sudipto Chatterjee argues in "South Asian American Theatre (Un/Re-)Painting the Town Brown" (115). However, since post-9/11 phase of the U.S.A., the mainstream audience has gradually connected with the South Asian theatre's socio-political themes related to race, ethnicity, religion like Islam and other political issues like the *Patriot Act of the U.S.A.*, which often associates the 'brownness' with 'racial otherness' (*ibid*. 114).

Although the initial phase of the history of Indo-American theatre performance may bring in mind the references to the theatrical adaptations of the English translation of Indian classics of Sanskrit literature, interestingly by all the white American casts, who used to don the brown-skinned Asian's attires to represent the ancient, magnificent, enigmatic, spiritual and exotic grandeur of the orients through their performances[4], in reality the actual Indian American theatre performances like dance-drama, music-drama or any traditional theatre by the immigrant Indian themselves began in the early twentieth century, but that too in close doors for the communities' own entertainments and also in either Punjabi or Hindi or any such regional language. Even the second quarter of the twentieth century does not offer mentionable record of any diasporic theatrical performances. From the 1960s' onwards, mostly the young migrant-Indians or the immigrants now completely settled in U.S.A.—or born in the

U.S.A. — began to look for alternative career options like working in television, media houses, radio and also in theatre. The first generation of the America born Indians develop a new experimental and critical theatre of 'interculturality' (Chatterjee 114). Although New York City becomes the epicentre of theatrical production houses, entire U.S.A. witnesses the South Asian American circle of (professional) theatre groups and companies such as New York's *Desipina and Company* or *SALAAM Theatre*, Boston's *South Asian American Theatre* (S.A.A.Th.), Chicago's *Rasaka's Theatre* and *Silk Road Theatre*, Minneapolis's *Pangea World Theatre, EnActe Arts* located in California and Texas, and also *Lark Theatre, Disha Theatre, Shunya Theatre*, and many others, all of which produce and stage South Asian diasporic experiences majority of which connect with Indian diaspora.

Whereas the British counterpart of South Asian diasporic theatre is privileged in getting/having funds, active and collective organisations, appropriate stage and other technical accessories and also expertise to train in the theatre-productions, the same cannot be said in case of America. Among the South Asian American playwrights, Indian diasporic playwrights like Shishir Kurup (b. 1961), Aasif Mandvi (b. 1966), and Anuvab Pal (b. 1976) continue to do years of hard work in theatre life to get the desired recognition of reputed playwrights/actors as they work in different marginal northern environments of the U.S.A. (Bose, *Beyond* 10). Born in Mumbai (in India), raised in Kenya, and now a U.S.-settled-actor, composer, playwright and director, Shishir Kurup naturally shows a multidisciplinary approach to theatre life. He wrote and directed plays several times for *Cornerstone Theatre Company*. He is so unique among other playwrights not only for adapting the European classics especially of Shakespeare's through the lens of his Indian/ South Asian diasporic aesthetics, but also for his special treatment with language in the text as part of his training. One such fundamental Kurup work is his pioneering play, *Merchant on Venice* (first professionally produced in 2007), that he adapted from the original Shakespearean *Merchant of Venice*. His appropriation of the Shakespearean plot, characters and language, use of iambic pentameter verse to retain the original flavour, mark his play as the "first attempt to comprehensively South Asian Americanise Shakespeare" (Bose, "Sharuk" 241). In "*Sharuk and Shylock*: The Creation of a South Asian American Aesthetic", Neilesh Bose writes his observation on the play thus:

> "Set in Culver City's intersection of Venice and Claringdom, the play's action begins in present-day, post-9/11 America, with names, characters and conflicts that would be immediately recognisable to a South Asian diasporic audience: wealthy, privileged elite young women, low-caste Hindu subordinates, marginalized Indian Muslims, grumbling elders, and thoroughly Americanized youth" (244).

In an online interview given to Neilesh Bose, Kurup sounds vocal and confident about his Indian diasporic existence in America as he comments on the use of iambic verse that 'if you have the iamb, the way language comes out is unique and it forces your brain to work in a particular way, and it is how Indians or South Asians talk', which is actually a legacy of (post)colonial English education (qtd. in Bose, "Sharuk" 241). Kurup's play differs from the original in many respects, and also it does not follow any strict nationalist agenda or written in any postcolonial frame, but it definitely captures well the South Asian/Indian American aesthetic. Among his other representative plays, *Assimilations* (2002) deals with racial issues of the immigrants of South Asian descent in the West, and *Ghurba* draws on the immigration stories. The other plays by Kurup include *Exile: Ruminations on a Reluctant Martyr* (1992), *Everyman in the Mall* (Co-authored in 1994 with William Rauchas, which, in effect, is an adaptation of the medieval morality-English-play *Everyman*), *Sid Arthur* (adapted Herman Hesse's novel *Siddhartha* in 1995), *An Antigone Story* (2000), *Vishnu Dreams* (2004), *Birthday of the Century*, *Sharif don't Like It*, *Skeleton Dance*, and so on.

The South Asian American aesthetics is also beautifully captured in another prolific American playwright cum actor (comedian) of Indian descent, Anuvab Pal's play like *Chaos Theory* (2013), which depicts the postcolonial conditions of the students of

South Asian origin in America, within the framework of love, romance, academics and colonial-modernity. Neilesh Bose argues:

> "Pal manages to show the unresolvable colonial modern in all its complexity. The colonial modern strikes at the moment an Indian knows that English is his key to a higher-paying job, when he realises that in diaspora, he needs to have separate identity from the masses of South Asians 'stuck' in their vernaculars" (*Beyond* 13).

Other plays written by Anuvab Pal include *Life, Love, and EBITDA* (2003), *Fatwa* (2004), *The President is Coming* (2006), *1-888-Dial-India* (2008), *Disco Dancer* (2011), and *The Bureaucrat* (2011), among others.

Born in Mumbai and based at New York City, the actor-playwright Aasif Mandvi made headlines with the 1998 one-man-show, *Sakina's Restaurant*, which explores the Indian diasporic experience through the American culture of owning a restaurant by making it a wonderful document of the working-class South Asian American ethnic community. Although Mandvi makes it clear that he does not intend to politicise the South Asian diaspora with such terms like 'immigrants' or 'the ethnic others', he also mentions that '[t]he play shows the community in a phase where racism, ignorance, and the problems of being a minority formed its major points of social departure' (Bose, *Beyond* 14).

Sudipta Bhawmik, another such prolific U.S.-based actor, cartoonist, director and playwright (hailing from Kolkata), has started unravelling his immigrant experiences through theatre productions when he failed to connect that through the Bengali plays he still was acting in. The most notable play *Ron*, written in between 2005-06, when the Iraq War was at its peak time, wonderfully captures a 'subtler layer of conflict in the minds of those immigrant parents whose American- born children were fighting in Iraq and for the U.S.A.' (Sengupta 845). The play problematises the complicated issues like *Islamophobia*, the diaspora's allegiance to the homeland and newly found patriotism for the host land. Allusions to the Indian epic sequences from *The Mahabharata*, the Hindu rituals like Baby shower ceremony, the references to Rabindra Sangeet all colour *Ron* with the hues of

Indian American diaspora. His theatre house *Ethnomedia Centre for Theatre Arts* (E.C.T.A.) produces many such Indian diasporic plays since 2003 like *Ekalavya, The Redemption, Taconic Parkway, The Curious Case of a Casual Terrorist, The Protector, The Last Flames, Shikhandi, Agnes* all of which connect directly the Indian experience, culture, memory, food, culture with the American aesthetics.

Mrinalini Kamath, a noted Indian-American playwright, is mostly known for her diasporic play *Boom* (2006), which explores how the U.S.-born second generation Americans with Indian descent feel when they visit India during the economic boom of the country in between 1991 and 2001. Ashis Sengupta writes:

> "The play explores the notion of 'home' in multiple perspectives, provided by the varying relationship between 'subject' and 'location' in a globalised world, and how that impacts the seemingly inviolate category of nationality. It also becomes clear early in the play that the Indian diaspora in the U.S.A., [...] is not a homogenous group with a singular notion of 'home'" (842).

Other plays of Indian diaspora by Kamath include, *Term Limits, The Nava Jeevan, Celestial Motions,* and so on.

Besides them, the other playwrights from the community, producing plays of Indian diaspora across the wide trajectory of the U.S.A., include Gargi Mukherjee (*Our Voices*), Rajiv Joseph (*Bengal Tiger at the Baghdad Zoo* in 2009, *Guards at the Taj* in 2015), Rohina Malik (*Yasmina's Necklace, Unveiled*), Dolly Dhingra (*Unsuitable Girls* in 2002), Sourabh Chatterjee (*Thakur's Nostalgia* in 2002), Sarovar Banka (*The Moral Implications of Time Travel* in 2002), Vinita Sud Belani and Ajay Chowdhury (who jointly authored *The Case of the Vanishing Firefish* in 2019), Madhuri Shekhar (*Nice Indian Boy, Queen*), Salil Singh and Anurag Wadehra (co-authored *The Parting* in 2017), Shane Sakhrani (*A Widow of No Importance*), Sujata Bhatt (*American Exports, Queen of the Remote Control, Invisible Hand, The Aunties*), Aditi Brennan Kapil (*The Adventures of Hanuman, King of the Monkeys, The Deaf Duckling, Love Person*), Sharbari Ahmed (*Bombay Duck, Raisins Not Virgins*), Dhan Gopal Mukherji (*The Judgment of Indra*), Lina Patel (*Perfect Fit, Sankalpan*), Nandita

Shenoy (*Lyme Park: An Austonian Romance of an Indian Nature, Marrying Nandini*) and so on. It is also important to talk about the South Asian Sister's Community, formed in the year 1999, that sees the South Asian American diasporic experience of female sexuality. Ashis Sengupta refers to the performance of "Yoni ki Baat" (Y.K.B.)-series starting in 2003, perceptively modelled on Eve Ensler's *Vagina Monologues* (1996); *yoni*, Sanskrit for 'vagina' symbolises female body with full of ambiguities, and the Y.K.B. performs the 'solo exploration of [the women's] own body and sexualities, dreams and desires, maladies and sufferings, often by combining spoken word with dance and music' (850).The musical solo monologues break the stereotypes and unmask the taboos by exploring such issues, directly connected with female sexuality and femininity, such as- sex, pleasure, desire, abuse, violence, (bodily)hair, bodily functions, menstruation, homosexuality, abortion, motherhood, female foeticide and so on. Vandana Makkar, Sapna Sahani, and Maulie Dass are among the Sister-groups who initiated the shows quite diligently. *Helpline* (2009) and *On-Truck* (2010) are two such *yoni* tales by Anita Chandwaney, a founding member of *Rasaka Theatre Company*, that not only identify the marginalised situation of the sister community, but also question the normative gender roles imposed upon the women of brown/black skin.

It is thus evident that the corpus of Indian diasporic theatre in the U.S.A. is not minimal in context of production and performance, but most of the playwrights/directors/actors are aware of the fact that the assimilation of the ethnic theatre with the mainstream American theatre is the need of the hour. Sudipto Chatterjee sounds anxious about the existence of the 'Desi theatre', which, as he thinks, would lose its vitality and validity unless it is 'self-interrogated stringently and more creatively, making it worthwhile for all sorts of audience, not merely the diasporic' (116). In an interview given to him by the Indian-American actor and composer, Samrat Chakrbarti on 2nd December 2007, the latter talks about organising their own *desi* voices so that they can "paint the town brown" (qtd. in Chatterjee 117).

The Indian Diasporic Theatre in Canada:

The opening of the trans-Canada rail route to the eastern port in the last decade of the 19th century accelerated the first notable emigration of the Indians to Canada. From 1904 onwards the Punjabi-Sikh population was gradually increasing in Canada, but they were not given the proper civil rights, and not being able to speak either in English or follow the Western manners, 'they were easy victims of economic exploitation by their fellow white workers' (Chandrasekhar 18-19). Different stringent laws and bills were passed to curb normal rights of the Indians and restrict their participation in any public office, judiciary, pharmacy, cremation and many more. With the establishment of the first Gurudwara[5] in Vancouver in 1908, followed by the registration of the *Khalsha Diwan Society* in 1909, the Sikhs felt a temporary solace of securing their own identity, and community (Hans 222-23). The exclusionist laws of the early European settlers in Canada were quite gruesome, and led to—among others—the widely-condemned *Komagata Maru*-incident of 23 May 1914. In order to challenge the imperial laws, a renowned Punjabi businessman, Gurdit Singh, chartered a Japanese steam-liner named *Komagata Maru*, with around 376 Punjabis on board. Only 22 of these hapless individuals were allowed to enter Canada, while the reset were repatriated because the local White Canadian people, out of insecurity, showed their racial animosity towards the Indians, resulting in the subsequent passages of more anti-Indian/ anti-subaltern laws. Once the ship was back to Budge Budge, repression by the English officers culminated in utter chaos, riot, leading to a mass homicide, leaving only a very few injured. Whereas, in India this incident is like the native's struggle against their colonisers, in Canada it is reminiscent of the brutish-racial Canadian discriminatory policy of the Sikh migrants' exclusion till the mid-twentieth century (Sahoo 112-13). However, the situation began to change from the period of the Second World War when the Canadian government gradually drew out the immigration restrictions in order to compensate the labour shortage between 1962 and 1967. Since the second half of the twentieth century, immigrants of all sexes, religions and states from India, started gathering in Canada. In 1971, the federal government of Canada declared the first 'multicultural policy' in the world, unlike the 'assimilation policy' or 'melting plot theory' as adapted by the U.S.A.; and because of this adoption of 'multiculturalism', Indians or all the 'Immigrants could retain their [pluralistic] cultural and ethnic identities' from then onwards (*ibid.* 115).

Just like what happened in the U.S.A., lots of trained Indians with job expertise of all professions set off for Canada, and many of them settled there permanently. However, the euphoria of racial discrimination did not evaporate completely, rather the educated and skilled proficiency of the Indians and other South Asian immigrants attracted a severe racial animosity among their European counterparts, especially in the 1970s', because by that time the South Asians, with the genial assurance of future by the Canada-government, had already started settling in the suburban areas of the country. This constant discrimination and the harassment took a much longer time to create a collective corpus of non-Anglophone, especially South Asian literary cultural traditions. The dominant English-speaking Canadian did not approve even the Francophone province of the eastern Canada, Québec in the Eastern Canada. To quote Swagata Bhattacharya:

> "As a result of this English supremacy, Canada has always remained a part of something-first, of the wilderness, then of the British Empire and North America, and finally of the global world. [...] Canadian literature itself is a problematic category. [...] [H]undreds of native Canadian writers born and brought up in the snow were never considered to be writers enough simply because they were not white" (192-93).

In such position, the South Asian diasporic writers' situation in Canada seems even more precarious because they are both immigrants and dark/brown/black-skinned ethnic people. Bharati Mukherjee, an Indian diasporic Canadian author, has written on this weird feeling of being classified along with the marginalised communities of the country, as she writes, "I cannot describe the agony and the betrayal one feels, herein oneself spoken of by one's *own country* [Canada, her new home] as being somehow exotic in nature" (33). In fact, within the 'ghettoisation' of the diasporic South Asian community (Parameswaran 143), the 'otherisation' within the Indian diaspora in Canada is also clear from the *group-ism* between the dominant migrant Indians and those who are doubly migrants, as they emigrated from India to another country before settling in Canada. This leads a diasporic writer to some of the select (and clichéd) diasporic themes such as memory, nostalgia, pain of separation, racism, quest for root, theme of belonging, discrimination of all sorts, violence, gender issues, identity issues, and so on.

Although Indian diasporic Canadian literature has created a considerable space in literary world through the fictions, non-fictions and poetry by Bharati Mukherjee, Uma Parameswaran, Rohinton Mistry, M. G. Vassanji, Lakshmi Gill, Anita Rau Badami, Himani Bannerji, Suniti Namjoshi, Surjeet Kalsey, Saros Cowasjee and so on, drama has got comparatively a late attention till in 1992 with the publication of McGifford's *The Geography of Voice*, where only two plays, along with two paragraphs to South Asian Drama in Canada in the introductory part, found a space. In most of the cases, the Indian diasporic Canadian playwrights are the first generation immigrants, and hence their writings do not necessarily always entail the tales of diasporic stereotypes such as the narratives of trauma, nostalgia, loss, concern for home and so on. As Nandi Bhatia writes:

> "Rather many of the concerns regarding issues of racism, multiculturalism, job discrimination and violence against women and other marginalised groups, concerns that constitute the subject of the plays by Rahul Varma, Rana Bose, Ajmer Rode, Sadhu Binning, and Uma Parameswaran, Surjit Kasley, Anosh Irani, and Anusree Roy, among others, are propelled by their links to the playwrights' homes of origin. Even though this home may not be the physical site of action in many of the plays, it appears in multiple dimensions and gets reproduced in terms of a productive tension that serves as the springboard for the thematic/activist content of the plays, content that negotiates the interests of minorities and migrants across home and diaspora" (216-17).

Theatre activity in Canada by the South Asians, majority of which are Indians, basically began as means of cultural protest against their dissatisfactory lived experience in a hostile host-land. Thus, many playwrights have chosen theatre as means of political queries by addressing such issues on stage through actors, lights, props, music that often connect the spectators with the fictional territories or, in words of Salman Rushdie, the 'imaginary homelands' even in a distant socio-cultural space. This theatre is ideologically much more serious than its American counterpart as the struggle for identity shaping undergoes a long run because of the unwelcoming attitude of the people of Canada. D. Sudha Rani writes on this:

> "The journey of this genre of art started as a protest theatre, then it started displaying the issues of their counterparts in homeland (*Bhopal*) and gradually it consolidated itself as a mainstream theatre and well recognised by both the governmental agencies and people of Canada" (270).

In the 1980s', three South Asian theatre companies took the responsibility of driving the wheel of the theatre movement in Canada. These were Rahul Varma's *Teesri Duniya* (Third World), co-founded by Rana Bose in 1981 in Montreal; *Vancouver Saath*, as initiated in 1982 by Sadhu Binning and some other Punjabi activists; and *Montreal Serai*, founded by Rana Bose in Montreal in 1985.

Teesri Duniya has already received mentionable amounts of monetary supports from the three separate *Councils of Canada Arts*, *The Québec Arts* and *The Montreal Arts*, and it has announced its vision and mission that they intend to stage politically conscious plays to voice for visible minorities and marginalised people living inside Canada, and promote multiculturalism. In 1998 — to promote the company's vision — Rahul Varma (b. 1952) initiated a quarterly theatre magazine titled *Alt. Theatre: Cultural Diversity and the Stage*. Initially, the theatre company used to stage plays in Hindi (such as *Bhanumati Pitara* in 1983, and *Ghar Ghar ki Kahani* in 1984 by Rahul Varma) meant for specific Hindi-speaking diasporic audience. However, since the mid-1980s', and especially after Varma became the artistic director of the company, the group started focussing on plays written in English, mostly written by Varma himself, which include, among others, *Job Stealer* (1987),

Immigration Game (1988), *Isolated Incident* (1989), *Equal Wages* (1989), *Land Where the Trees Talk* (1990), *No Man's Land* (1992), *No Man's Land* (1992), *Trading Injuries* (1993), *Counter Offence* (1996), *Truth and Treason* (2009), and *State of Denial* (2012). What makes Varma an eminent Indian diasporic theatre person is his 2001 production of *Bhopal*, as directed by Jack Langedijk. In India, the play was staged in Hindi as *Zehreeli Hawa* (Poisonous Air) in 2002 under the direction of Habib Tanvir. *Bhopal* is based on the historical Bhopal gas tragedy of India in 1984 which not only took thousands of lives but also left deformed more than that with a continuing after-effect even to the next generations and the unborns. The play includes the journey of some fictional characters, local (like the village men and women), development freak diasporic N.R.I. (Devraj Sarthi), minister (Jaganlal), as well as Canadian doctor (Sonya Labonte) and many more. Bhatia argues:

> "While showing the complicity of local politicians with American multinational corporations, a complicity that facilitated the disaster with fatal consequences, the play [*Bhopal*] forcefully references the malformed bodies at home that continue to be affected by the policies and practices of multinational corporations with little or no accountability. Such a lack of accountability and the motivations of greed on the part of American corporations that amass their fortunes through exploitation of Third World subjects and through the complicities of local politicians interested in accruing political gains highlight the asymmetries of power between First and Third Worlds by displaying for the audience bodies that do not matter" (225).

Varma creates his play as a critique of developmentalism, the murder of the poor as legitimised in the name of progression, politics and state, environmental crises and the stark division between the inhabitants of the First and Third world. Thus the idea of home, in this play, is used as a concept to explore, in words of Varma himself, "poverty's relationship to development" (188), and thus making *Bhopal* as 'a play against forgetting' (*ibid*. 189).

Vancouver Saath was initiated in the 1980s' by Sadhu Binning (b. 1947) and other politically-conscious activists, being inspired by the *Saath* community in the villages of Punjab, in order to advance the ideas of community bonding and solidarity through theatre with the vision of 'raising issues pertaining to Punjabi immigrants, namely, employment, B.C.'s anti-labour legislation, the divisive impact of the movement for self-determination in Punjab on the Punjabi community in B.C. in the 1980s', and the rights of women, youth and the elderly at home and in the workplace' (Bhatia 218). The *Saath*-activists preferred theatre because they were doubtful about the impact of the journals like *Watna Dur* or *Canada Darpan* on the general audience. Sadhu Binning comments:

> "We realised that most of the Punjabis were not in the habit of reading serious articles in the best of times, let alone at a time when they were simply too involved in their daily struggles to establish themselves in a new land. This realisation led us to experiment with theatre" (23).

So their mandate was clear from its inception. The activists were initially inspired by the Punjabi playwright Gursharan Singh (1929-2011) when his theatre group, *Amritsar Natak Kala Kander*, went for stage shows in Canada, and then with the collaboration of *Punjabi Cultural Association*, these theatre activists finally produced their first play in 1984. The first few plays were based on the issues of Punjab like—Makhan Tut's *Punjab di Awaz* (The Voice of Punjab; 1984), Gursharan Singh's *Kursi, Morcha, te Hawa Vich Latke Log* (Chair, Battlefront and People Dangling in the Air; 1984), Gursharan Singh's adaptation of Sohan Singh's Sital's partition-novel, *Tootan Wala Khoon* (A Well with Mulberry Trees; 1985). In 1984 November, Saath staged its another play, *Picket Line*, written by Sadhu Binning and Sukhawant Hundal, and it was staged along with Gursharan Singh's *Haval Gole* (Air Balls). *Picket Line* was later staged in English in 1986, and this gave the space for the entry of new activists such as Pindy Gill, Nick Sihota, Sital Dhillon and Bhavna Bhangu along with already-established activists like Makhan Tut, Jagdish Binning, Sadhu Binning, Inderjit Rode, Anju Hundal, Sukhwant Hundal, Paul Binning and others. In 1987, female writers like Anju Hundal, Jagdish Binning, Harjinder Sangra and Pindy Gill produced *Different Age Same Cage*, on different stages of the life of Punjabi women, and in this play even the male characters were performed by the women.

Other *Saath*-plays include, *A Crop of Poison* (1988), *A Lesson of a Different Kind* (1989) by Sadhu Binning (it explores the exploitation of the immigrant janitorial workers), *Not a Small Matter* (1989) on gender violence, written by Anju Hundal, Jagdish Binning, Harjinder Sangra, Sukhwant Hundal and Sadhu Binning among others (Binning 25-26).

Taking a cue from the revolutionary theatre crafts and ideologies of Utpal Dutt and Badal Sircar, the 'stalwarts of the avant-garde Indian theatre of the 1960s' and 1970s" (Bose, *Beyond* 162), Rana Bose (b. 1966) formed another South Asian Canadian theatre company in Montreal called *Montreal Serai* in mid-1980s' with the mandate to challenge discrimination in art and society on the whole. 'Multiethnic in its orientation', the theatre company stages radical political plays, with 'radical dramaturgical techniques of absurdist and non-realistic modes of presentation' (*ibid*. 163). For the *Serai*-members, 'multiculturalism against ghettoisation became a looming concern' (Bhatia 219). Rana Bose's *The Death of Abbie Hoffman* (1999), based on Badal Sircar's Bengali play, *Micchil* (Procession), is 'a protest theatre, a performance manifesto, and a novel inclusion of innovative performance aesthetics into a politically diasporic space' (Bose, *Beyond* 166). Though Bose's play does not deal with typical Indian diasporic concerns, undoubtedly he is the first to include absurdist, non-realistic and political drama in the corpus of South Asian diasporic theatre. His play blurs the lines between colour, race, nation and identity. Bose's theatre of politics, as he said in an interview given to Neilesh Bose on 28 April 2006, is meant to introduce 'a lot of Asian contemporariness into the mainstream of Canadian culture by exposing the larger white audience to many things South Asian' (qtd. in Bose, *Beyond* 166). His other plays include *Nobody Gets Laid, On the Double* (1992), *Baba Jacques Dass and Turmoil at Côte-des-Neiges Cemetery* (1996), *Five or Six Characters in Search of Toronto* (1997), *Prairie Fire, Some Dogs, The Sulpician Escarpment,* and *Who to Please,* which often question or criticise the Indian immigration experiences in Canada or the Canadian cultural outlook towards the South Asia, or embark upon transnational issues as in *Nobody Gets Laid,* or highlights a different type of patriarchy within the South Asian-Canadian setting as in his second play like *On the Double*. A believer in multiculturalism, Rana Bose does not believe in the existence of borders, rather his play shows, as he says in his own words in an interview given to Uma Parameswaran, how he extends 'the borders, extending and blending them to the centre, of blending', and thus acquires a distinct political position that he holds as a diasporic theatre artist (qtd.in Chougule and Paricharak 76).

Other than the Indian theatre-companies in Vancouver and Montreal, those in Toronto such as *Rasikarts* also produce plays of South Asia/India since 2000. Such theatre-houses even produce plays like the Indian playwright Mahesh Dattani's *Tara* or Gurucharan Das's *9 Jakhoo Hill*, while also producing other English diasporic plays such as Tanika Gupta's *The Waiting Room* or Dinesh Narandas's *Inmates* (Bose, *Beyond* 163). While Saros Cowasjee's *The Last of the Maharajas* (1980), a screenplay adaptation of Mulk Raj Anand's *Private Life of an Indian Prince*, deals with a small private segment of Indian history of kingship, Anosh Irani's *Matka King* (first premiered in 2003), *The Bombay Black* (2006), *Men in White* (2018), *Buffoon* (2021) often touch the concept of home, both in India and Canada. Among others, mention must be made of women-centric plays of Indian diaspora in Canada, such as Surjeet Kalsey's *Daughters Behind the Palace* (1982), *Nirlujj Saman* (Shameess Times, 1994), *Poh de Agan* (Holy Fire, 1998), *Vijay ton Baad* (After Getting Visa, 1997), *Chetna* (Awareness, co-authored with Ajmer Rode, first staged in 1982), *Dhian Pardesnan* (Daughters Abroad, 1997), *Saat Pariyaan Ghar da Supna* (Distant Women: Dreaming of Home, 1996). Uma Parameswaran (b. 1938), on the other hand, while dealing with the feminist issues, often deals with the problem of home of a woman placed within a repressive patriarchal culture through the mythical and historical stories of India. Such themes are highlighted in her plays like *Meera: A Dance Drama* (1971), *Sons Must Die* (written in 1972 on 1947 Indian partition and the maternal sensibility of three women), *Rootless but Green are the Boulevard* (1987), *Dear Deedi, My Sister* (1989), *Sita's Promise* (2004), and so on. Nandi Bhatia observes that:

> "Over time, the annihilation of the idea of a mythical (Hindu) India led to a plurality in the way home came to be represented and drama took on an activist dimension in the 1980s' and onwards in order to address concerns shaped by multiculturalism, transnational capitalism and its local effects, violence against women, and the effects of war and displacement on women and their families" (222).

Many such feminist plays of Indo-Canadian literature are also visible in the Toronto-based South Asian Women's Theatre productions like the British-Sikh playwright, Gurpreet Kaur Bhatti's *Baysharam* (Shameless, 1991), or Cahoot's Theatre Project such as *A Canadian Monsoon* (1993), Company of Sirens' *All Whispers/ No Words* (1995) and so on (*ibid.* 222).Thus, in the gradual attempt to be a part of Canadian mainstream theatre, Indian diasporic plays in Canada continue to highlight issues of the South Asian/Indian communities through socio-political concerns of both the homeland and host-land.

Indian Diasporic Theatre in (South) Africa:

The entire continent of Africa, which 'houses' several countries that are erstwhile-English-colonies, shares the similar kind of socio-political consciousness like that of the common peoples' and intellectuals' of India/South Asia. Still Indian diaspora in Africa does have a non-linear and arbitrary relationship with the so-called 'host-country'. The 'Indian diasporic periods' in Africa can broadly be categorised into four parts: from 1860-1914, 1914-48, 1948-94, and post-1994 period. Most of the Indian migrants in present South Africa are the descendants of those labourers who came to the region around 1860-1914. Majority of them, belonging either to Southern India (like Tamil speaking people) or the Hindi-speaking north-Indian regions, or to Bengal, landed on the shores of Natal to work as indentured labours. As the Indians too were direct English subjects, the Afrikaaner government could not overtly subdue them, but devised different measures and tricks to encourage Indians to leave Africa or curb their power and rights. Things got more complicated with the activism and activities of Mohandas Karamchand Gandhi (1869-1948). M.K. Gandhi, during his two decades' sojourn in South Africa as a lawyer, put forth non-violent civil disobedience and *Satyagraha*-movement against the colonisers to resist the unjust laws against the Indians, which finally ended with an agreement between him and the South African statesman, Jan Smuts (1870-1950), with certain conditions applicable to both the sides. From 1914 to 1948, a gradual consolidated process of urbanisation of the Indians could be noticed. In 1920s, the birth of South African Indian Congress appeared as an impediment to the government's measures to restrict the resistance of all sorts by the Indians. In fact, a gradual development in education, art and culture among the Indians brought them closer to the rulers. With the independence of India in 1947, the Indians in Africa remained no more the British subjects. The apartheid-period of South Africa, from 1948 to 1994, witnessed the participation of many Indians to fight along with the natives against the unjust and inhuman apartheid practices in the country. Anti-apartheid Indian activists like Ahmed Kathrada, Mac Maharaj, Ismail and Fatima Meer, and many others participated in every possible way to end the apartheid system. In the history of this long, fifty years' apartheid system, formally ending in 1994, a 'complete indigenisation of Indians in South Africa' (Vahed 229) could be traced. According to Neilesh Bose, "As residential segregation grew more prominent, the ethnic insularity and attention on solely 'Indian South African' culture grew within Indian communities" (*Beyond* 365). The post-apartheid period in free South Africa presents a completely different scenario within a multiracial context that witnesses the growth of the Indian community now more firm and stable after years of hardships on a foreign soil.

With the increasing population of the Indian migrants in Africa, gradually develops the cultural practice of different art forms in a multi-racial ambience. While tracing the theatre history of the Indian diaspora in Africa, Neilesh Bose notes that '[b]efore the late-1950s', Indian South African theatre and performance was encompassed under traditional Indian dance-drama forms such as *Therakutu*, a popular performance deriving from Tamil Nadu in South India' (*ibid*. 365). Dramatic adaptation of Indian epics like the *Ramayana*, the *Mahabharata*, or historical/ mythic stories such as *Nallatankal* or *Satyavan-Savitri*, or even Kalidasa's *Sakuntala* were staged in regional languages like Tamil, Telegu and so on. But during the apartheid phase, theatre in English replaced that in the indigenous languages. The educated Indians and liberal English performers started performing the British plays. Even if the British produced Indian classics by Kalidasa or Rabindranath Tagore, they promoted 'Orientalist versions of Indian culture', and such theatre could not address the local, indigenous concerns (365).

Since 1960s, however, the Indian theatrical tradition in Africa started shifting its interest and patterns by focussing on the community concerns and involving local casts. When Krishna Shah visited Durban in 1962 for staging Rabindranath Tagore's *The King of the Dark Chamber*, a host of Indian theatre-enthusiasts residing at Durban, like Muthal Naidoo, Ronnie Govender, Welcome Msomi, and others formed the *Durban Academy of Theatre Arts* (D.A.T.A.), which produced many English and American plays such as R. B. Sheridan's *The School for Scandal* and Edward Albee's *Who's Afraid of Virginia Woolf*, especially at the initial stage (Bose, *Beyond* 366). To honour Krishna Shah, Naidoo and Govender founded another theatre company called the *Shah Theatre Academy* that produced plays like Arthur Miller's *All My Sons*, among many others. Gradually, the founders and actors of these theatre companies started writing their own scripts on socio-political issues for the stage performances as they 'identify themselves with native Africans and joins hands in voicing against racial discrimination' (Rani 274).

During the apartheid-phase, playwrights like Muthal Naidoo, Ronnie Govender, Kessie Govender, and Kriben Pillay formed a completely new corpus of *indigenous South African Indian theatre* that deals with the issues concerned with socio-political satire and also the use of patois and native dictions. The best example of this tradition, arguably, is Ronnie Govender's *The Lahnee's Pleasure* (1972), the 'first theatrical exposure of working class Indian South African life on stage' (Bose, *Beyond* 366). The *Black Consciousness Movement* during 1960s' and 1970s' was led by some Indian theatre-activists, including Saths Cooper and Strini

Moodley, to create a political space for *black-theatre*. Although, it left less impact on Indian South African theatrical tradition, it definitely raised some vital political questions that the time demanded. Thus, Indian South African theatre got a new momentum and acquired its own aesthetic space. Set within the apartheid regime of South Africa, *The Lahnee's Pleasure* documents the contemporary socio-cultural lives of the Indians situated in a world dominated by racial segregation. As Bose writes, "[a]esthetically, Govender successfully introduced an Indian patois into a show that spoke to all South Africans" (*ibid.* 370). Other important plays written by Ronnie Govender on diverse socio-political issues include, *Beyond Calvary, The First Stone, His Brother's Keeper, Swami, At the Edge, Off-Side!, In-Side!, Back-Side!, 1949, Too Muckin' Futch, The Great R31M Robbery, Who or What is Deena Naicker?, Your Own Dog Won't Bite You, Blossoms from the Bough* and so on.

Like Ronnie Govender's political satires, Muthal Naidoo's *The Master Plan, We 3 Kings,* **Kessie** Govender's *Working Class Hero* and Kriben Pillay's *Looking for Muruga* document not only the socio-political role played by the Indian communities in South African apartheid regime, but also capture the Indo-African relations and the whereabouts of the dominant working class people through the aesthetics, poetics, idioms, expressions and patois of indigenous performances. Such plays deal not with the theme of displacement but with the deep rooted pain of racial segregation and discrimination that the coloured migrants experienced in the so-called 'host-lands'. Other mentionable plays written by the trio include Muthal Naidoo's *Flight from the Mahabharata, Ikyalethu,* and *Mask;* Kessie Govender's *Alternative Action, Black Skies, The Decision, God Made Mosquitoes Too, Herstory, Injured on Duty, Ka-goos, On the Fence, Ravana, The Shack, Stable Expense, Trump-You, Trump-Me, Underground* among others; Kriben Pillay's *Coming Home, FM Stereotype, Mr. Bansi is Dead, Mr. O's Story, Side by Side Masisizane,* and so on.

The post-apartheid scenario of free South Africa has been wonderfully captured in the plays of Rajesh Gopie (*Martial Blitz,* 1996; *Out of Bounds,* toured 1998-2003; *A Coolie Odyssey,* 2002) covering a wide range of issues of 'import to post-apartheid Indian communities, such as gender, spousal abuse, and youth in Indian South Africa' (Bose, *Beyond* 366-67). Yugan Naidoo's 2003 play *Latas FM* is a "humorous demonstration of the liberal bourgeois indictment of ethnicised 'lowbrow' humour that pervades the Indian South African theatre community" (367). In plays like *Cheaper than Roses* and *Purdah*, Ismail Mahomed mirrors the socio-cultural lives of the Muslim communities. Krijay Govender's *Women in Brown* deals with the situations of women in the newly born South Africa. With the increasing power of the black communities in post-apartheid South Africa, the Indians face new challenges at the community levels, which are dealt with utmost sincerity in the plays like *Spice 'n Stuff* and *To House* by Ashwin Singh. Besides these, Dinesh Narandas's *Inmates*, Geraldine Naidoo's *Chilly Boy*, Vivian Moodley's *Hambha Kahle Mr. Moodley*, too, contribute to the corpus of Indian diasporic theatre in South Africa.

The Curtain Call:

Indian diasporic theatre, of course, is not restricted to the four nations discussed earlier. The researcher could not discuss the theatrical productions in places like Fiji, Malaysia, Singapore, Trinidad and Tobago, and other such countries for constraints of space. That does not, however, narrow down the growing corpus of Indian diasporic theatre, which shares some fundamental commonalities, as reflected through the theatrical texts and performances. The most important struggle is to be assimilated with the mainstream theatre of any nation, along with the funding and patronising issues. Indian diaspora, among those of the other South Asian-nations, is most vibrant in its cultural form, and theatre, being a direct connecting medium with the audience, can create a cathartic response among them. This is how the multicultural ethnicity and indigenousness of the Indian theatre can survive in the overseas and create a distinct diasporic aesthetics with both local and global touches.

Notes:

1. Consisting of 36 Chapters, the ancient Indian *Natyashastra*, written by Bharat Muni between 200 B.C. and A.D. 200/ 500 B.C.–A.D. 500, is a dramatic treatise on different facets of theatrical tradition as well as a manual for the performative aesthetics of ancient Indian arts.
2. In an interview given to Sarah Qari for Qari's undergraduation-thesis (titled *Identity in Play: An Ethnography of South Asian Theatre in London*, 2016), Jatinder Verma, while talking about the 'cultural contour of the migrant' (30), also talks about the dual existence of the immigrant, in memory as well as in the present lived experience. This has been referred to in Qari's (*Academia.edu*-uploaded-article), "Identity in Play"-paper, which was accessed by the author on 15 April 2022 <https://www.academia.edu/26155690/Identity_in_Play_An_Ethnography_of_South_Asian_Theater_in_London>
3. Rasa, in the Indian aesthetics, is the essence of heart, different emotions, usually evoked within a reader/listener/spectator whoever is experiencing a piece of art and performance.
4. Arthur William Ryder, a Harvard English scholar of Sankrit language and literature had translated into English the Sanskrit classics like *Mrichchhakatikam* by Shudraka as *The Little Clay Cart*, and *Shakuntala* by Kalidasa, both of which were staged multiple times in the first decade of the twentieth century and also later, but interestingly neither the translator/director(s) were Indian, nor any one of the large crew of the performers.
5. Gurudwara, meaning 'gateway to guru', is the religious place of gathering for the Sikh communities.

Works Cited:

Alam, Mohammed Badrul. "Situating Asian Indian Diaspora in the United States: An Exploratory Study". *Indian Diaspora: Trends and Issues*. Eds. Ajaya Kumara Sahoo and K. Laxmi Narayan. New Delhi: Serials Publications, 2008. Rpt. 2019. 64-77.

Bhatia, Nandi. "Diasporic Activism and the Mediations of 'Home': South Asian Voices in Canadian Drama". *South Asian Diasporic Cinema and Theatre: Re-visiting Screen and Stage in the New Millennium.* Eds. Ajay K. Chaubey and Ashvin I. Devasundaram. Jaipur: Rawat Publications, 2017. 215-237.

Bhattacharya, Swagata. *"Re-defining 'Can. Lit.' Or 'Indian Writing in English'?*: English Writings and the Indian Diaspora in Canada". *Journal of Comparative Literature and Aesthetics* 44.2 (Summer 2021): 191-198. Accessed on 15 June 2021 <*http://jcla.in/wp-content/uploads/2021/06/JCLA-44.2_Summer-2021_Swagata-Bhattacharya.pdf*>

Binning, Sadhu. "Vancouver Saath: A Profile by Sadhu Binning". Rungh: *A South Asian Quarterly of Culture, Comment and Criticism* 2.1&3 (1993): 22-26. Accessed on 15 June 2022 <*https://www.tru.ca/cicac/readings/Rungh_v2_n1-2.pdf*>

Bose, Neilesh. *Beyond Bollywood and Broadway: Plays from the South Asian Diaspora.* Ed. Neilesh Bose. Bloomington: Indiana University Press, 2009.

---. ""Sharuk and Shylock: The Creation of a South Asian American Aesthetic". *South Asian Diasporic Cinema and Theatre: Re-visiting Screen and Stage in the New Millennium.* Eds. Ajay K. Chaubey and Ashvin I. Devasundaram. Jaipur: Rawat Publications, 2017. 238-264.

Chandrasekhar, S. (ed.). From India to Canada: *A Brief History of Immigration; Problems of Discrimination; Admission and Assimilation.* La Jolla-California: Population Review Books, 1986.

Chatterjee, Sudipto. "South Asian American Theatre (Un/Re-) Painting the Town Brown". *Theatre Survey* 49.1 (May 2008): 109-117. Accessed on 25 June 2022 <*https://www.cambridge.org/core/services/aop-cambridge-core/content/view/B87F62F2245D67F4B7415ADF84C74332/S0040557408000069a.pdf/south-asian-american-theatre-un-re-painting-the-town-brown.pdf*>

Chaturvedi, Ravi. "Preface". *Contemporary Indian Theatre: Theatricality and Artistic Crossovers.* Eds. Ravi Chaturvedi and Tapati Guha. Jaipur: Rawat Publications, 2017. xi-xiii.

Chaubey, Ajay K. and Ashvin I. Devasundaram. "South Asian Diasporic Cinema and Theatre: A Critical Introduction". *South Asian Diasporic Cinema and Theatre: Re-visiting Screen and Stage in the New Millennium.* Eds. Ajay K. Chaubey and Ashvin I. Devasundaram. Jaipur: Rawat Publications, 2017. 1-20.

Chougule, Ramesh and Paricharak D.S. "Transnational Culture in Rana Bose's *Nobody Gets Laid*". *Lierary Endeavour* 8.3 (July, 2017): 75-79. Accessed on 12 July 2022 <https://www.researchgate.net/profile/Ramesh-Chougule/publication/327882286_Transnational_Culture_in_Rana_Bose's_Nobody_Gets_Laid/links/5baafbd792851ca9ed25e923/Transnational-Culture-in-Rana-Boses-Nobody-Gets-Laid.pdf>

Dattani, Mahesh. *Final Solutions and Other Plays*. Chennai: Manas, 1994.

Dharwadker, Aparna. "Diaspora and Theatre of the Nation". *Theatre Research International* 1.3 (2003): 303-25.

---"Diaspora, Nation, and the Failure of Home: Two Contemporary Indian Plays". *Theatre Journal* 50.1 (March 1998): 71-94. Accessed on 12 April 2022 <https://www.jstor.org/stable/25068484>

Griffin, Gabriele. *Contemporary Black and Asian Women Playwrights in Britain*. Cambridge: Cambridge University Press, 2003.

Gupta, Surendra K. *Indian Diaspora: Study of Emerging Sandwich Cultures*. New Delhi: Atlantic Publishers and Distributors, 2013.

Gupta, Tapati. "Introduction". *Contemporary Indian Theatre: Theatricality and Artistic Crossovers*. Eds. Ravi Chaturvedi and Tapati Guha. Jaipur: Rawat Publications, 2017.1-11. Hans, Raj Kumar. "Gurudwara as a Cultural Site of Punjabi Community in British Columbia, 1905-1965." *Fractured Identity: The Indian Diaspora in Canada*. Eds. Sushma J. Varma and Radhika Seshan. New Delhi: Rawat Publication, 2003. 207-216.

Hussain, Asaf. "The Indian Diaspora in Britain: Political Interventionism and Diaspora Activism". *Asian Affairs: An American Review* 32.3 (Fall 2005): 189-208. Accessed on 8 June 2022 <http://www.jstor.com/stable/30172878>

Lahiri, Himadri. *Diaspora Theory and Transnationalism*. Ed. Allen Hibbard. Hyderabad: Orient Blackswan, 2019.

Mistry, Cyrus. *Doongaji House*. Ed. Alok Bhalla and Anju Makhija. New Delhi: Sahitya Academy, 2006.

Mukherjee, Bharati. "An Invisible Woman". *Saturday Night* 96 (March 1981): 30-39.

Parameswaran, Uma. *SACLIT: An Introduction to South Asian-Canadian Literature*. Madras: East- West Books, 1996.

Qari, Sarah. *Identity in Play: An Ethnography of South Asian Theatre in London*. A U.G.-thesis submitted to the Department of Anthropology, Princeton University, 2016. Accessed on 20 July 2022 <https://www.academia.edu/26155690/Identity_in_Play_An_Ethnography_of_South_Asian_Theater_in_London>

Rani, D. Sudha. "South Asian Diasporic Theatre: A Critical Overview". *South Asian Diasporic Cinema and Theatre: Re-visiting Screen and Stage in the New Millennium.* Eds. Ajay K. Chaubey and Ashvin I. Devasundaram. Jaipur: Rawat Publications, 2017. 265-276.

Sahoo, Ajaya Kumara. "Some Reflections on Indian Diaspora in Canada". *Indian Diaspora: Trends and Issues.* Eds. Ajaya Kumara Sahoo and K. Laxmi Narayan. New Delhi: Serials Publications, 2008. Rpt. 2019.110-121.

Salusso, Daniela. "The 'Diasporic Theatre' from nostalgia to contemporary socio-politics: reimagining identity in some contemporary Black and Asian British playwrights". 2020: 87-76. Accessed on 25 June 2022 <*https://ilcastellodielsinore.it/index.php/ Elsinore/article/download/135/117/*>

Schechner, Richard. *Performance Theory.* New York and London: Routledge, 1988.

Sengupta, Ashis. "Staging Diaspora: South Asian American Theatre Today". *Journal of American Studies* 46.4 (November 2012): 831-54. Accessed on 9 June 2022. <*https://www.jstor.org/stable/23352467*>

Thakur, Priyam Basu. "Theatre for Development in Indian Context: An Introspection". *South Asian Diasporic Cinema and Theatre: Re-visiting Screen and Stage in the New Millennium.* Eds. Ajay K. Chaubey and Ashvin I. Devasundaram. Jaipur: Rawat Publications, 2017. 277-289.

Ubersfeld, Anne. *Reading Theatre.* Toronto-Buffalo-London: University of Toronto Press, 1999.

Vahed, Goolam. *The Making of Indian Identity in Durban, 1914-1949.* Ph.D Dissertation. Indiana University, 1995.

Varma, Rahul. "Teesri Duniya Theatre: Diversifying Diversity with Relevant Works of Theatre". *South Asian Popular Culture* 73.3 (2009): 179-94.

Whitton, David. "Foreword". *Contemporary Indian Theatre: Theatricality and Artistic Crossovers.* Eds. Ravi Chaturvedi and Tapati Guha. Jaipur: Rawat Publications, 2017.vii-ix.

The Indian Diaspora and the Short Story
Critical Reflections on Jhumpa Lahiri

–Lalan Kishore Singh

Stories, elaborate or brief, since antiquity, has always been intrinsic to how humans have expressed themselves. As R.C Feddersen, in tracing a genealogy of storytelling, points out, "[W]hether they bespeak the bases and values of culture in myth and folktale or foster a sense of right and wrong in fables, stories organize and transmit sequences of human events and experiences into meaningful units. The most fragmentary of tales still suggest some relationship between present, past, and future" (xv). Victoria Patea too, in tracing a history of storytelling, traces it to "myths and biblical verse narratives, medieval sermons and romances, fables, folktales, ballads", but as a form or genre, she states that it has been largely neglected in comparison to other genres, and theorisation about its form and nature has been "a long-deferred process" (1-26). The engagement with the nature of the form, in its modern avatar, was initially initiated not by literary critics, but 19th century practitioners of the form like Edgar Allan Poe, Herman Melville and Anton Chekhov, and early 20th century writers like Henry James, Flanner O'Connor and Eudora Welty. To Patea, Edgar Allan Poe's engagement with the nature of the short story marks its genesis as a unique genre, for "he brought into discussion issues of form, style, length, design, authorial goals, and reader affect" and devised a "framework" for the modern short story (Patea 2-3). For Edgar Allan Poe, the uniqueness of the form of the short story lay in its 'unity of effect or impression', a quality preserved because of its brevity 'requiring from a half-hour to one or two hours in its perusal' (ref. to Hays 19).

The short story in its modern form, while deriving much of its energy from the eternal human propensity to narrate stories, may be seen as an emergent form which seeks to define itself as a genre distinct from the novel. The distinction between the two narrative types has been a subject of critical debate. For Branders Mathews—as he states in *The Philosophy of the Short Story*—a short story is not one because of its brevity, but because of its "unity of impression", a unity which a novel does not possess. A 'Short-Story' *proper* is characterised by a "single effect, complete and self-contained" and hence it has the "effect of totality" or a "unity of impression" of a particular experience. The unity of impression of the genre is achieved through compression and conciseness rendering it a more difficult art than fiction. A short story is invariably narrated to a 'plan', a motive which is not necessarily what is termed a plot of a work of fiction. A sense of form, the ability to be logical and harmonious is an essential attribute a short story writer must possess (Matthews 1-30). This symmetrical juxtaposition of the short story and the novel is, however, criticised by Mary Louise Pratt. For her, the relationship between the two is asymmetrical and hierarchal "with the novel on top and the short story dependent". Conceptually, she asserts, mere brevity "cannot be an intrinsic property" and historically, "the novel has been …the more…prestigious of the two" (qtd. in Pratt 96). Nadine Gordimer, in analysing the relation between the two, however asserts that the short story is "more flexible and open to experimentation", requires "a stricter technical discipline" and the writer enjoys "a wider freedom than the novelist". The form of the novel, by its very nature, for her, "is false to the nature of whatever can be grasped of human reality". In a novel, the character is one while "each of us has a thousand lives"; the novelist may experiment with chronology and the narrative, but the "characters have the reader by the hand", and this relationship "cannot and does not convey the quality of human life". In contrast, the short story "sees by the light of the flash", engages with the certainty of "the present moment" and "how the characters will appear, think, behave […] is irrelevant" and is a form where "a discreet moment of truth is aimed at" and not the moment of truth, as in a novel, that is the culmination of actions that lead to it (Gordimer 264).

Indeed, discussions about the nature, history and development of the short story invariably leads to comparisons with the novelistic form and all that one can arrive at is a relative description of its nature without endeavouring to define it. However, certain deductions can be drawn that seem to describe its nature. One important deduction that can be drawn is that a short story, in endeavouring to achieve a unity in terms of impression through a plan or a motive, articulates a certain intension, and the motive that drives it is invariably a personal one, whether it be an emotional experience or a cultural/social experience that the author seeks to articulate. The relationship between the novel and the short story is relevant to an understanding of diaspora experience for both these forms have found acceptance as a form suited to articulate the uniqueness of the diasporic experience. Writers have used both the forms to represent diasporic experience, but it is in the short story form, where the emotions expressed is more immediate, that the richness and poignancy of the experience is best discernible. It is a suitable vehicle for chronicling the new cultural reality and the transformative changes that modernity brings into their experiences, the challenges of migration and displacement and the emergence of a new diasporic identity as an in-between space between home and host spaces.

The Indian diasporic experience finds articulation most intensely in short stories written by women. Some of the prominent diasporic Indian origin women who employ the form of the short story include Bharati Mukherjee, Chitra Divakaruni and Jhumpa Lahiri. Bharati Mukherjee's *The Middleman and Other Stories* (1988), which won the *National Book Critics Circle Award* in 1988, engages with the issues of immigration and its experience, while Chitra Banerjee Divakaruni, whose short-story-collection *Arranged Marriage and Other Stories* won the *American Book Award* in 1995, also delves into the intricacies of life away from home, and the complications of living in the U.S.A. as diasporic subjects. Jhumpa Lahiri's short-story-collection *Interpreter of Maladies* (1999) won the *Pulitzer Prize for Fiction*, and her other short-story-collection (until today), *Unaccustomed Earth* (2008), won the *Frank*

O'Connor International Short Story Award. Of the three mentioned names, Jhumpa Lahiri's identity as an Indian diasporic writer is complicated by her space and experience. Born to a Bengali immigrant couple in London, on 11 July 1967, she immigrated to the United States with her parents when she was a two-year-old child, to be raised in Kingston where her father worked as a librarian at the University of Rhode Island. Her status as a writer has been a subject of intense debate. The objective of this study is to understand her short stories through the prism of her identity and the nature of her cultural heritage. The purpose is to investigate if and how, in spite of her hyphenated identity, and her cultural experience the Indian cultural experience continues to influence her writing.

'Diaspora' as a historical experience has had a long history and the meaning of the experience has also evolved with time. The understanding of the term 'Diaspora' has migrated beyond its restricted meaning related to the dispersal and exile of the Jews. Today, the propensity is to denote any kind of migration as diasporic. The term itself traces its genealogy to the Greek noun *diaspora* derived from the verb *diaspeirein* signifying the idea of dispersal. In its origin sense, the term was a theological concept relating to the exile of the Jews from Israel for disobedience of God's Laws within which was enshrined the possibility of a return as a reward for obedience to God. However, the idea of the diaspora, as employed today, does not, for William Safran, conform to the "ideal type" of the Jewish diaspora. Instead he delineates certain characteristics of the modern diasporic experience: (a) Ancestral dispersion from a 'centre' to foreign regions. (b) Retention of "a collective memory, vision, or myth about the original homeland—its physical location, history and achievements; (c) The experience of alienation and insulation from the host society ; (d) The vision that the ancestral homeland is "their true, ideal home" and "the place to which they or their descendants would (or should) eventually return"; (e) A collective commitment to the "maintenance or restoration of their original homeland and its safety and prosperity"; (f) a continuous relationship with the homeland as a means to sustain "their ethnocommunal consciousness and solidarity" (Safran 83). Moreover, today, as James Clifford observes, numerous descriptive terms wrestle to describe the intermediate zone "of nations, cultures, and regions", terms like "border, travel, creolisation, transculturation, hybridity, and diaspora", rendering it difficult to maintain "exclusivist paradigms" in "attempts to account for transnational identity formations" (Clifford 303-04). Indeed, in the age of globalisation diasporas are, as Robin Cohen states, "in a continuous state of formation and reformation", responding to events, either tumultuous or subtle "in religious epicentres, homelands and hostlands". In the present age, Cohen highlights four aspects that are noteworthy in comprehending the continuous transformation of the idea of diaspora: (a) the globalised nature of the economy, connectivity, growth of "new professional and managerial cadres" which creates new opportunities for the diaspora. (b) new forms of global migration, which unlike the past which necessitated a permanent residency and adoption of the host country, now evolved into "limited contractual relationships, family visits, (and) intermittent stays abroad" (c) the growth of a cosmopolitan sensibility as a consequence of the "multiplication […] of transactions […] between the different peoples of the world", and (d) Religion as a tool for social cohesion through "renewed pilgrimage and translocation" (Cohen 141).

The trajectory in which the idea of the diaspora has evolved through its historical growth as well as the immediacy of experience that migration and travel from the homeland to the hostland entails, seeks articulation of the experience through narrative forms that may convey the intensity of the experience with a unity and immediacy. The short story form with its penchant to relay with unity and immediacy in brevity makes it's a useful form for the articulation of experiences of travel, cultural assimilation or ostracisation, pangs of memory of the homeland and the longing for a return, besides other experiences. The range of experiences and the nature of the emotions tangled with the concept of diaspora, necessitates a form that enables a clear and uncomplicated expression of the experience. The form of the short story, more than the novel, provides, through its conciseness, a suitable mode for the articulation of the diasporic experience.

An examination of the history of the Indian diaspora would reveal the myriad forms of experiences that are enshrined within it. The history of the Indian diaspora has been shaped by the nation's experience of historical forces—colonialism, nationalism and globalization. Radha Sarma Hegde and Ajaya Kumar Sahoo in the *Introduction* to their edited-work *Routledge Handbook of the Indian Diaspora* describe the historical trajectory of the Indian diaspora. Indians, they state, constitute after the British and the Chinese, the third largest diasporic group residing outside the homeland with nearly 25 million Indians settled in over 100 countries, and in some cases as in Fiji, Mauritius, Trinidad, Guyana and Surinam, constituting nearly 40 percent of the local population. In the pre-colonial period, trade and religion were the chief reasons for migration. Historically, they trace the global mobility of Indians to the first century A.D. with myriad classes of people like merchants, princes, priests, poets and artisans migrated to East Africa and Southeast Asian countries forging cultural ties in these spaces. The Indian sub-continent, because of its strategic location, was an important central space for the traffic of people and ideology between the kingdoms of the Coromandel Coast and South East Asia. With colonisation in the nineteenth and twentieth centuries, conditions necessitating migration of Indians to other parts of the world increased manifold for "European imperialist expansion depended on both the movement and regulation of the bodies of the colonized". During the nineteenth century, Indian workers found themselves transported to British Guiana, Trinidad, Jamaica and South Africa owing to the abolition of slavery and the demand for workers in the "sugar, tea, coffee, cocoa and rubber plantations in the colonies." The situation in India—colonial rule, famine and natural calamities—destroyed cottage industries, forcing workers to migrate under the indenture system. Post the two World Wars, following India's independence, the nature of migration altered; the movement was largely to the West and labour force in the diaspora consisted largely of skilled professionals, under the influence of the economic changes. This situation "significantly reworked the Indian diasporic narrative in the post-independence context" (Hegde and Sahoo 3-6).

The literature of the Indian diaspora follows the curve taken by its history and expectedly so as the lived experience of a subjectivity would logically correspond to its historical experience. Vijay Mishra's *The Literature of the Indian Diaspora* is an important intervention in the understanding of the historical and theoretical understanding of the Indian diasporic experience. His cryptic comment—"All diasporas are unhappy, but every diaspora is unhappy in its own way"—points to the dilemma of the diasporic experience. Diasporic subjects, he states, are not "comfortable with their non-hyphenated identities", and seek to explore the significance of the hyphen, but do not wish to "press the hyphen too far" for fear of reprisals away from home. Displacement, and "self-imposed exile" is fundamental to its experience. Vijay Mishra bifurcates narratives articulating the Indian diasporic experience into the old (that is, early modern 19th century indenture experience) and the new (or, the late modern or capitalist), which, he states, "traverse two quite different kinds of topography". The old narratives are where the Indian subject interacts largely with "other colonized peoples" in a "complex relationship of power and privilege". These old spaces are, he states, Fiji, South Africa, Malaysia, Mauritius, Trinidad, Guyana and Surinam. The new narratives articulate experiences of migrations to the metropolitan centres of the erstwhile Empire and other white-settler countries like Australia, Canada, New Zealand and the U.S.A. "as part of a post-1960s pattern of global migration". But as he points out, this bifurcation is not uncomplicated, for the 'old' can become part of the 'new' through "re-migrations such as Fiji-Indians to Vancouver or Trinidadian-Indians to Toronto" (Mishra 1-3).

Jhumpa Lahiri is a subject of just such a double hyphenated identity. Lavina Dhingra and Floyd Cheung in their *Preface* to their work *Naming Jhumpa Lahiri* ask, "Is she a Bengali, Indian, Asian American, American, or a postcolonial writer?" (Dhingra and Cheung). In "My Two Lives", a short piece, which incidentally is not part of any of her two collections of stories, but finds its presence in a collection of narratives edited by Donald McQuade and Robert Atwan titled *The Writer's Presence: A Pool of Readings*, Jhumpa Lahiri addresses the complication with regard to her identity after having lived for thirty-seven years in the United States where she anticipates "growing old". Although "Indian-American" has been the way she has been identified, she states, "less constant is (her) relationship to the term", for growing up in Rhode Island in the 1970s, she "felt neither Indian nor American". This, she states, was complicated for her, like many other immigrant children, by "the pressure to be two things, loyal to the old world and fluent in the new", and thereby being approved of neither of the two worlds "on either side of the hyphen". Growing up as a young girl, she observes, was "That I fell short at both ends, shuttling between two dimensions that had nothing to do with one another". Hence, while at home she followed the Bengali customs, speaking the language, "eating rice and dal with (her) fingers", while when with her American friends, she realized that "these ordinary facts seemed part of a secret, utterly alien way of life" which she was careful to conceal from her American friends. Home, for Lahiri's parents, was Calcutta (or, Kolkata), memory for them was "the family they missed", Bengali attire was "the clothes (her) mother wore" that was not to be found in any American mall, "at once as precious and as worthless as an outmoded currency" and music was "Nazrul songs". But there was another world, of which the writer was a part and of which her parents "had little knowledge or control of", the world of her "school, books, music, television" that quietly "seeped in and became a fundamental aspect of who (she) was". Yet as her name or appearance did not sound American, since she did not attend "Sunday School", had not expertise in ice-skating and "disappeared to India for months at a time", she was aware that she was not perceived as "entirely American". As a child growing up, she observes, she was aware that unlike those who proudly called themselves Irish-American or Italian-American because their roots "had descended underground", her ethnic roots "were still tangled and green". This predicament was complicated by her parents highlighting that she was not American, but Indian, leading her to gradually become defiant and assertive about who she thought she was. But in spite of her best efforts to define who she was, her "conflicting selves always (cancelled) each other".

The duality of the experience of Lahiri's identity is what motivated her to write. What drew her to her craft, she meditates, "was the desire to force the two worlds... to mingle on the page" as she had maturely allowed to mingle in her life. She "was not conscious that (her) subject was the Indian-American experience". The term "Indian-American" had gained currency in the United States around the time that her first collection of short stories *Interpreter of Maladies*, was published in 1999, and she began conveniently using the term to avoid explaining the complications around her identity, so that she did not "have to explain further", to bring to temporary closure the dilemma of her childhood "when there was no such way to describe me, when the most I could do was to clumsily and ineffectually explain". From that point on, though her middle age, "one plus one equals two", both sides of her hyphenated identity dwelling in her "like siblings" asserting themselves, "one outshining the other depending on the day", and she accepts "that a "bicultural upbringing is a rich but imperfect thing". But this admission of the bicultural nature of her identity is not an acceptance of her hyphenated identity. If anything, it seems to imply an acceptance of how she has been identified culturally rather than an assertion of such an identity. She asserts that she is American as "she was raised in this country" and if she feels Indian, it is not because of any experience of being Indian or "because of (her) genetic composition", but because of her parentage. After they are gone, "an anchor will drop, a line of connection will be severed" and by implication the duality of her identity would find resolution by the assertion of her American identity. "Their passing away" will for her mean the loss of "a singular struggle", the fading of "the immigrant's journey... founded on departure and deprivation", but for the next generation like herself, this would denote "a sense of arrival and advantage". For her, the "Indian-American" experience of the diaspora is the substance of her narratives because her parents lived that experience and she had emotionally undergone the intricate complexity of it as the next generation subject grappling with her identity in that in-between space (Lahiri 256-58). Lahiri here seems to provide a context to her engagement with the diasporic experience. The context hinges on her bicultural subjectivity, where the narrativisation in her short stories and fictional works of the Indian experience of displacement and acculturation appears to be her parents experience largely and her negotiation with it, while the American cultural assimilation or the difficulty of it, would seem to be of her own personal experience largely and her parents' negotiation with the new reality. But more significantly, her engagement with her subjectivity and cultural heritage, her endeavour to explore the hyphenated "Indian-American" experience, gains much of its impetus from her own experience as such a subject. In that sense, what she considers the moment of arrival for her generation, when they can begin to live an unhyphenated subjectivity would appear to be unrealistic, for the consciousness of the experience of being hyphenated would remain. As Salman Rushdie observes, "Literature is an interim report from the consciousness of the artist, as so can never be 'finished' or 'perfect'. Literature is made at the frontier between self and the world, and in the act of creation that frontier softens, becomes permeable, allows the world to flow into the artist and the artist to flow into the world" (Rushdie 427). This appears true for Jhumpa Lahiri, for even as she endeavours to be objective in her short stories, the experience of the reader is of the artist being between her subjectivity and her world.

Indeed, the stories that form the corpus of the two collections of short stories, *Interpreter of Maladies* and *Unaccustomed Earth* demonstrate the duality of Lahiri's engagement with her identity. In the collections, can be found stories that deal with both parts of her hyphenated identity as some with the hyphen itself. Certain themes and settings are constant within her stories—the Bengali characters, the reference to materials that invoke her cultural roots and the inter-personal relations or the complications thereof. Within the collections are (a) stories that engage with her cultural roots, (b) stories that have settings in India as 'home' and (c) stories that present the Indian-American encounter as forms of interpersonal bonding or the lack of it thereof. This engagement with the duality and the attendant difficulty of negotiating that dichotomy of identity by Jhumpa Lahiri raises a few questions with regard to authorship, representation and cultural consciousness. The diasporic experience being historical in nature, chained to politics and economics, as much as to culture, how is one to read Lahiri's stories because she has neither the consciousness of a diasporic subject nor the experience of it? If, as she states, the "Indian-American" experience is what she seeks to represent in her narratives, while at the same time confessing her lack of any immediate intimacy with that experience or culture, how is the reader to comprehend her stories—as a representation of the experience of diasporic 'going away' or the hyphenated moment of 'arrival'? Could the cultural memories and consciousness be severed, as she states with regard to her parentage and the erasure of it?

If, as Rushdie states, literature is the report of the consciousness from the artist, Lahiri's short story "When Mr. Pirzada came to dine" which is part of *Interpreter of Maladies* demonstrates her continuing identification with the historical significance of her Bengali cultural heritage. The story is narrated as a recollection through the memory of a character named Lilia, about incidents at her home in Boston when she was ten years old, and how these incidents which involved the regular visits of one Mr. Pirzada for dinner to listen to the television news about incidents at Dhaka in 1971 as East Pakistan was in the midst of violent clashes in is painful transformation into the modern state of Bangladesh, transformed her understanding of her culture and its history. This story begins with a historically important timeline in the lives of the Bengali society -autumn of 1971. This was at the height of the Bangladesh Liberation War that took place between March and December 1971. The war was against the Pakistani state for the liberation of the Bengali dominated East Pakistan and the formation of the new state of Bangladesh. A 10-year-old child, Lilia, is the narrator of the story. The story is narrated through memory of the visit of a certain Mr. Pirzada who is Bengali but hails from East Pakistan, at that point at war with the Pakistani state. She belongs to a Bengali family with roots in India. Mr. Pirzada, a lecturer in Botany at the university at Dhaka, was in Boston during the period of the war with his wife and seven daughters caught up in the violence at home. Hence what the story indicates is a present understanding of historical events that had been lived through as a child as part of a cultural experience, the import of which the narrator comprehends as an older person and narrates through memory. He had been awarded a grant, ironically by the Pakistani government to "study the foliage of New England" and he was writing a book on his discoveries and research. The story begins with a sketch of the war—Pakistan in a civil war, Dhaka "fighting for autonomy", Dhaka "invaded, torched, and shelled by the Pakistani army", and teachers shot dead, women raped, "three hundred thousand people" killed. Mr. Pirzada, while in Boston visited Laila's family every day hoping to ascertain, through the television-news, the "life or death of his family" from whom he had not heard for over six months, in spite of writing to his wife every passing week. As he had not enough money to procure a television, he visited Laila's family each evening "to eat dinner and watch the evening news".

Lilia, who was then a child of ten, did not understand the reasons for his daily visits. The narrator here seems to indicate her present understanding of the historical events. She felt that it was because of the cultural affinity that he was regularly invited for dinner. There is in this story a juxtaposition to two historical timelines, the 1971-Boston, the world to which Laila as a child belonged, and the conflict in the Indian sub-continent, to which her parents and Mr. Pirzada culturally identified, and as such was a historical reality for them. Throughout the story, these two historical realities, played out simultaneously is juxtaposed to expose the irony of the situation for Laila who recollects the story of her childhood and the tragic cultural experience of her being a Bengali. Laila recalls how Mr. Pirzada was discovered by her parents who "used to trail their fingers [...] through the [...] university directory" searching for "surnames familiar to their part of the world". Mr. Pirzada was discovered through the directory and invited to her home. Mr. Pirzada's initial visits did not attract Laila's visits much, but by September end when the war back home was intensifying, his visits became frequent enough for her to grow Pirzada's presence at her home. She had always thought of him as Indian as her parents who were Bengali and Indian, till her father shatters her ignorance by telling her one evening as she tries to arrange a "glass for the Indian man", that since 1947, Mr. Pirzada was "no longer considered Indian". Jhumpa Lahiri through a few sentences, poignantly brings out the consciousness of being a Bengali when she shatters the young Lilia's understanding of the history of her community. The young Lilia narrates the memory of her confusion as she questions her father about dates and her father tells her how their community had been "sliced" by history—"like a pie. Hindus here, Muslims there. Dhaka no longer belongs to us"—and the girl's innocent understanding of her culture is broken through her father's account of the Partition after which the enmity between the Hindus and the Muslims (both of which form part of the Bengali community) was such that "the idea of eating in the other company was still unthinkable".

At a young girl, all this "made no sense" to Lilia. Mr. Pirzada and her parents conversed in "the same language", shared a similar sense of humour, physically resembled each other, ate "pickled mangoes", " rice [...] with their hands", "chewed fennel seeds [...] as a digestive" and "took off their shoes before entering a room", all highlighting her Bengali cultural practises. She, then as a child, was perplexed and her father skilfully, through a map of the world points out to her how, although Mr. Pirzada and they were similar, were yet not of the same nationality. The map makes the young girl notice that Pakistan had "two distinct parts to it", one larger than the other, "separated by an expanse of Indian territory". Then her father tells her how, the smaller part of Pakistan (that is, East Pakistan), from where Mr. Pirzada, a Bengali Muslim hails, is fighting for its sovereignty. As a child, the implied now adult narrator, felt puzzled by the complications of her culture and identity. Lilia's father is annoyed that her school education in Boston does not teach her history that would make her aware of her culture or geography that would enable her to have a sense of the location of her identity. But unlike him, Lilia's mother is glad that she does not know about Partition, was proud that her daughter was born in the United States, was assured a good life, and education. Her reflections on the comfortable life they have managed to secure for themselves makes her remember that unlike them, Lilia would not need to "eat rationed food", "obey curfews", hide "neighbours in water tanks to prevent them from being shot".

The young Lilia, having been made to understand a difference between her and Mr. Pirzada as Bengalis but different, began "to study him with extra care" to locate what it was that "made him different". Mr. Pirzada carried a pocket watch by which he would make himself aware of the time it was in Dhaka and imagine what his family might be doing at that time. This was a significant difference between Lilia and him, she realized. While her family was unmindful of their cultural space, Mr. Pirzada, even while in Boston, "lived in Dhaka first", imagining what his daughters would be doing as they get ready for school like Lilia, and she comprehends that "our meals, our actions" were but a "shadow of what had already happened there" like a "lagging ghost of where Mr. Pirzada really belonged". The narrator announces her comprehension of the imitative nature of the performance of her culture in the United States, which just like the time lag that Mr. Pirzada keeps himself aware of through his watch, they simply performed daily while Mr. Pirzada actually lived his culture even in a different space and time through the immediacy of the memory of it. The visuals on the television as Mr. Pirzada along with Lilia and her family watch the pictures from the geography of their culture brings home to the narrator's consciousness what she had seen as a ten-year-old child. Lilia sees "tanks rolling", "fallen buildings", "East Pakistani refugees" fleeing to the Indian border, "barricaded university", "newspaper offices burnt", and looking at Mr. Pirzada's expressions she understood how, unlike her family, these images were so familiar to him. When Lilia's father points out to her the difference between her life and the lives of children her age in Dhaka—"See, children your age, what they do to survive"—she could not eat and admired Mr. Pirzada's stoic expression, and thought he must be thinking of his daughters who might suddenly appear on the television "blowing kisses" at him. At night, as she went to bed, Lilia could not imagine the relation of a suavely dressed Mr. Pirzada in Boston to the "unruly, sweltering world" they had seen. Her "stomach tightened" at the thought of his family being in the crowd of people she saw on the screen and whether they were dead. Identifying with him culturally, the narrator recalls praying for his family, although she had never been taught to pray by her parents.

The writer juxtaposes this cultural reality with the complete lack of awareness of the situation as it was evolving in the Indian subcontinent in Boston. Lilia recalls that at school, no one "talked about the war" and her education centred on the American Revolution, taxation and "memorized passages" from the Declaration of American Independence and its romantic enactment by students supervised by teachers. On one such occasion, when she was asked to write a report through research in the library on "a particular aspect of the Revolution" with "a slip of paper with the names of three books" given to her by her teacher, she finds it difficult to concentrate for her mind is on the tragic circumstances in the Indian subcontinent. So instead of working on her assignment, she picks out a book "titled *Pakistan: A Land and its People*" trying to understand her cultural roots better through pages "filled with photos of rivers and rice fields and men in military uniforms". She discovers a chapter on Dhaka in the book and, as she recalls, she began to read about "its rainfall", "its jute production", and its demography. But as news coming out from Dhaka began to be censored, she recalls how she was puzzled as a child wondering how her parents and Mr. Pirzada continued to spend their evenings enjoying "long leisurely meals", discussing Pirzada's book, her "father's nomination for tenure", playing "Scrabble until the eleven o'clock news" while all she wanted to do was "console Mr. Pirzada" and pray for his family by "eating a piece of candy" given to her by

Mr. Pirzada each day, as a form of prayer for his family. But as she dozed off to sleep each night, she would hear the "anticipating the birth of a nation on the other side of the world". The narrator recalls how, when October comes and while the American society was preparing for Halloween, news about the plight of Bengali refugees from East Pakistan to India kept pouring in, unsettling Mr. Pirzada as he tries to help young Lilia in her preparations for Halloween. She remembers how, as she dressed as a witch for Halloween, to participate in the traditions associated with it, the American society being oblivious of the tragedy happening to her community, she noticed, on returning home, Mr. Pirzada with "his head in his hands" with the news that war was inevitable, it was to be waged "on East Pakistan soil", the United States, their present space, ironically, "siding with West Pakistan" while the Soviet Union was "with India and what was soon to be Bangladesh". The war began, she recalls and in twelve days, the Pakistani army "surrendered in Dhaka". She emphasizes that she now knows these things she experienced as a child, not because she was aware of the experiences as a child, but because as an adult, she has read them in a library. What she remembered from memory of the incident as a child was that she was not allowed to watch television, "Mr. Pirzada stopped bringing (her) candy" and dinner was no longer a lavish affair. She remembered Mr. Pirzada not returning to his dormitory room and sleeping on the sofa at her home, her parents frantically calling up "relatives in Calcutta to learn details about the situation". She remembers the united manner in which her parents and Mr. Pirzada worked thought that period as if "they were a single person, sharing a single meal, a single body, a single silence, and a single fear". By January, the war having ended, Mr. Pirzada left Boston for his home at Dhaka "to discover what was left of it". She states she does not remember his leaving them, but she recalls the evening news narrating how 'Dhaka was repairing", the new leader Sheikh Mujibar Rahaman seeking help from countries for the reconstruction of Bangladesh, refugees returning from India only to be greeted "by unemployment and the threat of famine". She imagined Mr. Pirzada "perspiring heavily" in search of his family. Soon news arrived from him through a postcard stating his family was fine, "having survived the events of the past year" by escaping to an estate "belonging to his wife's grandparents" in Shillong which is in India close to the borders with Bangladesh. At the end of the story, the adult narrator recalls how she identified with Mr. Pirzada's experience which was accentuated now with his absence. His missing his family was metaphorically an acknowledgement of the experience of his community which the narrator hints at identifying with and being conscious of as her experience of her culture too (Lahiri, *The Interpreter* 23-42).

If, "When Mr. Pirzada came to dine" reveals Jhumpa Lahiri's consciousness as an artist about the trails and travails of her Bengali heritage as it has historically been moulded by the machinations of nationalism and separation, "The Third and Final Continent" which is the concluding story of *Interpreter of Maladies* displays her conscious of the Bengali diasporic travel out from 'home' and the journey involves a gradual blending of Bengali roots and the new environment in the space of 'arrival'. This story narrates the experience of modern experience of migration and dislocation by tracing, through the story of a young Indian, his story of travelling away from home and his arrival at the diasporic space or spaces. This story has a peculiar similarity with Jhumpa Lahiri's parents' journey, which only serves to emphasise how consciousness gets translated through experience in literary production. The narrator of the story begins with a definite timeline—"I left India in 1964". He narrates how he left India on a ship, in a third-class cabin and finally arrived in England, living in a house "occupied […] by penniless Bengali bachelors […] struggling to educate and establish (themselves) abroad". Typical of the struggles of migrants, he had to work and study at the same time, sharing a room with three other people, taking turns in cooking and eating "on a table covered with newspapers" besides sharing "a single, icy toilet". This balance was disturbed when one of them moved out to prepare for married live when the family in Calcutta had found a groom for him. In 1969, our thirty-six years old narrator informs that his marriage was too arranged and he simultaneously around the same time "was offered a full-time job in America" in the M.I.T.-library with a salary generous enough to "support a wife". Armed with a green card and the honour of serving in a renowned university, he "prepared to travel farther still". After his marriage, armed with *The Student Guide to North America* as a reading guide, he flew to Boston, learning on the flight about American driving conventions, and also that unlike his stay in Britain, live in North America would be much busier, and on landing he is greeting by the announcement by President Nixon that two Americans had set foot on the moon and the cheers of "God bless America". Having occupied a small room as a temporary accommodation, the narrator notes the difference he perceives from his earlier quite experience in England through the shrill sound of car horns and flashing sirens. Unlike the meals he had with his friends in England, which were largely of an Indian nature, here he had to make do with cornflakes, milk and bananas in the initial phase of his arrival till his wife reached America. In anticipation of her arrival, he rents a room "in a house on a quiet street" for eight dollars owned by a very old lady named Mrs. Croft who was over a hundred years old. Mrs. Croft typifies, in keeping with her age, the American character, bold, assertive and full of the American pride after the successful landing on the moon, who only rents "rooms to boys from Harvard or Tech" and one who expects punctuality with the rent and into whose premises lady visitors were not permitted.

The narrator's wife, he tells us was Mala, twenty-seven years of age, and daughter of a school-teacher in Beleghata (Kolkata, West Bengal) and their marriage had been arranged by his brother and his wife, with the narrator being largely indifferent to it, for, in keeping with Indian/Bengali customs, obedience to the choice of his elders was "a duty expected of (him)". Like any Bengali girl, Mala could "cook, knit, embroider, sketch landscapes, and recite poems by Tagore". Talented as she was, yet her not possessing a fair complexion led to rejections of proposals of marriage, and her parents fearing that she would never get married, were ready to "ship their only child halfway across the world in order to save her from spinsterhood". After their marriage, the narrator notes how, each night for the "five nights we shared a bed" she would go through the routine of "applying cold cream", "braiding her hair" with "black cotton string" and turning from him and weeping at the thought of her parents. Before leaving for America, the narrator notes how he did not console her or take her back to her parents, for as "custom dictated" she was now a member of his household and hence had to live with his brother and his wife "cooking, cleaning, serving tea and sweets to guests". Sleeping on the bed with her, the narrator does not console her, but remembers his own dead mother, whom he had watched die, before he had left for London. He remembers how he had cleaned her dead fingernails and had "touched the flame to her temple, to release her tormented soul to heaven". Jhumpa Lahiri, in this depiction of the typical Indian/Bengali tradition of marriage dynamics in India and its attendant patriarchal nature, displays her consciousness of aspects that form an important aspect of her hyphenated identity.

Lahiri displays this consciousness in the depiction of the juxtaposition of the closely structured Bengali family with the typical American family. Unlike the narrator who undertakes the care of his mother as a sacred duty, Mrs. Croft's daughter Helen lived away from her mother and only visited her every Sunday to bring her groceries. On their first meeting, Helen, herself an elderly woman of sixty-eight, notices that the narrator was "the first boarder she's ever referred to as a gentleman". Mrs. Croft displays age old American traditions, which are unlike the present American values and hence, when she finds her daughter engaging in a conversation with the narrator, she promptly calls for them and let them know that "it (was) improper for a lady and a gentleman who are not married […] to hold private conversations" even if the lady be an aged eighty-eight-year-old. She objects to Helen's wearing "a dress so high above her ankle" and when Helen reminds her that it is 1969, and girls were wearing mini-skirts, Mrs. Croft would have none of it. Helen reveals the independent nature of Mr. Croft how liked to do things herself, and how after the death of her father, she had raised her children giving piano-lessons.

It mortified the narrator that Mrs. Croft, old as she was, lived alone, and reflects on how widowhood had driven his mother to insanity. Lahiri here seems to juxtapose two family structure—the Indian/Bengali and the American as a means to represent the two sides of her hyphenated consciousness. The comparison between the narrator's mother and Mrs. Croft as widowed individuals in two different family structures is a means to demonstrate a difference in terms of culture and society. The narrator laments how, unlike the strong Mrs. Croft, after the death of his father when he was sixteen, his mother "refused to adjust to life without him", "sank [...] into a world of darkness" and depression that neither him, his brother, and nor his relatives could save her from. He recalls how after his father's death; his brother gave up his education to support his family by working in a jute mill and how he (the narrator) sat by his mother's side as she battled insanity. On learning from Helen that Mrs. Croft no longer ate solid food, but only soup, the narrator, out of a typical Indian sense of duty towards elders, volunteers to warm her soup each evening, but Helen discourages him from doing so, for if she was alive even at a hundred years or more, it was because of her independent nature and any kind of dependence "would kill her altogether". Yet, the narrator felt responsible for Helen's mother, but it puzzled him that Helen never worried about her mother, the way he did his. She would come and go each Sunday, to replenish her grocery without being too concerned about her.

In his six weeks of stay in Mrs. Croft's house, before the arrival of his wife from India, he would spend his evenings with Mrs. Croft trying to imagine how much of the history of the U.S.A. was before him in her person. He "tried to picture the world she had been born into, in 1866", a world he imagined that was "filled with women in long black skirts, and chaste conversations". Soon he receives a letter from his wife Mala about her impending arrival. Reading her letter with queries about the place, he wonders how little he knew his wife. They had only spent "a handful of days" together, and yet "were bound together", his duty being to guide her and protect her in an alien space. In anticipation of her arrival he rented a furnished apartment "with a double bed and a private kitchen and bath" for forty dollars a week. Mala soon arrives with things from 'home', but the narrator records how they even after a week of her arrival, she seemed a stranger to him, for he was no longer accustomed to "coming home to an apartment that smelled of steamed rice" and being served the typical Bengali breakfast assuming that, unlike the cornflakes and milk he ate each morning, he "would eat rice for breakfast, as most Bengali husbands did". Soon they decide to meet Mrs. Craft as a couple. Unlike how family structures are in the Bengali psyche, Mala is disturbed to learn from her husband that Mrs. Croft is over a hundred years and lives alone with none to care for her. When they visit her, Helen happens to be around and is greeted by her who informs them that Mrs. Croft has had a "little accident" and she could not be left "alone these days, not even for a minute". When he introduces Mala to her, Mrs. Croft looks at her minutely in her saree and typical Bengali demeanour, and finally, to the surprise of the narrator, declared that his wife was "a perfect lady". Mala's smile and her acceptance by an ancient American lady, suddenly lessened the distance between him and his wife and soon they began to explore other Bengali families in the town, "some of whom are still friends today". But soon the sad news of Mrs. Croft death arrives to them through an obituary in the evening news paper. It was a depressing news for the narrator, and it "was the first death (he) mourned in America", for she was the first person she admired in the U.S.A.

If Mrs. Croft was the narrators first introduction to the idea of America and her accommodative acceptance of the beauty in Mala as a 'perfect lady' as a Bengali lady, in having the compassion to mourn her death, the narrator experiences his final 'arrival' in America, the third and final continent of his diasporic migration. As he states, they were now American citizens now, and although they do visit 'home' in Calcutta, "bring back more drawstring pajamas and Darjeeling tea", America was they "have decided to grow old". But their Bengali cultural roots are still deep for, though "Mala no longer drapes the end of her sari over her head" they still worry that their son, who is studying in Harvard might lose connections with his Bengali background. Hence, they visit him every weekend to ensure "he can eat rice with his hands", "speak in Bengali", things the couple worry their son "will no longer do after (they) die". Meditating on his life, the narrator knows he is not alone in seeking a life elsewhere, but each step, each meal, and each room he lived in, which while it may seem ordinary now, "there are times when it is beyond (his) imagination" (Lahiri, *The Interpreter* 173-98). This story, in juxtaposing the nature of family relations of the narrator with that of Mrs. Croft's family highlights the independent, though insecure nature of American families and the desire of Mala and her husband to hold on to their traditional roots inspite of assimilation into the American society, betrays an uneasiness with the nature of American family structures. The typical Bengali family and the mother's dependence on her husband's presence is contrasted with the strong independent nature of Mrs. Croft who had the courage to live alone beyond the death of her husband. In this juxtaposition, Jhumpa Lahiri appears ambivalent and it is in this ambivalence that is discernible both her consciousness of her Bengali cultural heritage and her journey to assimilate into the American way of life. The ambivalence reveals the difficulty of mobility beyond the hyphenated status of her identity.

While *Interpreter of Maladies*, the earlier of the two short story collections of Jhumpa Lahiri dwell on themes like migration, cultural difference and the memory of 'home', her later short story collection *Unaccustomed Earth* engages with cultural assimilation and a broader understanding of the hyphenated identity. The first story in this collection titled "Unaccustomed Earth" narrates the story of a Bengali/Indian-American father who has retired from his job and his daughter Ruma, the former celebrating the independence he has gained through a fresh understanding of life and relationships after the death of his wife, while the latter caught between memories of her own Indian upbringing by her late mother and her struggle to assert an American way of life as she oscillates between concern for her father who, now that he was alone would stay with her and seek to assert her Bengali cultural mores and her own American family as she is pregnant with a second child, having quit her job for it. Ruma, we are told, has lived her life in the American way since she was a child, much to the displeasure of her parents. So after her mother's death, she is worried that taking care of her father would bring back the cultural conflicts she encountered in her childhood. Her American husband Adam's constant absence from home, and her memory of home with her parents and her brother Roma, is a constant refrain in the story. With Roma away abroad, she instinctively realises that it was her duty as a Bengali to care for her father, and hence she constantly communicates with him as he tours Europe living a life finally freed of all familial concerns. When her father finally visits her, she is surprised that he looked more American now then he did earlier, while her father, through the period of his stay with her, is disturbed that she was no longer the independent girl she was as a child. The story, in oscillating between the past and the present is an interesting meditation on both the American and the Bengali way of life and the gradual assimilation of a blend of it into the American environment. However, even here, the travel to either side of the hyphen is not achieved by Jhumpa Lahiri, and her consciousness remains caged in her hyphenated consciousness. Other stories of this later collection continue to explore the nature of this hyphenated identity and therein lies the poetic nature of the experience that the stories of Lahiri, a poetic blend of two cultures that seeks articulation even as it struggles to resolve the nature of the tension that the hyphen entails.

In conclusion, the poetic nature of the tension that punctuates Jhumpa Lahiri's diasporic identity, a poetry that finds its intensity in the unity that the short story form provides, is perhaps best expressed in her work *In Other Words*. In this autobiographical work, in comparing her mother she poetically expresses the irony of her identity. Her mother, who wrote poetry in Bengali, cannot, after "almost fifty years after moving there", find "a book written in her language" because Bengali "is foreign in America". She states that she has got accustomed to this "linguistic exile", "a continuous sense of estrangement". But for her, the circumstances are further aggravated because she does not speak Bengali perfectly either, she does not "know how to read it, or even write it", perceives "a disjunction between it" and her, and as a result her "mother tongue" is, for her "a foreign language" too (*Lahiri, In Other* 23-24). Indeed, it is between these two extremes that her stories must be located in terms of the experiences it seeks to articulate, and it is in her short stories that the reader experiences the intensity of the poetry that her ruminations on her identity entail.

Works cited:

Clifford, James. "Diasporas". *Cultural Anthropology* 9. 3 (August 1994): 302-38.

Cohen, Robin. *Global Diasporas: An Introduction*. New York and London: Routledge, 2008.

Dhingra, Lavina, and Floyd Cheung. *Naming Jhumpa Lahiri: Canons and Controversies*. Lanham: Lexington Books, 2012.

Feddersen, R. C. "Introduction: A Glance at the History of the Short-story in English". *A Reader's Companion to Short-story in English*. Eds. Erin Fallon *et al*. New York and London: Routledge, 2001.

Gordimer, Nadine. "The Flash of Fireflies". *The New Short Story Theories*. Ed. Charles May. Athens: Ohio University Press, 1994.

Hays, Kevin (ed.). *The Cambridge Companion to Edgar Allan Poe*. Cambridge: Cambridge University Press, 2002. Rpt. 2003.

Hegde, Radha, and Ajaya Sahoo (eds.). *Routledge Handbook of the Indian Diaspora*. New York and London: Routledge, 2018.

Lahiri, Jhumpa. "My Two Lives". *The Writer's Presence: A Pool of Readings*. Eds. Donald McQuade and Robert Atwan. Medford: Macmillan Learning, 2018.

---. *Interpreter of Maladies*. London: Harper Collins, 1999 (Kindle).

---. *Unaccustomed Earth*. London: Penguin Books, 2013 (Kindle).

---. *In Other Words*. London: Penguin Books, 2017 (Kindle).

Mathews, Brander. *The Philosophy of the Short-story*. New York: Longmans, Green, and Company, 1901. Rpt. 1917.

Mishra, Vijay. *The Literature of the Indian Diaspora: Theorising the Diasporic Imaginary*. New York and London: Routledge, 2007.

Patea, Victoria. *Short Story Theories: A Twenty-first Century Perspective*. Amsterdam: Rodopi, 2012.

Pratt, Mary Louise. "The Short Story: The Long and the Short of it". *The New Short Story Theories*. Ed. Charles May. Athens: Ohio University Press, 1994.

Rushdie, Salman. *Imaginary Homelands*. London: Granta Books, 1991.

Safran, William. "*Diasporas in Modern Societies*: Myths of Homeland and Return". *Diaspora: A Journal of Transnational Studies* 1.1 (Spring 1991): 83-99.

Cultural Encounters and Feminine Identities
A Re-Reading of Short-Stories by Select Indian Diasporic Writers

—Neha Swarnakar

The concept of 'diaspora' is an evolving one, and is synonymous to migration, dispersal and exile. Apart from the theological overtones of the term 'diaspora' in the Ancient Greek period—chronotopically—it has acquired multiple meanings. 'Diaspora' is generally referred as an alternative for any concept of expansion and dispersing away from the centre (Tölölyan 10). In a broader sense—as Steven Vertovec mentions in his "The Political Importance of Diaspora"- diaspora is, "a term of self-identification among many varied groups who themselves or whose forbearers migrated from one place to another or to several places" (2). Therefore, it is pertinent that the discourses of diaspora—including the novels and short-stories by Indian diasporic authors—posit a dichotomy between 'homeland' and 'host land'. A consciousness of belonging to the 'homeland' and the attempts for assimilation in the 'host land'—in turn—gives birth to a consciousness of 'in-betweenness'. Therefore, this status of *in-betweenness* becomes the site of cultural encounter of the home/host land and challenges the assumption of established rigid diasporic identity: this becomes perceptible in both the diasporic novels and short-stories.

Stuart Hall, in *Cultural Identity and Diaspora*, defines diasporic experience "not by essence or purity, but by recognition of a necessary heterogeneity and diversity; by a conception of 'identity' which lives with and through, not despite, difference, by hybridity. Diaspora identities are those which are constantly producing and reproducing themselves anew, through transformation and difference" (235). In this context, identity—which is determined by the socio-cultural-economic environment—becomes a matter of discussion. As Homi K. Bhabha in *The Location of Culture* (1994) argues, "[T]errain[s] for elaborating strategies of selfhood—singular or communal—initiate new signs of identity, and innovative sites of collaboration, and contestation, in the act of defining the idea of society itself. It is in the emergence of the interstices—the overlap and displacement of domains of difference—that the intersubjective and collective experiences of *nationness*, community interest, or cultural value are negotiated" (2). These aspects deserve utmost attention whenever any diasporic writing (including the short-stories by diasporic Indian writers) is to be read or studied. A very recent development in the studies of women's experience within the diaspora has been gaining attention. 'Woman'—as Chandra Talpade Mohanty points out—has become a cultural and ideological composite 'Other' constructed through multiple representational discourses, and has been charged with maintaining the edifice of 'home life' at micro or macro level (53). Therefore, the gendered study of diaspora (including the studies of diasporic novels and short-stories) questions not only the heteronormative construction of the nation but investigates the traditional, patriarchal rather hegemonic assumptions associated with the discourse of diaspora.

The questions whether (a) the notion of the diaspora imparts agency to women who embarks from the nationalistic narrative to transnational experience, and (b) whether they discover themselves in a more marginalised or stigmatised situation due to race, ethnicity, and gendered cause, are very much important ones. In this context, one can observe that female identity is intricately linked to diasporic writings. From the women's representation as custodians of cultures (which retain their submissive positions in family, society and nation) to their participation in the 'transnational spaces' and questing for identities, diaspora studies (including those focussing on the diasporic novels and short-stories) present another subversive narrative which challenges and interrogates the stereotypical representations of women and imposes an identity in the midst of 'hybridity'. South Asian diasporic writings—including the short-stories by Indian diasporic authors—document this cross cultural encounter and different tropes of alienation, displacement, memory, in perpetuating the identity of the female subjects. In this context, it is noteworthy to mention that India has the largest diasporic community in the world and population of approximately 18 million people moves in all famous areas over the world.

One may remember what Amitav Ghosh has written: "the Indian Diaspora is one of the most important demographic dislocations of modern times and each day is growing and assuming the form of representative, significant force in global culture" (Ghosh 243). The *International Migrant Stock 2019* provides the report—as published by *The Economic Times*—that "the top 10 countries of origin account for one-third of all international migrants. In 2019, with 17.5 million persons living abroad, India was the leading country of origin of international migrants. Migrants from Mexico constituted the second largest diaspora (11.8 million), followed by China (10.7 million), Russia (10.5 million), Syria (8.2 million), Bangladesh (7.8 million), Pakistan (6.3 million), Ukraine (5.9 million), the Philippines (5.4 million) and Afghanistan (5.1 million)" (*The Economic Times* 2019). Members of these migrants, Indian writers like Bharati Mukherjee, Chitra Banerjee Divkaruni, Jhumpa Lahiri, Anjana Appachana, Padma Hejmadi, Shauna Singh Baldwin, Vijay Lakshmi, Neela Vaswani, and Rishi Reddi have presented the issues of diaspora in their writings—including their short-fictional-narratives. This paper intends to briefly explore the issues of cultural conflicts and identity-construction as represented in the short-stories of diasporic Indian writers—especially, those by the female litterateurs.

The Kolkata-born Bharati Mukherjee (1940-2017), who first migrated to Canada and then permanently to the U.S.A., is (arguably) one of the better short-story writers of the Indian diaspora, and in her highly-appreciated stories, she could be found dealing with the themes of immigration, displacement, exile, return, identity, and cross-cultural conflicts. Her first volume of short-stories—*Darkness* (1985)—comprises of twelve short narratives, and focuses on the difficulties in the process of cultural assimilation in Canada and the U.S.A. the collections in her *The Middleman and Other Stories* (1988) focus on the theme of immigration from different perspectives. The entangled ties between Indian and American cultures, the constant clash between binary identities, and the challenge of assimilation have been variously showcased through her short stories. To Sharmani P. Gabriel, the distinctive quality of Mukherjee's work in the tradition of diaspora literature in general and American literature in particular lies in her ability to draw the tension or conflict that holds in balance her consciousness 'as a condition of loss or unhousement', involving a split in that link between cultures, peoples or identities and places, on the one hand , and on the other, her acknowledgement of it 'as a condition of gain or re-housement', of recreation, re-imagination and re-generation in new socio-political, cultural and geographical landscapes (Gabriel). Her assertion about her stories as 'it is about conquest not about loss' and her concept on, "the fact of being 'in between' of having a fresh angle on the narrative of remaking the self in the new world, that keeps the immigrant writer, the naturalized American writer, at her or his most fervent, intense and sensitive" (Gabriel 127) presents the female characters such as Nafisa in "The Lady from Lucknow" [from the *Darkness* collection], Maya in "The Tenant" [from *Middleman and Other stories*] and Jasmine of the short story or of the novel who are confined in terms of gender, making choices for their empowerment in sexual terms, is like escaping out of that sphere of taboos and smudging multiple borders of language, history, race, time and culture.

Jhumpa Lahiri's *Interpreter of Maladies* (1999), an anthology of nine short-stories, collects narratives that capture diverse Indian diasporic experiences and brings out the complexities and nuances. It talks about the characters that are entangled in cultural tension, anxiety by being displaced from one place to another and striving of the characters for survival. Though varied in theme and setting, these nine stories are united by one leitmotif- exclusion, loneliness and quest for identity and fulfilment (Mandal 18). Addressing the criticism of Gayatri Gopinath—as quoted in Williams—whose lamentation over the "centrality of [male-male or father-son] trope as the primary trope in imagining diaspora invariably displaces and elides female diasporic subjects" (Williams 70), this paper intends to focus on the construction of female identity through her short stories which "deals with the suffering, pressure and possible failure or success in the adaptation-process of these female characters in (re-)constructing their subjectivity, (re-)asserting their agency or negotiating their identities through either silence, resistance, negotiation, acculturation or assimilation" (Bahmanpour 44).

The story entitled "Mrs. Sen's" represents Mrs. Sen, first generation of immigrants, who is dwindling between two cultural values, takes up the job of caretaker of an eleven year old boy, Eliot. It projects her struggle in the process of adaptation in a new culture of United States. Her complain about the exotic land where Mr. Sen has brought her and insomnia due to utter silence of that exotic atmosphere, reflects her trapped condition. On one hand, her obsession with the culture and values of homeland and on the other, the culture of alien land poses a threat to her ethnic identity. Her recourse to the past memory of her homeland, her way of life in that land and her constant retelling of having a driver at home or her telling to Eliot about people in Calcutta, their fascination with fish as it is the first thing to eat in the morning, and last thing before bed, and also using it as snack (Lahiri 66), weaves an 'escapist narrative' where she feels a connection to the root. Her assertion to the ethnic identity through her keeping of Indian practices of cooking, buying interest, having fish and wearing of colourful collection of saris from her homeland in one way forms an unconscious resistance to the new culture of America which blocks the 'acculturation' process which Esman defines as "acceptance and adaptation of basic elements of the local culture, its language and life style" (Esman 103). On the other hand, her broken English, "Is it Beethoven? She asked once, pronouncing the first part of the composer's name not 'bay' but 'bee', like the insect" (Lahiri 65), and her courage to drive to be independent can be read as her attempt to accept the culture of host land and an attempt to liberate herself from the patriarchal grid of her husband which always places her in a subordinated and submissive role. Mrs. Sen, therefore, can be read as cite of cultural clash and asserts a 'hybrid identity' which is a cultural artefact and conceived as "a process, as performed, and as unstable" (Pratt 154). Her desire to be independent subverts her role of 'home making' doll and 'custodian of culture' in the host land and provides her liberating agency of 'be-coming'.

"This Blessed House" unfolds the experiences of a second generation female immigrant, Twinkle who have already fashioned herself in the hybrid diasporic identity. It unfolds a narrative which embraces the multiplicity and conflicted aspects of blended culture. Sanjeev and Twinkle, a newlywed couple who moves from Boston to Connecticut, to a new house, represents the cultural dichotomy of two generation of immigrants. While Twinkle belongs to the second generation and has moulded herself in the hybrid spaces, Sanjeev belongs to the first generation, therefore it represents the ever conflicting mindset of the couple. The scattered pieces- a white porcelain effigy of Christ, a wooden cross key chain, a small plastic dome containing a miniature Nativity scene etc. found in this house are treasured by Twinkle, provides her interest in Christian paraphernalia, on the other Sanjeev's searching for a chance to throw everything in the garbage, "he hated it because he knew that Twinkle loved it" (Lahiri 82) represents the cultural conflict. Even the general food habits of the couple represent this conflict, "She detested chopping garlic, and feelings ginger, and could not operate a blinder, and so it was Sanjeev who, on weekends, seasoned mustard oil with cinnamon sticks and cloves in order to produce a proper curry" (*ibid.* 76). Thus, Twinkle becomes a fluid identity whose cultural assimilation therefore compelling and constructive force. Her acceptance of different cultures as reflected in her choice of Irish poet for her Master's thesis, interest in foreign artefacts, or her positive negotiation of identity as an American of Indian decent, her uttering, "we're good little Hindus", or her kissing "on top of Christ's head" (*ibid.* 73) therefore presents the 'impurity', 'fluidity', 'openness' which provides her identity 'of becoming' which is the most important feature of diasporic experiences in the Postmodern world.

In the next story entitled "The Treatment of Bibi Haldar", Lahiri projects a woman who breaks the stereotype and resists the construction of 'Othering' process and asserts her own identity. Bibi is a 29-year-old poor Indian girl living in Kolkata, and has been the victim of politics of exclusion, suffers from an unknown disease. The story talks about her constant strife to overcome her ailment, and her recurring perception of 'becoming woman'. Alienation from her own 'home' and her non affiliation to the construction of the Indian version of female identity, her curing of disease forms a resistance to the *Otherness* in the culture she has been brought up which "confined her world to the unpainted four story building" (Lahiri 83) and makes her someone unusual. At the end, her giving birth to a child and her emergence as an immigrant in her own land empowers her with the identity of being a woman and liberates her from that confined world. In making a new life she says, "The world begins at the bottom of the stairs, now I am free to discover life as I please" (*ibid*. 88). Her journey from a 'Girl, unstable' to a 'cured mother' and a 'self sustained women' can better be described in the words of Ling Yun, "[The] narration of their story serves as counter-memory to speak their own voice and shows that they are 'woman warriors' against the yoke and prejudice of patriarchy as they finally throw off the shackles and live an independent and brave life" (6). Bibi Halder, therefore, in the words of Savita Patil, "It sounds to be the feminine voice in this story to prove the abilities of woman in the society where male appears as an escapist and female a daring entity. Bibi Halder is an individual who maintains her individuality against all odds" (212).

Only the immigrant 'Other' do not fall prey of the cultural clash, rather the native self can also experience the diasporic identity crisis. And such theme reverberates through the short story 'Sexy'. It unfolds a narrative where Miranda, a female American in Boston, her fascination for exotic culture which culminates in her affair with Dev, an Indian, opens up herself to experience the thrill of Indian culture which is exemplified by her visit to the Indian grocery shop or her visit to Indian restaurant. She opens up herself in knowing the other in such way which

Spivak calls "ethical responsibility"; "ethics are not just a problem of knowledge but a call to a relationship" (Landry 5).

Simone de Beauvoir, in her *The Second Sex*, writes that "[h]umanity is male, and man defines woman, not in herself, but in relation to himself; she is not considered an autonomous being... She is determined and differentiated in relation to man, while he is not in relation to her; she is the inessential in front of the essential. He is the subject; he is the absolute. She is the Other" (26). This discourse of 'otherness' — in Lahiri — weaves another narrative, where the female characters have their own way of survival. Resistance or acceptance, escapist attitude or the process of acculturation provides them the means for attaining or ascertaining their own identity, their own individuality.

The ever-changing concept of culture has also been showcased by Jhumpa Lahiri in her *Unaccustomed Earth* (2008) — a collection of eight short-stories that focus on the life of two separate cultures. The cultural disparity between the American-born second-generation Indians and their parents who immigrated to the U.S.A in the 1970s' and 1980s' becomes one of *leitmotifs* of this collection. The polyphonic voices of characters attempt to find an identity of their own. All the stories explore the cultural trauma and suffering which carries the connotation of deep suffering, solitude, and alienation resulting in a residual melancholy. Lahiri shared her experience — at a conference in Kolkata in 2001 — of homeland and sense/absence of belongingness: "No country is my motherland. I always find myself in exile whichever country I travel to, that's why I was tempted to write something about those living their lives in exile" (Large and Quinn). Similar cultural identities of her female characters can be found in the stories of *Unaccustomed Earth* — in a daughter from the first story named "Unaccustomed Earth", and a wife from second story "Hell-Heaven".

Yasim Hussein observes that the south Asians, "may be connected by a common race, a national origin" shared a history but the subsequent generation, who are brought up in "a country that is culturally, socially and religiously different from their ethnic culture maintained within the home environment" will have a different perception on "the individual's conception of self' (25-26). To the first generation women, it is difficult to forget the culture and value system of the previous world and to get assimilated to the new world while it is easier to the second and third generation women. To them, the distance from tradition, the proximity in time and place to modernity can be traced as reason for their success.

In "Unaccustomed Earth", Ruma, a lawyer by profession, marries Adam (a White American), and gives birth to a bi-racial child Akash. In Lahiri's brilliantly-poignant story, she is represented as a representative of the conflicting self. Her moving to the U.S.A. results in her utter isolation. On getting pregnant for second time, she gives up the job to take care of her son. She is caught between her desire to walk out of the door to sense the free air and her responsibilities as an Indian mother. Her journey from growing up to moving to a foreign land for the sake of marriage, taking care exclusively for children and a household reveals her suppressed condition. Caught between American modernism and Indian traditionalism, Ruma suffers from an ambiguous identity. It may be observed here that Edward Said in *Relfections on Exile* articulates that the migrants voluntarily living in the foreign country suffer from isolation and 'estrangement of exile'. And in this process, some are benefitted by their ambiguous status while others — surrounded by the perpetual feeling of vagrancy on being settled in the West — try to mimic the ideologies that channelled their lives in their homeland.

"Hell-Heaven" narrates the story of Aparna who lives a life of solitariness and silence. Her marginality has been asserted by her apathetic husband and her conception about marriage. Usha's perception about her mother who leads a desolate life exposes the patriarchal construction of female identity which assigns the role of women in the domestic affairs. But the resistance to that role is quite apparent which, according to Yasmin Hussain, "arise from exposure to the integrating services of the majority society from birth. Experience of education system and with the employment sphere influences their attitudes and relationships. The child is confronted with both cultures at the same time and beings to absorb totally different values of family life and society" (26).

Chitra Banerjee Divakaruni describes the cross-cultural ethos, the experiences of female immigrants, and their search for individual identity through her anthology of short-stories, *Arranged Marriage* (1995). Debjani Banerjee in her essay "Home and Us": Re-Defining Identity in the South Asian Diaspora through the writings of Chitra Banerjee Devkaruni and Meena Alexander", suggests that for female protagonists, clothes, education, thinking about their own rights and pleasures become a signifier of modernity and identity of modern women is often associated with an elite "westernization", and a repudiation of an ancient and supposedly timeless traditions (Banerjee 14). Divakaruni, in an interview with Metka Zupančič says,

> "My characters are mostly Indian women growing up in India in a very traditional family. In *Arranged Marriage*, many come from a background similar to my own. I grew up with very definite notions of womanhood, of who is considered a good woman and how she is to behave, especially within the family context. Much of that was based on the notion that a good woman makes sacrifices. As a result of immigration, when we find ourselves in the West, there is quite a different notion of what a good woman is and what she is expected to be. Many characters in 'Arranged Marriage' are dealing with this sudden change in worldwide, at once exhilarating and also terrifying. They have to make sense of the situation, which begins to transform them as woman. It begins to change their relationship with the people in family-their husbands, who are with them in the new country, and their parents, who are usually, back in India. There are children who are now born in new environment, still caught between two cultures, yet with a completely different worldview" (qtd. in Zupančič 94).

Through the tropes of alienation, assimilation, negotiation, past memory, the female characters raise their voice of resistance to the stereotypical and submissive role they have been taught to sustain and quest for an identity for their self empowerment.

The opening story of *Arranged Marriage*, "The Bats", is 'situated' in Kolkata, and portrays the domestic violence perpetuated on women by the patriarchal system. A young girl narrates her mother's crying at night—the mother who has been the victim of oppression by her chauvinistic husband. The girl notices the blotches on her mother's cheeks but remains ignorant of the reason of her mother's crying. Unable to endure the violence, mother and daughter manages to go to her old father's house. But the poignant criticism of the neighbour makes her situation difficult. She is conditioned by the norms of Indian womanhood, according to which she cannot break the marital bond. Her return to the husband's house can be read from the viewpoint of feministic discourse where she returns to confront the oppressive patriarchal structure.

In the story "Clothes", the sartorial symbol related to the different stages in the life of the protagonist Sumita, bears the stamp of continue cultural entanglement and her comment on her predicament, "caught in a world where everything is frozen [...] like a scene inside a glass paperweight. It is a world so small [...] I stand inside this glass world, watching helplessly [...] wanting to scream" (Divakaruni 24). She wears sari at every occasion, and this reflects her Indian identity. The gradual transformation of her identity is reflected in her wearing of saris—whether be it yellow, or pink, or be it red or white—and each colour has different symbolical meaning. After the death of her husband, her firm decision to stay in America and work there provides her the identity of independent, empowered and strong woman. "Clothes" therefore, symbolises her embracing of western culture with empowerment and her freedom of choices.

Divakaruni portrays the incompatible nature of two cultures—those of India's and U.S.A.'s—through the story titled "Doors". It depicts the attitudinal and cultural differences of a married couple: Preeti (an Indian living in the U.S.A. from her childhood) and Deepak (a new immigrant to the U.S.A.). The cultural conflict is apparent in perception: whether be its Preeti's mother's {"What do you really know about how Indian men think? About what they expect from their women?" (Divakaruni 143)}, or be its Deepak's friend's {"And you know how these 'American' women are always bossing you, always thinking about themselves... it's no wonder we call them ABCDs- American-Born-confused-Desis, quipped another friend as he took a swallow of beer" (*ibid.* 144)}. Though presented as a 'perfectly matched couple' (*ibid.* 146), "none of the guests had known, of course, about the matter of doors. Deepak likes to leave them open, and Preeti liked them closed" (*ibid.* 146). They try to live peacefully until the arrival of Deepak's childhood friend Raj. Arrival of Raj into their lives makes the cultural clash too apparent, as "the concept of doors did not exist in Raj's universe, and he ignored their physical reality-so solid and reassuring to Preeti-whenever he could. He would burst into her closed study to tell her of the latest events in his computer lab, leaving the door ajar when he left. He would throw open the door to the garage where she did laundry to offer help; usually just she was folding her underwear. Even when she retreated to her little garden in search of privacy, there was no escape. From the porch, he gave solicitous advice on the dropping fuchsias" (*ibid.* 151). Therefore his arrival causes her irritation, and intrudes into her private spaces. 'Closing of door' therefore symbolises private space without disturbances and intrusions, the story asserts that a women need to have a space of their own as Virginia Woolf preaches for this in A *Rooms of One's Own* . Along with the cultural conflict it brings out the issue of female assertion and self identity. Deepak's mind has been developed in a culture where a woman's privacy has not been considered. In one hand, Divakaruni portrays the diasporic dilemma through the character of Preeti as revealed in the statement, "A part of her cried out to go to him to apologize and offer to have Raj back" (Divakaruni 157) on the other she asserts female individuality by leaving her female character independent.

"Affair" narrates the story of two couples Abha and Ashok, Meena and Srikant. It exposes the futility of arranged marriages and self-realisation of female immigrants who give a boost to their life by breaking the futile knot and taking steps for their own happiness in life. After knowing her husband's having an affair with Meena, Abha's self-realisation, her grabbing of the offer from the *Indian Courier* for compiling a cook book of Indian Cuisine in the Bay Area Indian Restaurants renew her with an independent identity. Her experience in her new found happiness exhilarates her, "I felt a bit embarrassed when I saw myself in the hall mirror as I came down the stairs, a bit silly, a girl dressed up in her in her big sister's fancy clothes. But it did give me an added confidence. And when I spoke to the manager of the first restaurant on the list Suren had handed me, I was surprised at how pleasantly businesslike my voice sounded, as though I'd been doing this kind of thing forever" (Divakaruni 201). The questioning of the self, "Had I ever really been myself? I didn't think so. All my energy had been taken up in being a good daughter. A good friend. And of course a good wife" by Abha or the statement by Meena, "It's not wrong to want to be happy, is it? To want more out of life than fulfilling duties you took on before you knew what they truly meant? (*ibid*. 211) provides them liberating agency. Therefore, in liberal atmosphere of America, both Abha and Meena prepare to free themselves from the stifling and destroying marriages and make good use of their existence.

Divakaruni's second collection of nine short-stories—titled *The Unknown Errors of Our Lives* (2001)—explores the inevitable conflict of two cultures, of the two belief systems and of two different philosophies. The collected narratives explore the women emancipation and their constant struggle for identity through the stories. "The Blooming Season for Cacti" narrates two women who experiences violence, deception in the native land, uprooted from there and finally finds solace in each other. Whether it is "The Lives of Strangers", or "What the Body Knows", each story deals with the female immigrant experiences, results in their realisation of their potential identity.

In her diverse short-stories, Anjana Appachana—an acclaimed writer both in India and the U.S.A.—portrays modern women in their trials and tribulations, refuses to succumb to the existing manacles against the traditional, stereotyped women. Her maiden book, *Incantations and Other Stories* (1991), is a collection of eight short stories that deal with different themes like politics, the inimitable Indian bureaucracy, psychology, hypocrisy of traditional ways. The stories "Bahu", "Incantations" and "Sharmaji and the Diwali Sweets" presents female characters who claims to power by defying societal gender expectations and violence.

The cultural displacement also finds it expression in Padma Hejmadi's *Coigns of Vantage* (1972), *Dr. Salaam, and Other Stories of India* (1978), and *Birthday, Deathday, and Other Stories* (1985). The craftsmanship and the endings of her story remind us of an elegantly-embroidered Kashmiri Shawl as the stories are intertwined with meanings which provides them a multicoloured-shot-effect. Her stories have an epic stroke where the representation of so called family, different plots, incidents, and the innumerable cross-relationships suggests a wide canvas.

Another important name in this genre is Shauna Singh Baldwin's. Her most famous short-story collection is *English Lessons and Other stories (1996)*, a compilation of fifteen narratives that revolve round the experiences of Sikh women in three different countries—India, Canada and the U.S.A. The varieties of theme—from the mother-daughter relationships of "Simran", the loneliness of ageing and dying in an alien land of "Jassie", or the descriptions of young married women in "Devika" or "Montreal 1962"—bring out the experiences of cultural displacement.

The Kashmir-born and U.S.A.-settled Vijay Lakshmi—a comparatively-newer name in the ever-expanding group of Indian expatriate short-story-writers—describes the female-experiences and tension of family life in the West in her "Touchline", "Home", "Mannequins" and those compiled in *Pomegranate Dreams and Other Stories* (2002). These stories weave the narrative of confrontation between East and West, their lifestyle, beliefs, hope and dreams.

The collections in Neela Vaswani's *Where the Long Grass Bends* (2004) deviate from the usual focuses on Indian diasporic short-story writers. In the collection, she experiments with her short stories which focus on mythic quality by employing Indian folk lore, Gaelic fables and historical legends. The plots invite the readers to question fictional forms, cultural issues and relationship between fiction and fantasy.

Another 'recent' writer, Rishi Reddi—who holds both British and American passports—weaves the multigenerational tapestry of interconnected lives in her *Karma and Other Stories* (2008). This critically-acclaimed collection contains eight stories, and it won the 2008 *L.L. Winship-PEN/New England Award*. Themes touching home and other sensibilities, dichotomies of belonging, outlook of people of different generation towards migration and settlement, and the experiences of migrants in the host land engage the attention of Reddi's readers.

The Indian diasporic short-story writers reviewed above usually write about the lives of people and their experiences ranging from old generation to new generation, and explore various situations alien to the new settings of the immigrants. They re-define the notion of diaspora, and present it as a space where the transformation occurs and the female characters becomes a culmination of pastiches through which they paint, in the words of Annie John, "the vastness and complexities of home country which contains everything in multitudes—multiple truths, multiple crisis, multiple realities—and this diversity is portrayed for the world wide reading public and chiefly for the Indians" (30). To conclude, one could easily cite—in the context of short-story-writings by the Indian diasporic authors—the observations of Amba Pande's:

> "Indian women usually migrate within the patriarchal framework and cultural considerations, and are supposed to preserve it as the bearers of Indian tradition, yet the process of migration and economic self dependency give them an opportunity to assert independence, and redefine roles and perceptions of self. While many of the problems, women in the Indian Diaspora face, arise out of the patriarchal structures besides foreign settings, one can find innumerable instances of their struggles and triumphs over adversities and hostile situations. Standing 'in-between' the two worlds, with complex realities of unequal power dynamics of the home land and stereotypical spaces of the host land, women tend to experience conflicting subjectivities of freedom and subjugation. The space of the 'hyphen' often gives them a freedom for self-exploration and deliberation to conceive new identities and to move beyond the fixed definitions of humanity" (2).

Works cited:

"At 17.5 million, Indian diaspora largest in the world: UN report". *The Economics Times* 18 September 2019. Accessed on 22 March 2022 <https://m.econoicties.com/nri/nris-in-news/at-17-5-million-indian-diaspora-largest-in-the-world-un-report/articleshow/71179163.cms>

Bahmanpour, Bahareh. "Female Subjects and negotiating Identities in Jhumpa Lahiri's Interpreter of Maladies". *Studies in Literature and Language* 1.6 (2010): 43-51.

Banerjee, Debjani. "Home and US: Re-defining Identity in the South Asian Diaspora through the Writings of Chitra Banerjee Divakaruni and Meena Alexander". *The Diasporic Imagination: Asian American Writing*. Ed. Somdatta Mandal. Vol II. New Delhi: Prestige. 2000.

Beauvoir, Simone De. *The Second Sex*. Trans. Constance Borde, and Sheila Malovany Chevallier. New York: Vintage Books, 2009 <e-Books.1949-simone-de-beauvoir-the-second-sex.pdf>

Bhabha, Homi. K. *The Location of Culture*. New York and London: Routledge. 1994.

Divakaruni, Chitra Banerjee. *Arranged Marriage*. New York: Anchor Books.1996.

Esman, Milton J. *Diaspora in the Contemporary World*. Cambridge: Polity Press, 2009.

Gabriel, Sharmani Patricia. "Routes of Identity': In Conversation with Bharati Mukherjee". *ARIEL: A Review of International English Literature* 34.4 (2003): 125-138. Accessed on 22 March 2022 <https://www.academia.edu/1553776/-Routes-of-Identity-In-Conversation-with-Bharati-Mukherjee>

Gabriel, Sharmani Patricia. "Between Mosaic and Melting pot': Negotiating Multiculturalism and Cultural Citizenship in Bharati Mukherjee' Narratives of Diaspora". *Postcolonial Text* 1.2 (2005). Accessed on 22 March 2022 <https://www.postcolonial.org/index.php/pct/article/viewArticle/420/827%20/>

Ghosh, Amitava. "The Diaspora in Indian Culture". *The Imam and the Indian*. Ed. Amitava Ghosh. New Delhi: Ravi Dayal. 2002.

Hall, Stuart. "Cultural Identity and Diaspora". *Identity: Community, Culture and Difference*. Ed. Jonathan Rutherford. London: Lawrence and Wishart Ltd. 1990. 222-37.

Hancock, Geoff. "An Interview with Bharati Mukherjee". *Canadian Fiction Magazine* 64 (1987): 30-44.

Hussain, Yasmin. *Writing Diaspora: South Asian Women, Culture and Ethnicity*. Farnham: Ashgate Publishing, 2005.

John, Annie. *In Search of Greener Pastures*. Vol. II. Mumbai: Pencaft publications. 2012.

Lahiri, Jhumpa. *Interpreter of Maladies*. New York: Houghton Mifflin Harcourt. 1999.

Landry, Donna and Maclean, Gerald. *The Spivak Reader: Selected Works of Gayatri Chakravorty Spivak*. New York and London: Routledge. 1996.

Large, Jackie and Quinn, Erin. "Jhumpa Lahiri: A Brief Biography". *The Literature and Culture of the Indian Subcontinent (South Asia) in the Postcolonial Web*. Accessed on 5 April 2022 <http://www.post colonialweb.org/india/literature/lahiri/bio.html>

Mandal, Somdatta. "Oh, Calcutta! The New Bengali Movement in Diasporic Indian English Fiction". *Indian Diaspora – The 21st century- Migration, Change and adaptations. Anthropologist Special Issue* 2 (2007): 9-23. Accessed on 21 Mar. 2022 <https://www.academia.edu/40776545/Oh-calcutta-1-The-New-Bengal-Movement-in-Diasporic-Indian-English-Fiction>

Mohanty, Chandra Talpde. "Under Western Eyes: Feminist Scholarship and Colonial Discourse". *Third World Women and the Politics of Feminism*. Ed. Chandra Talpade Mohanty, Ann Russo and Lourdes Torres. Bloomington: Indiana University Press. 1991. 51-80.

Pande, Amba. "Women in Indian Diaspora: Redefining Self Between Dislocation and Relocation". *Women in the Indian Diaspora Historical Narratives and Contemporary Challenges*. Ed. Amba Pande. Singapore: Sringer Nature. 2018. 1-14.

Patil, A. Savita and Pawar, H. Kishan. "Human Relationships in *Interpreter of Maladies*". *Jhumpa Lahiri: The Master Storyteller: A Critical Response to Interpreter of Maladies*. Ed. Suman Bala. New Delhi: Khosla Publication House. 2002. 204-14.

Pratt, Geraldine. "Grids of difference: place and identity formation". *Cultural Studies: an Anthology*. Ed. Michael Rayan. Singapore: Blackwell Publishing Ltd., 2008.

Tölölyan, Khachig. "*Rethinking Diaspora(s)*: Stateless Power in the Transnational Moment". *Diaspora: A Journal of Transnational Studies* 5.1 (1996): 3-36. Accessed on 23 Mar. 2022 <https://doi.org/10.3138/diaspora.5.1.3>

Tyson, Lois. *Critical Theory Today: A Use-friendly Guide*. 2nd edn. New York and London: Routledge. 2006.

Vertovec, Steven. "The Political Importance of Diaspora". *Centre on Migration Policy and Society* (University of Oxford) 13 (2005): 5-13. Accessed on 23 March 2022 <*http://www.compas.ox.ac.uk/publications/papers/steve%Vertovec%20WP0513.pdf*>

Williams, Laura A. "Foodways and Subjectivity in Jhumpa Lahiri's *Interpreter of Maladies*". *Food in Multi-Ethnic Literature* 32.4 (2007): 69-79. Accessed on 21 March 2022 <*http://www.jstor.org/stable/30029832*>

Yun, Ling. "History and Counter-memory in Jhumpa Lahiri's Interpreter of Maladies". *Reviews of Literature* 1.7 (2014): 1-6.

Zupančič, Metka. "The Power of Storytelling: An Interview with Chitra Banerjee Divakaruni". *Contemporary Women's Writing* 6.2 (2011): 85-101. Accessed on 20 March 2022 <*https://doi.org/10.1093/cww/vpr023*>

From Text to Screen
Searching for the Roots of the Indian Diaspora in Select Films

—Subhrajit Samanta & Soumyajit Samanta

The term diaspora, especially during the decades of the 1960s and 1970s was used (apart from the classic Jewish experience) to denote the "ideology of separation from, and a longing for a return to, the homeland" (Knott 9). Bhabha in *The Location of Culture* has defined such "terms of cultural engagement", as activities, which are "produced performatively" in-between cultures (2).

In the present paper, an attempt is being made to understand the complexities of multi-racial relationships from varied theoretical standpoints, with particular references to films made by/on the Indian diasporic people. It requires mention here that numerous critics have tried to understand the very term 'diaspora' from the standpoints offered by, for example, Spivak (1996) and Homi Bhabha (1994): their perspectives offer a wholesome understanding of the complexities within the intercultural place.

To cite an example, Bhabha has explained that: "It is in the emergence of the interstices-the overlap and displacement of domains of difference-that the intersubjective and collective experiences of nationness, community interest, or cultural value are negotiated" (9). It is also true that "the social articulation of difference, from the minority perspective, is a complex, an ongoing negotiation that seeks to authorise cultural hybridities that emerge in moments of historical transformation. The borderline engagements of cultural difference may as often be consensual as conflictual" (*ibid.* 2). These hybridities and issues of cultural differences are reflected in both Indian diasporic writings and the films on/by the Indian diasporic people.

Analyses of the presentation of an immigrant culture in Indian diasporic cinema, and, to a certain extent, in diasporic literature might appear to be dated. However, in the present paper, an attempt is made to understand the complexities of these multi-racial relationships from varied theoretical standpoints. The most obvious critical approach, which has been used in the examination of diasporic literature and films, is—to iterate—in understanding diasporic literature and films from the point of critical view offered by Spivak and Homi Bhabha. However, this paper also offers a departure from the prevalent approaches in its research by having recourse to Michel Foucault's concept of *Heterotopia* and Edward Soja's (1996) idea of the "third space". Another theorist to be brought into analyses would be Henri Lefebvre. Their writings would be employed to explain and illuminate issues of hybridity, identity in transnational communities, especially, the Indian diaspora. Furthermore, we have also employed the insights offered by Bakhtin and Lacan to sift and understand the resulting spirit of 'jouissance' found in such cultural interactions.

This paper attempts to answer the following questions: (a) how does diasporic cinema, as an example of transnational cinema, challenge the idea of consciousness, experience and lived-in experience of diasporic people, who float between two cultures in time and space? (b) why and how do socio-economic as well as cultural exchanges broaden the mental and physical ambience of the Indian diaspora? (c) how do diasporic communities live in-between spaces of inter-cultural ambiences?; and (d) how do transnational cultural liaisons lift inter-cultural communities to a position where they can frame their heterogeneous identities through a process of migration and dislocation?

While trying to answer these questions, the present essay charts a chronological sequence of Indian diasporic films and texts within a vertical examination of diasporic issues in time. The complex issues in diasporic communities in terms of space would also be explained. The objective, in simple terms, would be to explore the tension between unity and disunity, between home and beyond, to refer to Higson's take on these issues (Higson 16).

In both films and literature by/on the diasporic people, new diasporic identities are constructed relationally, and they gloss over national differences. In other words, culture and identity become a product of negotiating differences in-between spaces, which may be physical, cultural and psychological. It cannot be denied that the diasporic cinema is an essential part of diasporic literature. But the focus and ambience of cinema have a lot to tell about visual culture especially when we witness spatial and temporal sequences of cross-cultural representations. These areas naturally call for interpretation vis-à-vis analyses of the domain of third space through Edward W. Soja's (1996) spatial theory and ideas in cultural geography, along with the French Marxist sociologist Henri Lefebvre's (1991) concept of spatial trialectics, including third-space, or spaces both real and imagined.

Throughout his 1991-publication, Lefebvre has considered space as a social construct where meaning is constantly produced by social interaction, always in the process. We have found that this approach helps to explain various dimensions of diasporic experiences from multi-cultural viewpoints. This becomes particularly relatable when we take into account the dramatic nature of intercultural conflicts in the merging of Bollywood and Hollywood visual cultures. Hence, the inferences of our paper may perhaps enrich research findings in the field of studies in the Indian diaspora, especially where films are concerned. To this extent, we have also tried to understand diasporic films and their vibrancy and ethos through Bollywood as well as Hollywood extravaganza in terms of Bakhtin's (1984) idea of the 'carnivalesque' and, to iterate, Lacan's (1992) exposition of 'jouissance".

Foucault (1986) has described the 'third space' as a transgressive practice of space often in imagination, usually underground, that includes a re-conceptualization of time that is at home in the space or topography being imagined. In addition, 'heterotopia' represents "counter-sites, a kind of effectively enacted utopia in which the real sites, all the other real sites that can be found in the culture, are simultaneously represented, contested, and inverted" (24). He says that "places of this kind are outside of all places, even though it may be possible to indicate their location in reality" (24). Foucault locates heterotopia in the place which is outside of all places and time. Edward Soja also finds that "the assertion of an alternative envisioning of spatiality [...] directly challenges (and is intended to challengingly deconstruct) all conventional modes of spatial thinking" (154-163).

This 'decisive shift' of focus in diasporic studies has been noted in one of Khachig Tololyan's essays published in "*Diaspora*: A Journal of Transnational Studies" (1991), which deals with "immigrants, ethnic minorities, exiles, expatriates, refugees, [and] guest workers" (qtd. in Knott 9). The notion of these *multicultural citizenship[s]* "tends to become a *continuous dialogue*" (*ibid*. 53). Thus, Knott writes, "As the parties to these dialogues are many, not just two, the process may be described as multi-logical. The multilogues allow for views to qualify each other, overlap, synthesise, for one to modify one's view in the light of having to coexist with that of others, hybridise, and allow new adjustments to be made, and new conversations to take place" (*ibid*. 53). Such 'multilogues' and the idea of hyphenated co-existence with other cultures within a hybrid framework, forms the basis of the present paper. We shall begin our discussion with the notion of 'multicultural accommodation' in Indian diasporic cinema, which, like 'integration', is likely to refer—as Knott says in his 2010-publication—to a "sense of solidarity with people of similar origins or faith or mother tongue, including those in a country of origin or a diaspora" (53).

The 'sense of solidarity' becomes perceptible in Indian diasporic cinema, which—perceptively—has its origins in the community's angst for their homeland as well as their romance with the adopted country. Diasporic cinema—in other words—presents the travails and problems of the Indian community in both, temporal and spatial dimensions. The racial memory of the immigrant Indian has its origins in the roots of the homeland. Most of the studies on Indian diaspora and cinema have focused on this aspect of immigrant culture with the themes of return specifically in films like *Dilwale Dulhanya Le Jayenge, The Namesake*, and so on. It is important to understand the Indian diaspora through a cinematic presentation of spectacle, narrative and

Bollywood extravaganza. Foucault has explained the dialogues between cultures as follows:

In his famous 1984-publication, Michel Foucault states: "We are in the epoch of simultaneity: we are in the epoch of juxtaposition, the epoch of the near and far, of the side-by-side, of the dispersed. We are at a moment, I believe, when our experience of the world is less that of a long life developing through time than that of a network that connects points and intersects with its skein" (1). He amplifies the considerations of space (which are routinely explored in the diasporic films) further and says that we live, as Bachelard says, not "in a homogeneous and empty space, but on the contrary in a space thoroughly imbued with quantities and perhaps thoroughly fantastic as well (*ibid*. 2).

Such notions of deviation from homogeneity, and the emergence of spaces within heterotopia, which may be the site of several contesting spaces, are liable to be termed—following Foucault's observations—'heterochrony' in diasporic cinema (*ibid*. 1-9). However, it is essential to discover the concept of heterotopias within cinema itself.

Demirkan, in his essay "The Representation of Heterotopias in Cinema" (2018), has analysed the filmic space in context of 'Foucault's heterotopia', which—in turn—corresponds to 'Soja's concept of third space or Lefebvre's space production diagram' (Demirkan 50). In this sense, "Third space is both intersection and combination of perceived and conceived space based on trialectics of being and trialectics of spatiality developing on Lefebvre's three moments of space production (perceived, conceived, lived)" (*ibid*. 50). Demirkan, further, writes, "In the heterotopia concept, although heterotopia appears as more real space than utopian spaces, this boundary is blurred. The heterotopian void prevails not only as a physical space but also as a perceived and lived space in which the desires, hopes, thresholds, and bounds occur" (*ibid*. 50).

In diasporic cinema, we find several such intersections of time as well as space when immigrants shuttle from their mother culture to that of the adopted country. As they re-consider their roots and childhood there is a steady shift in cultural panorama in time, which oscillates between times past and present. Whereas, when we witness their inter-cultural dilemma in the present space, we see a collision and coalescing of space in their multi-cultural dress and habits, especially in their love relationships and marriages. Indian diasporic films are attempts to realise these concepts. Hence, such filmic spaces may be said to illustrate Foucault's heterotopia in space and time.

To cite an example, Mira Nair's (*M.G.M.*-distribution) *Mississippi Masala* (1991) has been defined by Ray as of race, rather, as a socio-political discourse spread over rural Mississippi (155). It focuses on a multi-cultural milieu in which, both African-Americans and Indian Americans become embroiled in inter-racial love affairs. Focusing on the *desi* immigrant community in the U.S.A., the film records how identity is formed and reformed in the light of immigration practices. Changes in time and spaceare recorded as the scenario shifts from Uganda (Kampala) to the U.S.A. in the early 1970s'. Jay's antagonism to his daughter's liaison with Demetrius, an Afro-American, invites the audience to understand the issues behind the rift between Indian and African communities. But the blending of cultures is yet to occur in the third space where hybrid identities are formed.

This 'heterotopic space' has been imbued with a clash of cultures as the search for a collective identity remains to be realised behind a sole self. Indeed, the search for Indian roots and culture dominates the film's exploration of several identities in the protagonists. This is seen in the weddings, which are conducted according to Indian traditions, hailing the question-Who is an Indian? As Jammu Bhai opts for his patriotic devotion to his roots, the ambience of heterotopia becomes riddled with "inherited memories". Jammu never forgets his roots in Indian culture and tradition.

The rift between the Africans and Indians is seen when Demetrius's father asks Meena, "How did Indians arrive in Africa" (*Mississippi* 0:51-1:25). Meena replies, "The British brought them here to build the railway" (*ibid*. 0:55-1:25). At once, his father quipped, "like slaves" (*ibid*. 0:56/-1:25). Again Demetrius confesses that he is just a carpet-cleaner and blames Meena for his loss of job. Also, he discovers that her family had trouble with black folks (*ibid.* 0:42-2:50). Jay is forced to accept that Uganda is not his home anymore despite having spent all his life there (*ibid.* 1:03-1:14). Finally, he is told that "Africa is for Africans, Black Africa" (*ibid.* 1:08-14-1:14).

As different identities clash, they also coexist at the same time, creating a third space. So, we never find anything utopian or homogenous. Racial issues become dystopic and heterogeneous. Thus, both Jammu and Jay are reminded of their origins and keep searching for their roots.

Gurinder Chadha's *Bhaji on the Beach* (1993) — distributed by F.I.F. — raises the issue of hybridised identities which co-exist at the juncture of transnational cultural flows, oscillating between Birmingham, Blackpool, and Mumbai. It focuses on cultural clashes in an area of multiple inscribed loyalties between cities, identities and cultures. In this context, identity becomes hybridised subjectivities, multiple inscribed loyalties in transnational cultures. Spanning three generations, British Asian women struggle at the intersection of ethnic, gendered trajectories among deep generational conflicts. The search for roots results in the collusion of divided loyalties, spanning three generations. Asha, Pushpa, Rekha, Ginder, Hashida, Ladhu, Madhu, and Simi (the organiser), travel from Birmingham to Blackpool. They arrive at a seaside resort and reach an intersection of transcultural flows that define their hybridised subjectivities, held in suspension in the third space.

Mendes, in her essay *"Triangulating Birmingham, Blackpool, and Bombay*: Gurinder Chadha's Bhaji on the Beach" (2010), has explored how identity is negotiated through cultural antinomies in the ambience of the seaside, illustrating a 'collusion of divided loyalties, weaving together the lives of this group of women from different backgrounds and generations'. At Blackpool, the characters inscribe multiple identities, at the intersection of ethnic and gendered lines. They are relegated to a position where they are forced to reconcile conflicting dichotomies in English and Indian cultures. It is at this juncture of transnational cultural flows that hybridised subjectivities in-between coexist and are held in suspension (Mendes 327). The beach provides an intercultural scenario (*Bhaji* 0:45-1:50).

Cultural hybridity, it is understood, may be theorised and interpreted on several planes. Mendes highlights the "intentional hybridity" of a cosmopolitan filmmaker like Chadha whose approach is likely to focus on transnational preoccupations. An *avant-garde* film, it focuses on issues of pregnancy which are highly debated (*Bhaji* 1:00-1:50). It also has a striptease show (*ibid.* 1:20-1:50). In this context, Chadha constructs ethnic identity only to deconstruct it from a transnational viewpoint (Mendes 328). The director's penchant might be to create an ambience of cultural shock by bringing into conflict an older mythical identity of the diasporic community with the new Western cultural artefacts, thereby producing a "dissenting discourse" (*ibid.* 328). This movement may be understood in the context of the 'third space' in terms of diasporic identities.

In an "*Interview with Edward Soja*: Third Space, Post-metropolis, and Social Theory" by Christian Borch, Soja has explained that his use of *Third Space* refers to "a particular way of thinking about and interpreting socially produced space. It is a way of thinking that sees the spatiality of our lives, the human geographies in which we live, as having the same scope and critical significance as the historical and social dimensions of our lives" (Borch 113). Soja, further, opines that the trajectory of Western critique has been to privilege historical discourse and thereby insisting on the primacy of time over space. Rather, he wishes to balance both time and space in a triple dialectic of a "Third Space perspective". In his book *Third Space* (1996), he refers to both Henri Lefebvre and Michel Foucault as preferring a similar argument in the late 1960s' and the early 1970s'. If human lives and ideology is mapped by "things in space", it is also possible to map "thoughts about space" (113). History, according to Soja, is constructed through our lived-in experience, in our individual lives and social relations: "what Lefebvre called lived space, an all-embracing and never fully knowable spatiality that was directly comparable to our lived time, Foucault called *des espaces autres*, not just simply translatable as 'other' but as 'significantly different' spaces, and invented a new term to describe how to look at this space in this new and different way: heterotopolgy" (qtd. in Borch 113).

To relate to the above observations, *Bhaji on the Beach* (1994) focuses on what it is like to live in England as a second-generation British-Asian. *Bhaji on the Beach* does not attempt to give expression to what Hall has indicated as one "authentic" or "essential" South Asian experience but rather places the stress upon heterogeneity and the "living" of "identity through difference" (Hall, *Old* 57). Thus, the British Asians are neither assimilated into the mainstream British culture; nor do they adhere to traditional immigrant culture, but remain with a pulsating, open, bilingual identity. Mendes comments: "Against a monolithic understanding of diasporic experience, *Bhaji on the Beach* offers a multiethnic reading in its deployment of gendered migrant identities" (329).

Finally, this feeling of diaspora as both insiders and outsiders in the intricate relationships of time and place, along with Chadha's usage of travel as a trope, "belies the configuration of deterritorialised female subjectivity within the framework of a home journey binary at the heart of the diaspora" (Mendes 330).

Aditya Chopra's *Dilwale Dulhaniya Le Jayenge* (A.A. Films, 1995) is a critique of Indian traditions and orthodox values, especially where marriage is concerned. The Indian society is shown to be restrictive and prescriptive (*Dilwale* 2:40:40-3:07:54).). Even love-relations must be guided by parental blessings (*ibid.* 1:30:50-3:07:54). Baldev's anguished cry to Simran in allowing her to go with Raj is in the spirit of the carnivalesque. Nothing matters where the spirit of joy in love is concerned: in this sense, this Bollywood extravaganza highlights the dialogue between modernity and traditional cultural symbols, especially around the position of women as well as issues of marriage. Here, the third space becomes a discursive space, enacting a tension between modesty and sexuality.

Referring to the classic ethos of Indian women, this film questions the dynamics of control and the power of men over women. Weddings, dances and cultural extravaganza become 'carnivalesque' in spirit and act. Such cultural extravaganza may be understood through Bakhtin's theory of the 'carnivalesque'. Its uniqueness lies in positing pulsating love relations in the context of many picturesque European scenarios. Clinging to Indian roots just like Baldev goes against modern European values (*Dilwale* 2:56:15-3:07:54). Yet, the contradictions are resolved and enriched in the pulsating romance between Simran and Raj. We may understand the dimensions of Bakhtin's 'carnivalesque' — with reference to its presentation in the diasporic Indian films — in different terms.

For instance, Clark and Holoquist, in their 1984-publication, explain Bakhtin's concept of the carnivalesque as follows:

> "Carnival is not a spectacle seen by the people; they live in it, and everyone participates because its very idea embraces all the people. While carnival lasts, there is no other life outside it. During the period of carnival, life is subject only to its laws, that is, the laws of its freedom. It has a universal spirit; it is a special condition of the entire world, of the world's revival and renewal, in which all take part. Such is the essence of carnival, vividly felt by all its participants" (7-8).

Large-scale participation in weddings in Bollywood style — the perfect example of this 'carnival' — incarnates the passions and emotions of youth with its roots in globalisation as well as tradition. The 1995-film does not offer any cultural shock to the audience since it heightens the merging of inter-racial cultures and celebrates the rise of the modern liberal Indian woman. Indeed, much in the spirit of the 'carnivalesque', the film uses the classic romantic formula to free women from the dynamics of male control. Granted, the film highlights the personalities of immigrant Indians in Western cultural contexts with the proverbial dualities of home and beyond. They do not exclude themselves from the influence of modern Western cultural influences but attempt to bridge gaps in culture through the third space, which, of course, is the site of cultural exchange and appropriation.

In *Dilwale Dulhaniya Le Jayenge*, Raj and Simran not only connect the different segments in Indian society by promoting the values of family. Gay abandon in dance sequences has a certain positive character, along with an abundance and a suggestion of fertility. But apart from the display of physical romance in exotic Switzerland scenarios, the abundance of the body and spirit in the spirit of joy and gay relativity suggests a cross-cultural dialogue in transnational settings. Finally, the love between Simran and Raj prevails (*Dilwale* 3:06–3:07:54). Such romance, therefore, becomes symbolic of the liberation of the traditional Indian woman in global terms.

The locale of Damien O' Donnell's *East is East* (1999) (distributed by *Miramax*) is Salford, Lancashire. The Irish director — presently fifty-five years old — focuses the action on a multi-ethnic British household with George, a Pakistani father, and Ella, who is an English mother. It had been staged in the *Birmingham Repertory Theatre*, and derives its cue from Rudyard Kipling's "The Ballad of East and West" (1889). But, as Kipling indicates, the wholesome nature of the world, prefigured by God, is inclusive of the four dimensions in nature. He had celebrated the oneness of man and nature by saying that there is neither *East* nor *West* in consideration of borders, birth, breed or directions. Indian diasporic cinema is a witness to such multiple considerations of time, and space in the arena of several cultures.

In *East is East*, Khan's children are frustrated since their father wants them to be paired off in arranged marriages. When George is presented with portraits of Muslim girls to be married off to his children, there is general consternation (*East* 37:30-35 and 96:50). The dystopic character of the family is underlined in cultural clashes between British customs and Pakistani culture. The household is in shambles as none of them harmonises with any other.

Like Osborne's *Look Back in Anger*, the characters, in *East is East*, are motivated by anger. Curses have an Asian flavour (*ibid.* 39:09-96:50). George attacks his British wife and tells her that she fails to behave like a proper Muslim wife (*ibid.* 61:40-96:50). She, in return, calls him a bastard and tells him that for all those married years he had never listened to her (*ibid.* 62:19–96: 50). George calls his children 'bastards', and they, in turn, respond by demeaning him as a 'Paki' — presently considered to be an extremely offensive term. His children are frustrated because they can never understand their father, and this is due to their dual identities of being British (White) as well as Muslim and Pakistani.

The Irish director, in his 1999-film, has raised the issue of mass-migration, with its consequent emphasis on the struggle for identity. At the site of dislocation is George's inter-racial marriage which raises the issues of racial rivalry, especially against the backdrop of 'holocausts' like the 9/11 and 7/7 conflicts. The theme of the film may be explained in the context of Stuart Hall's explanation of, the "challenges" of "fixed binaries which stabilise meaning and representation and show how meaning is never finished or completed but keeps on moving to encompass other, additional or supplementary meanings. Without relations of difference, no representations could occur. But what is then constituted within representation is always open to being deferred, staggered, serialised" (Hall, *Cultural* 229).

In this context, the film comments on tenets of multiculturalism, which indicates a shift from the palpable sense of being Asian or Muslim or Pakistani, with its perpetual and endless search for home and return in reverse gear. Finally, the film preaches that the alienation of Asians in Britain was a subject of consideration in the 1970s'. When the film was released there was a palpable change of attitude in Britain. The Asians, identifiably, were no longer victims of torture or racial discrimination. Manzoor, a British (Pakistani) journalist, in his 2021-article, has noted that the scenario changed during the early 21st century. The film was shown, without any incident, for the first time from 4 October 2014 to 3 January 2015, at the *Trafalgar Studios*, London.

Mira Nair's *Monsoon Wedding* (U.S.A. Films, 2001) presents the *A.B.C.D.-Generation* (that is, the *American Born Confused Desi*-generation), in the ambience of Bhabha and Lefebvre's *Third space*. Nair's film enacts a honeymoon between the East and West in the scenario of New Delhi. The epilogue of the film-"We are like that only" contextualises the splendid display of "Musti", which, in Nair's terminology, describes the "intoxication with life" in a carnivalesque manner. *Ghazal*-s, Punjabi *bhangra*-s, Indian popsongs as well as jazz resound with the 'jouissance' of life. Owen Hewitson—it demands mentioning—has asked, "What does Lacan say about Jouissance?". According to Lacan, "Jouissance is an excess of life" and "as an enjoyment beyond the pleasure principle". In other words, it denotes "an excess of life", which Lacan means "superabundant vitality" (94).

Monsoon Wedding challenges the Western concepts of arranged marriage, and portrays Indian values as of family holding on to their origins against assimilation. It comments on the changed role of a woman in Aditi, who has an extra-marital affair with her office-boss, but is not shunned by her would-be husband. It is a critique of the Western stigma of love marriages as incompatible and doomed. As Indian women return to their roots they incur respect and are portrayed in an *avant-garde* fashion. Incarnating the voice of the modern woman in Aditi highlights the decolonisation of women in India. This idea of liberation in terms of gender, class and nationality has been influenced by the Western culture, especially in the ambience of the would-be husband, 'Hemant from Houston', Tej Puri from the U.S.A., and Shashi's husband from Oman.

With monsoon showers, the traditional formulas of Bollywood weddings merge with their symbolic release from traditional bonds. This cultural shift explores the role of the middle-class woman. Aditi takes her own decisions. When her would-be husband comes to know of her erstwhile liaison with her boss, he becomes angry but adjusts himself to his new situation. Aditi tells him, "You have every reason to be angry (*Monsoon* 1:14-1:52-24). "I know we can put this behind us", says Hemant (*ibid.* 1:15:21-1:52:24) in the voice of the new Indian diaspora. The director has positioned the new woman in Aditi, thus obliterating traditional beliefs (*ibid.* 1:15:55-1:16:02). Aditi becomes the pivot around whom the feeling of 'jouissance' circulates.

Anurag Mehta's *American Chai* (D.M. Pictures, 2001) explores the ambitions of Sureel, a first-generation Indian-American, in the context of his Indian heritage. His father wants him to become a doctor. He thinks that he is in the pre-medical course. But he is bent on gaining recognition as a musical artist and that is how he wants his father's blessing. Sureel formed his American musical band, and his song- "We used to be together all the time" (*American* 0:16 - 2:28). His father dictates that he wants to see his son as a medical practitioner. He commands: "And no girlfriends, no music, no parties, no drinking, no R-rated movies, nothing" (*ibid.* 0:40-2:52). But Sureel confesses, "All my life I've been hiding from my parents. It makes me crazy" (*ibid.* 0:27-2:39).

This prepares the scenario for a generation gap and clash between traditional values and modern Western values. Here, the formation of a 'desi' identity is challenged on a global level and a hybrid identity emerges as a product of negotiating differences. His father plans an arranged marriage for him (*ibid.* 1:09-1:11 and 2:12). On the other hand, Sureel and his friends exult: "In America, you can do anything you want: that's why I am here" (*ibid.* 1:31-3:33).

The 'Third Cinema' or the filmic portrayal of 'Diasporas in the West' is the subject of Stuart Hall's *Cultural Identity and Diaspora* (1990). Hall questions, "Who is this emergent, new subject of the cinema? From where does he/she speak?" (222). Hall has problematised identity by saying that "identity" as such may be seen as something "which is incessantly produced or in a state of production, never static" (*ibid.* 222). In fact, identity is "always constituted within, not outside, representation. This view problematises the very authority and authenticity in respect of the term "*cultural identity*, to which he has laid claim" (*ibid.* 222).

Mehta's 2001-comedy-drama film attempts to answer the question of how diasporic communities live in-between spaces of inter-cultural ambiences. As the film resonates with the issues behind cultural and generational differences it highlights how a new diasporic identity is constructed relationally, glossing over national differences. In other words, culture and identity become products of negotiating differences in-between spaces, which may be physical, cultural and psychological. As Sureel's father comes to his dormitory, he finds textbooks on medical science strewn all over the place. On the other hand, Sureel not only excels in his relationship with Maya but also creates his musical band, *American Chai*.

In this context—that is, with reference to the different aspects of *American Chai*—one may mention that Stuart Hall has noted how diasporic communities produce and reproduce themselves through incessant transformation (Hall, *Old* 58). According to the Jamaican-born British Marxist sociologist, cultural identity may not be singular but a product of "critical points of deep and significant difference which constitutes 'what we are; or rather, since history has intervened -'what we have become' (*Cultural* 225). We cannot speak for very long, with any exactness, about 'one experience, one identity, without acknowledging its other side-the ruptures and continuities which constitute, precisely, the Caribbean's 'uniqueness' (*ibid*. 225). Cultural identity, in this second sense, is a matter of 'becoming' as well as of 'being'. It belongs to the future as much as the past. It is not something which already exists, transcending place, time, history and culture. Cultural identities come from somewhere and have histories. But, like everything historical, they undergo constant transformation. Far from being eternally fixed in some essentialised past, they are subject to—to refer to Hall—the constant 'play' of history, culture and power" (*ibid*. 225).

This study—as we have already mentioned—re-values and re-validates the cultural assumptions of the diasporic community in 'the constant play of history, culture and power' (*ibid*. 225). Spatial theory re-positions the diasporic community in the context of the 'third space' (to refer to Soja's 1996-publication), as well as Foucault's notion of 'heterotopia' (about which he discusses in his 1984-writing). Our research attempts to telescope both the time as well as spatial dimensions in history and geographical places.

In such a context and situation, our next film to be discussed is Gurinder Chadha's *Bend it like Beckham* (Searchlight Pictures, et al., 2002), which focuses on the socio-politics of football with the (former) English footballer, David R.J. Beckham (b. 1975), as its icon. The inter-cultural nexus finds its exponent in Jesminder (*Jess*) Bhamra, daughter of a British Sikh family, especially in her infatuation with football, which is looked down upon in her family. Her attitude raises some fundamental questions regarding her roots. Visitors to her house say that soon Jess will be married and that all mosquitoes will be juicy mangoes after marriage (*Bend* 00:50-1:52). Can she be termed an obedient Indian girl? Her father cautions her that she must start behaving like a proper woman (*ibid*. 0:28-11:52). Jess's mother tells her–"no more football" (*ibid*. 0:49-1:52). She is expected to dance to the tunes of English music. But she hides in the lavatory to escape acting in conformity with her parents. Jess's parents say that they cannot tolerate their daughter who kicks football all day but cannot make *chapatti*-s. The film iconises her dual role between the intersection of English football practices and wedding scenes wherein she attempts to integrate her heritage with her adopted country.

Jess has a penchant for locating herself in-between cultures. She cannot forget *pakora*-s in the vicinity of Aero-chocolate bars and mixes fizzy drinks with a concoction named 'volcano'. She merges her passion for soccer with Indian food and ceremonial dance at her sister's wedding ceremonies. Her cultural hyphenation in the third space has been symbolised by Beckham's curling football kick. As the ball twists and turns to deceive the defenders in the game, similarly, Jess learns to twist and bend the social rules to confirm her multi-cultural heritage. The film is about bending all the rules (*ibid*. 1:41/1:52).In this sense, her passion for football merges with her ethnicity, which is re-formulated, re-aligned and re-positioned in the context of third space. The visual clues to Sikh cultural practices like the *kara* or bracelet and turban have been re-aligned with her father's airline uniform. Throughout, we find that Jess seeks an identity which coalesces both her ancestral roots and her adopted home in the 'third space' of her unique identity. Her ambitions curl through the wall of her parents' taboosin an attempt to re-read her personality through the trope of the game of football.

In this instance, the spatial theory positions the diasporic community within the related notion of Foucault's heterotopia (1984), or Soja's 1996-notion of 'third space', as we take into account the evolution/revolution of spatial customs and practices in the ethos of the diaspora.

Gurinder Chadha's *Bride and Prejudice* (*Pathe Distribution*, 2004) follows the story of Austen's 'Pride and Prejudice', and is centred on the Bakshi family. It is a tale of a modern woman in a traditional family (*Bride* 0:23−2:40). Lalita Bakshi and her three sisters, Jaya, Maya, and Lakhi meet Balraj Uppal and William Darcy. These characters are from two completely different worlds (*ibid*. 0:31-2:48). Marriages are arranged (*ibid*. 1:10-3:27). Among the would-be husbands is Darcy (an American) and Uppal, a barrister and British citizen. Functioning largely as a hypertext, the film is also a transnational cinema, bringing in the nuances of three continents (North America, Europe, and Asia), as well as narratives of different nations. Aware of these socio-cultural-economic differences, Darcy constantly cautions Uppal. He warns him not to sell himself in terms of marriage.

The film challenges the idea of consciousness as a monolith since it experiments with socio-economic and cultural exchanges of different nationalities (Higson 168). It also illustrates how the ambience of the 19th and 21st centuries can be paralleled in various means of reduplication to show that identity can never be a monolith and can be variously interpreted. The song by the sisters iconises unity in diversity (*Bride* 14:20-15:22-1:46:49). Again, if cultures clash in Goa (*ibid*. 26:40/1:46:49), there is also scope for mutual understanding. Its multilithic interpretation of diasporic cultures challenges the ideas of nationalism linked to cultures and one's roots. The film attempts to return to its roots through elaborate wedding parties and Indian dance numbers. At last, Lalita and Darcy come to love each other (*ibid*. 1:22-27: 32/ 1:46:49). In this sense, the film departs from stable notions of cultural sites in Austen and verges toward a plural society, where identity becomes plural. Chadha's blending of two similar scenarios in England and India illustrates that gender and ethnicity, as well as class relations, can always be re-formulated, and re-conceived in different cultural contexts. Hence, in the film, identities become variously constructed in different specificities of time and space. The 'third space' here is the site of cultural formulation where national boundaries are effaced and a truly transnational cinema emerges.

Such a transnational cinema becomes a unique experiment when the director presents a cultural confrontation between Darcy (representative of the so-called 'West') and Lalita Bakshi ('East'). On the other hand, Balraj Uppal and Kiran Uppal, the siblings, project the British images of upper-class cultures. The director's experiment verges towards a climax when Indians are posited against diasporic Indians. Here, the strains of Hollywood and Bollywood merge in an essentially hybrid drama where romance and its paraphernalia are used as experiments to overcome cultural prejudices as well as pride in acts of subversion. Racial prejudices are overcome in the experience of love affairs where characters are permitted to see and witness a different culture from the eyes of the other.

In Chadha's film, the 'third space' is compounded by several echoes of cultural hybridity. Hindus, Muslims, Sikhs, Americans, and British enact a multi-cultural harmony in the context of Ashanti and Afro-American singing in Goa. Lalita Bakshi plays cricket with 'desi' children on the beach in Goa amidst merry-making and laughter has suggestions of Bakhtinian carnivalesque:

> "Laughter is essentially not an external but an interior form of truth---it liberates from the fear that developed in man during thousands of years: fear of the sacred, of prohibitions, of the past, of the power. Laughter opened men's eyes on that which is now, on the future" (Bakhtin 94).

Diasporic movies illustrate this spirit of joy in a multicultural setting with a promise of a new order of things, transcending the orthodox, traditional ways of life.

The American writer/director Paul M. Berges's direction, and Gurinder Chadha's screenplay make *The Mistress of Spices* (*Rainbow Films*, 2005) a unique film. It uses the techniques of magic-realism to present the problems of migrants living in America. Varieties of Indian spices have been anthropomorphised, and are used as metaphors to co-relate the symbolic and the actual in the domain of myths, magic as well as a historical phenomenon. The epigraph of the film—understandably—reads, "India is an ancient land for its myths, magic and traditions. But when the people leave to start new lives in the faraway lands of America and Europe, what happens to the magic left behind? This is an immigrant's tale about keeping the magic alive" (Jain 184). The film also provides several such answers.

In the 2005-film, Tilottama, a clairvoyant, is the so-called 'mistress of spices', and acts as the proverbial 'medicine-woman', dispensing each spice for a particular ailment or mental state. Supervised by the mysterious 'First Mother', the salesgirls are directed not to leave their shops all around the world. Tilottama runs a store named *Spice Bazaar* in the San Francisco Bay Area. Her customers include Haroun, Geeta, Kwesi and Jagjit. As Doug crashes his motorbike outside her store, she rushes to nurse him, while falling in love. But the spices shun human emotions and have their dimensions of existence. The chillies warn her from falling in love with Doug. But she realises her mistake and sets the store on fire. In the sequel, the 'Mother' of spices acknowledges Tilo's sacrifice, and blesses her. Doug and Tilo, at the end of the film, restore the shop and spices.

In this 2005-production, the dramatic character of spices becomes obvious in the matter-of-fact assimilation of the fantastic into a realist scenario. In the film, each spice becomes animated with a distinctive characteristic of its own. Fenugreek ameliorates digestion, red chilli destroys evil spirits, turmeric stands for panacea, and lotus root signifies long-lasting love whereas asafoetida is an antidote to love. This anthropomorphising of Indian cuisine and medicine reaches its climax when women and spices become complimentary. The uniqueness of this movie lies in the fact that man-woman relations are metaphorically presented through the language of spices. Language, culture, cuisine and history have been re-defined in a diasporic setting. Gurinder Chadha and Berges have done a wonderful job in integrating familial, social and national issues through the paraphernalia of spices. Hence the title, 'Mistress of Spices', becomes extremely significant.

The theme of the film becomes clear when we attempt to understand the Indian diaspora through the persona of 'The Mistress' of the Spices. Tilo (that is, Tilottoma) is shown to become a prisoner of her culture and traditions, illustrated metaphorically in the drama of spices. One of the characters in the film, Geeta's grandfather, does not approve of late hours in the office with male youngsters. But he also says, "This America is not so bad" (*The Mistress* 16:17–16:36).

Finally, this film challenges the fixed binaries of representation in diasporic cinema. It presents an avant-garde method to illustrate the complexities of Tilo's emotional urges, dreams and performance in the context of America, the land of opportunities. The world of spices has an enchanted odour and fantasy, incarnating the realm of Indian traditions and yet they become alien in America. The Chillies warn her against softening her heart concerning Doug (*ibid.* 18:30-18:36).

Spices depend on inner needs, Tilo tells Doug. Through the metaphor of spices, the director positions the immigrant in a foreign country. Yet in the third space, there is the danger of cultural clashes. The spices can make people happy as well as satisfy their desires (*ibid.* 76:40 onwards).

Through the strains of magical realism, Tilo has been positioned and re-positioned within the norms of the Indian diaspora by the director. Her marriage to Doug confirms her inalienable presence in the plethora of multi-cultures. The film positions itself in the third space as seen in Tilo's response to Geeta's grandfather, who — as already mentioned — does not approve of late hours in the office with male youngsters.

Indeed, Tilottama — in the film — must break out from her imprisonment within her roots and liberate herself from the control of spices. Indian spices also metaphorically illustrate gender relations where men have power over women. The ultimate desire to transgress her own culture, traditions and forms of male control forms the journey of the diasporic Indian woman in a foreign country. Ultimately, she finds her freedom in her liaison with Doug, and successfully deconstructs her fascination for spices. In the end of the novel, the spices clear the doubts in Tilo's mind:

> "And a voice: By tomorrow night Tilo, you will be at beauty's summit. Enjoy well. By the next morning, it will be gone.

Ah spices, why should I worry about the next morning. By then will I too not be gone.
And will you be happy going, or will you come to us with your heart stained with the colours of regret?
For myself I have no regrets, I say" (Divakaruni 263).

Mira Nair's *The Namesake* (*Fox Searchlight Pictures*, 2006) is built on the complex theme of immigrant identities at cross-cultural intersections. Gogol faces a complex problem regarding his name. Named after the famous Russian novelist, Gogol refuses to accept his nomenclature and would rather be known as Nikhil. The film is about a sense of belonging to one's own culture, roots and origins. He feels a sense of alienation in the American scenario (*The Namesake* 0:40-2:35). He merges very well with his American girlfriend, Maxine and feels more attuned with her family than with his. And yet, after his father's demise, he feels an urge to return to his origins in Calcutta.

The feeling of being displaced from one's roots and a lack of belonging in a foreign country is a distinctive feature of this film. And yet Ashoke Ganguly and Ashima, his wife try their utmost to balance themselves between American culture and social mores and their Bengali cultures. His father tells Gogol-"no kissing, no holding hands (1:16-18- 2: 35).Their son, Gogol is forced to engage in an incessant dialogue between his inner self and his American way of life. In this sense, his self as well as those of his parents are subject to a flux of cultures and identities without any sense of continuity. In other words, Gogol always questions his inter-cultural ambience and tries to position himself in-between through participation in music, school and college friends as well as the medium of language.

The story of Gogol and his family rotates around his affiliation with his namesake. His father tells the story behind his nomenclature (*ibid*. 1:39-2:35). His acts of coherence, as well as incompatibility with a foreign culture, enacts his struggle with his dispersal and fragmentation just like the conflicts faced by all enforced diasporas. By and large, the nucleus of his life is framed around his constructed identity. Here, we find, as explained by

Stuart Hall, "the traumatic character of the "colonial experience" (Hall, *Cultural* 225).

Hall, further, writes: "This inner expropriation of cultural identity cripples and deforms if its silences are not resisted, they produce, in Fanon's phrase, 'individuals without an anchor, without horizon, a colourless, stateless, rootless-a race of angels' [...]. In this perspective, cultural identity is not a fixed essence at all, lying unchanged outside history and culture. [...]. [I]t is not once-and-for-all. It has its histories — and histories have their real, material and symbolic effects. The past continues to speak to us — it is always constructed through memory, fantasy, narrative and myth" (Hall, *Cultural* 226). In this context, one may notice how Gogol feels free during his interaction with foreign cultures: "For the first time in life I felt free" (*The Namesake* 0: 11 — 2:46).

The Namesake not only positions cultures through the ramifications revolving around Gogol's pet name but also questions his adoption of a foreign culture. The film presents a constant dialogue between himself and other cultures. As Ashima Ganguly explains, "Being a foreigner is a sort of life-long pregnancy: a perpetual wait, a constant burden, a continuous feeling out of sorts. It is an ongoing responsibility, a parenthesis in what had been ordinary life, only to discover that that previous life has vanished, replaced by something more complicated and demanding like pregnancy" (quoted from *https://www.goodreads.com/quotes/61740-though-no-longer-pregnant-she-continues-at-times-to-mix*). Being a foreigner, Ashima believes, is something that elicits the same curiosity from strangers, the same combination of pity and respect.

Gogol, in *The Namesake*, re-formulates his identity by reaching out to his past roots and tradition and attempts to reconnect with his homeland through his realization of his new self which he feels is an evolving identity. He accepts that his new diasporic identity is a construction of social, material and essential selves. Nair's film re-situates and re-formulates Gogol's wholesome participation in life in his marriage with Moushumi. Re-defining names, therefore, contextualises differences within the notion of identity in itself. Nair's film does not merely present this "cultural play" in cinematic terms as a "simple binary opposition between past /present, them/us. Its complexity exceeds this binary structure of representation. They become differential points along a sliding scale" (Hall, *Cultural* 228).

Vipul A. Shah's *Namastey London* (*Adlabs Films*, 2007) is centred on Jasmeet or *Jazz*, an Indian girl brought up in London, with an *avant-garde* temperament. She is fond of social life in the city along with parties, and alcohol with a dash of casual affairs (*Namastey* 8:35-10:51). Jazz prides herself on being British (*ibid.* 3:38-5:54). While Manmohan regrets her daughter's fast life and especially becomes disenchanted with her daughter's affair with Charles Brown. Sometimes she melts into her Indian origins (*ibid.* 54:45-57:01) and feels comfortable with Arjun (58:11-1:00:27). Hence, she is persuaded to marry Arjun but she escapes to London to marry Charles. Amidst such complications, Jasmeet faces racial abuse by Charles and his family. Indian customs and traditions interlock with the British way of life (*ibid.* 1:25:40-1:27:56).

While Jasmeet wavers, Arjun feels connected with his roots (*ibid.* 1:52:17-1:54:33). Charles's family looks down on India as an ancient land full of castes and prejudice, where snake charmers are found along with rope tricks with *chicken tandoor*.

This film focuses on the problems of the diasporic community, who find it difficult to adapt to British culture and way of life as they are in the habit of holding on to their roots. Jasmeet loves flamboyance in the urban space of London but it is here that she meets with Arjun, who is suave, cultured and handsome. Arjun tells Jasmeet that she cannot abjure her Indian origins.

Such sites of cultural conflict determine the trajectory of this film as they undermine the idea of unity within the diasporic community. The locale of cultural interaction becomes a troubled space of dystopic encounters, undermining any Utopian amalgamation of identities as well as cultures. If the diasporic space becomes heterotopic where things, personalities and emotions operate differently in the system, there is a danger that history becomes responsible for present scenarios. Thus racialism is a by-product of colonial endeavours but such residual actions must be re-interpreted in the light of globalisation today. Diasporic movies like this one situate the Indian in cross-sections of time and space at home and abroad.

Indian diasporic community remains suspended in-between dual cultures. On the one hand, the cultural baggage of the diasporic Indian is contested or consumed by Western values. Finally, Jasmeet debunks her role as a wife in the marriage ceremony in the church and surprises Charlie by opting for Arjun as her husband (*ibid.* 2:11:11-2:13:27).

Released through *Netflix on* 27 April 2020, Mindy Kaling and Lang Fisher's *Never Have I Ever* attempt a parallel representation of two cultures in the scenario of San Fernando Valley. In the film/drama television-series, an American high school student's (Devi Vishwakumar's) childhood experiences have been brought to the foreground of the action. Vishwakumar attempts to understand her origins especially when her daughter is born. Her liaison with her friends, Eleanor Wong, Fabiola Torres and Praxton Hall-Yoshida position her affinity with Western cultures against her roots in Indian traditional values. Often, she feels lost in her school (*Never* 1:10-1:14). She even says that "the high school's a dick" (*ibid.* 18:22-20:23). Vishwakumar's conflict with Hinduism makes her insecure. She wants to re-configure and re-formulate her faith and culture in a unique, novel perspective.

But as she searches for the ideal husband she gets involved in a torrid love affair with Praxton-Hall. And yet, amidst all the complexities of living as a first-generation Indian-American teenager, she looks for obvious symbols like the elephant, Goddess Durga and Ganesh to celebrate her Indianness. Moreover, the film is quite self-explanatory as it presents a thirty-minute affair in the backdrop of celebrations of *Ganesh Pooja*. Teenage obsessions with skin, several cameos of Indian culture and several break-ups due to family tensions question the place of women in foreign cultures. Among other things, she hankers after "some steamy romance with boy-friends" (*ibid.* 1:36-1:39). She is called a "weird girl in school" (*ibid.* 1:31-1:34). This throwback towards Indian roots and its resultant tension with Western social mores occurs in the persona of women. She has a rabid affair with Praxton-Hall. Her relationships seem to matter more than anything else (*ibid*. 10:15-12:36). The director draws our attention to her "weird" personality, not only in her affair but in her advertising to her school friends: "Praxton kissed me in the park" (*ibid*. 6:51-7:03). She is even hauled up by Praxton: "Why are you lying to everyone about us having sex (*ibid*. 2:54—3:56). Her role breaks down the conventional Asian stereotypes of Indian women.

On the other hand, if we critically consider the status of another film/ reality-television-series like Smriti Mundhra's *Indian Matchmaking* (2020). we find how different is the scenario regarding the position of women. If *Never Have I Ever* is avant-garde, *Indian Matchmaking* positions the Indian women as stereotypes. It is interesting to find that the entire film is about all the requirements necessary for a marriage. If marriage is all about social obligation, it also concerns the issues of caste and notions of chastity and purity. It is required that the girl must be fair, educated and of a required height. In other words, the director of this *Netflix*-series has focused on romantic numbers dealing with the search for the perfect match. In many ways, both films question the sociology and rationale behind Indian marriages. They both offer critiques of Indian marriages as an institution in obverse and reverse manner. Both focus on women and their problems regarding marriage. The notion of reversing and getting back to roots is then fraught with danger. If we go back in time, then we lose our spatial positions in the present and which is untenable. Both the films, therefore, critique gender stereotypes as well as issues of adjustment in social marriages.

Finally, such films focus on preconceived notions of marriage and the obligation of parents as well as their high-handedness from a postmodern view of the woman abroad. On the one hand, we find career-driven women with their hyphenated identities and with niche-dating apps. On the other hand, there is also angst about the reverse journey to their roots but which is improbable. Hence, diasporic movies are not only preoccupied with traditions but simultaneously critique such attempts in the light of their hyphenated identity. Marriage as the ultimate signified becomes ephemeral and transient. To put it differently, identity, social contracts and marriages are always defined and re-defined continuously in time and space. It is here that Foucault's concepts of heterotopia and Lefebvre as well as Soja's notion of third space have become helpful and significant in making us understand such complex issues.

Filmography:

Mississippi Masala. Dir. Mira Nair. Black River Productions/ Mirabai Films (1991). *YouTube* <https://www.youtube.com/watch?v=cjt3z44UySI>

Bhaji on the Beach. Dir. Gurinder Chadha. Four Films/Umbi Films (1993).

DilwaleDulhaniya le Jayenge. Dir. Aditya Chopra. Yash Raj Films (1995). YouTube <https://www.youtube.com/watch?v=IbwjDTOvwG8>

East is East. Dir. Daniel O'Donnell. Film4 Productions (1999).

Monsoon Wedding. Dir. Mira Nair. C Productions/ Mirabai Films (2001). YouTube <https://www.youtube.com/watch?v=wvB-dokfP2Y>

American Chai. Dir. Anurag Mehta. Fusion Films (2001). YouTube <https://www.youtube.com/watch?v=BrPd8vDL1u0>

Bend it like Beckham. Dir. Gurinder Chadha. Kintop Pictures (2002). YouTube <https://www.youtube.com/watch?v=WDd-HnppQwM>

Bride and Prejudice. Dir. Gurinder Chadha. Miramax Films (2004). YouTube <https://www.youtube.com/watch?v=O6cs4hUxSAc>

The Namesake. Dir. Mira Nair. Mirabai Films (2006).

Namastey London. Dir. V. A. Shah. Pen Studios (2007). YouTube <https://www.youtube.com/watch?v=O6cs4hUxSAc>

Never have I ever. Dirs. Mindy Kaling and L. Fisher. Kaling International, Inc. (2020). *YouTube* <https://www.youtube.com/watch?v=O6cs4hUxSAc>?

Indian Matchmaking. Directed by S. Mundhra.*Netflix* (2020).

Works cited:

Aldea, Elena. "Gurinder Chadha's 'Bride and Prejudice': a Transnational Journey through Time and Space". *International Journal of English Studies* 12.1 (June 2012): 167-82.

Bakhtin. M. *Rabelais and his World*. Translated by H. Iswolsky. Bloomington: Indiana University Press, 1984.

Bhabha, Homi K. *The Location of Culture*. New York and London: Routledge. 1994.

Blake, Emma. "Spatiality Past and Present: An Interview with Edward Soja". *Journal of Social Archaeology* 2.2 (June 2002): 139-58.

Borch, Christian. "Interview with Edward Soja: Third Space, Postmetropolis, and Social Theory". *Distinktion: Journal of Social Theory* 3.1 (March 2011): 113-20.

Clark, Katerina, and Michael Holoquist. *Mikhail Bakhtin*. Cambridge: Harvard University Press 1984.

Demirkan, Özlem. "The Representation of Heterotopia in Cinema". Paper included online in *Moving Image – Static Spaces: Architectures, Art, Media, Film, Digital Art and Design* (Altınbaş University) 12-13 April 2018, pp. 49-57 <*https://acikerisim.karatay.edu.tr/bitstream/handle/20.500.12498/1202/20190709162445.pdf?sequence=1&isAllowed=y*>

Divakaruni, Chitra Banerjee. *The Mistress of Spices*. New York: Doubleday, 1997.

Foucault, Michel. "*Of Other Spaces*: Utopias and Heterotopias". Trans. Jay Miskowiec. *Diacritics*, 16.1 (1984): 22-27.

Hall, Stuart. "Cultural Identity and Diaspora". *Identity, Community, Cultural Difference*. Ed. J. Rutherford. London: Lawrence and Wishart, 1990. 222-37.

---. "Old and New Identities, Old and New Ethnicities". *Culture, Globalisation and the World-System: Contemporary Conditions for the Representations of Identity*. Ed. Anthony D. King. Basingstoke: Macmillan.1991. 41-68.

Higson, Andrew. *The Instability of the National*. Eds. J. Ashby and A. Higson. *British Cinema, Past and Present*. New York and London: Routledge, 2000.

Jain, Jasbir. *The Diaspora writes Home: Subcontinental Narratives* (e-book). Singapore: Springer, 2017.

Knott, Kim et al. *Diasporas: Concepts, Intersections, Identities*. London: Zed Books. 2010.

Lacan, Jacques. *The Four Fundamental Concepts of Psychoanalysis*. Ed. Jacques Alain Miller., and Trans. Alan Sheridan. New York and London: Routledge. 2004.

Lacan, Jacques, and Jacques-Alain Miller. *The Ethics of Psychoanalysis.1959-60 – The Seminar of Jacques Lacan. Book VII*. Trans. D. Porter. New York and London: Routledge, 1992.

Lahiri, Jhumpa. *The Namesake*. New York: HarperCollins, 2004.

Lefebvre, Henri. *The Production of Space*. Trans. D. Nicholson-Smith. Hoboken: Wiley-Blackwell.1991.

Landry, Donna, and Gerald McLean (eds.). *The Spivak Reader*. New York and London: Routledge, 1996.

Maier, Harry. "*Soja's Third Space, Foucault's Heterotopia and de Certeau's Practice*: Time-Space and Social Geography in Emergent Christianity". *Historical Social Research* 38 (2013): 76-92.

Manzoor, Sarfaraz. "East is back: being a British Pakistani has changed". *The Guardian* 4 October 2014. Accessed on 15 May 2022 <https://www.theguardian.com/stage/2014/oct/04/east-is-east-20-years-on-restaged-life-british-pakistanis-changed>

Mendes, Anna C. "Triangulating Birmingham, Blackpool, and Bombay: Gurinder Chadha's *Bhaji on the Beach*". *Anglo Saxonica* 3 (January 2010): 327-40.

Mishra, Vijay. *The Literature of the Indian Diaspora: Theorising the Diasporic Imaginary*. New York and London: Routledge, 2007.

Ray, Radharani. "Interrogating Race in *Mississippi Masala*". *Race, Gender and Class* 8.4 (31 October 2001): 155.

Soja, Edward. *Thirdspace: Journeys to Los Angeles and Other Real-and-Imagined Places*. Hoboken: Wiley-Blackwell, 1996.

Tololyan, Khachig. "The Nation-State and its Others: In Lieu of a Preface". *Diaspora*: *A Journal of Transnational Studies* 1.1 (Spring 1991): 3-7.

Mathematics, Motherhood and Migrations
Gyno-Film and Diaspora in Shakuntala Devi

—Saunak Samajdar

In a deleted scene of the 2020-Indian (Hindi) biographical-film *Shakuntala Devi*—not integrated into the principal video/film released by Anupama Menon (b. 1979)—Shakuntala Devi, a pregnant female, while travelling by car, notices the Ramanujan Number (that is, 1729) on the number-plate of the car going ahead, and the *mise-en-scène* of the film conflates a road accident with the code of recognition of a scientist who is none other than a mother-to-be, and the genres blur between tragedy and farcicality—as the female-scientist/mathematician laughs about the numerals she had seen, while her waters break and a mother is born soon through the birth of the daughter (Deleted Scene 1—*Shakuntala Devi—The Numeral Accident*). There is, identifiably, no abjection of the mother in the mathematical epiphany, and no homologation of the mathematician in the figure of the accident-victim, a mother-to-arrive. And the lady becomes/remains a repatriational figure, who has relinquished the diasporic tinsels for as a minimum, to marry, and to settle as a mother.

Yes—as the spectators see—she laughs before the accident as a mathematician, and, after the accident as a mathematician! It is that almost no disjunction or no dispositif is discernible on the screen between the comedy and the *Komos*, constituted by the choric voices of the policemen and by-standers. This may be interpreted as the straddling of two different worlds with equal ease, and negotiating all the gifts without a sacrifice –a symbolic combination of Derrida's *cosmopolitan* and Irigaray's *Mother*.

In the 2020-film on the mathematician, who spent most of her life in the West, molarities are on the surface tripartite: the mathematician, the migrant and the mother. Apparently, the issues named above do not have a cusp, or a chiasmus. Mathematics is a symbolic, quantitative model of the beings, doings and happenings in realities and possibilities. Migration—

as seen in case of Shakuntala Devi's—is a matter of new land, often involving corporeal, material and cognitive readjustments of the sense of self and community. Motherhood is an experience of the extra resourcefulness of the femaleness, in body, mind and matter. But in the various anecdotes of Shakuntala Devi's, and in the 2020-film, these have been put into an intersection, co-extending to each other in the trajectories of the *becomings* of Shakuntala Devi. Underneath, I want to explore the cinematic and narrative strategies of the film enmesh mathematics, migration and motherhood into a single figure, that of a Bengaluru-girl becoming an urbane Londonite and then becoming international, and successfully though not quite conventionally negotiating the otherness to her being-of-itself through her interventions and mediations with digits, diaspora and daughter. The migrant, the mathematician and the mother are rolled into one—not as a mere parallel performances or multi-tasking, but into a singularity of her self-authentication as a woman taking the leap. Like the protagonist of Margaret Atwood's *Surfacing* who is in tandem a female, an animal, a topography of the lake and a mother to a jellyfish, or Cathy is Heathcliff in *Wuthering Heights,* Shakuntala re-territorialises the different lines into *her-self.*

There are a number of elements and portals already in that energetics: firstly, when the Subject of all three, namely intervening into mathematics, into diaspora and into motherhood is a woman, she would be expected by social stereotypes to be the most natural in the third while largely remaining a margin or a minoritarian entity in the first two. This is where the film dramatises the transmutation. Shakuntala is not a mathematician by academic degree, research activity or even through pedagogic profession. She is an epiphanic mathematician, one who can see digits and results of complex sums hovering around her like butterflies, faster than the supercomputer of her contemporary technologies. Speed is definitely important, because if it is not a *techne* or an acquired skill, fast and swift would not imply expertise but spontaneity, naturalness and/or miracle (an event not explicable by conventions and stereotypes of knowledge and of sociology). The optics of the digits and signs of mathematics flying like sylphs around Shakuntala Devi's eyes, invisible to others, constitute an iconographic code as Umberto Eco would have put it: the creature whose epistemology is in excess to the disciplinary limits, whereby the ontic equippedness for invocation, oneiric knowledge, Imagination as valid means of wisdom and intimacy with the signifiers of the knowledge beyond learning, merge into the figure of female-magician, smiling with innocent friendliness to the visitors from the extraordinary realm, the arithmetical numerals. The iconography of fairies and/or butterflies absorb the marks we see in mathematical texts, as the small South Indian rural girl in front of her cottage (and later, in the film, in a number of shows here she demonstrates her powers) is cinematically represented as the woman with super-human abilities. The pattern is, at the abstract blueprint of ocular representation on the screen and in the narrative grids of spatial displacement, the same with the figure of the migrant: one who crosses the boundaries and is an arrivant elsewhere, but an excess that has left a space and an excess that has come into another space, likely to have a rhizomatic mnemonics as opposed to fixed addresses and belongings. The diasporic entity is a Subject already always in a becoming instead of remaining a being-in-itself. Shakuntala Rao's announcement on the boat that approaches the Western shores is unique: she is a solo female in a self-urged exile, escaping the plateaus of the patriarchal exploitation of her talent, of a male lover who betrays her dignity and finally, as she claims, of a homicidal leap she has taken back in her country. Viewers are reminded, across centuries and cultures of difference, and in spite of the incommensurability between Early Modern European Zeitgeist and the contingencies of a colonial India, and albeit a difference between the mechanics of self-fashioning anew (cross-dressing in the former case, and the naming of herself as a criminal-fugitive in the latter), of Viola asking after reaching unknown shores whether the ruler of Ilyria is unmarried. The point is, Shakuntala arrives abroad as to catharsise her mathematics from petty and rustic mode of commercialisation by a greedy father, and to evade the plateaus of androcracy, which had been her *dasein* in the homeland. And her femaleness quickly exudes intimacy and hospitality and welcome to the stranger, Javier [Xavier], who himself is a diasporic mathematician in London. So, the migrant arrives at London with mathematics but also with the extra resources of *femaleness*—the ethics of love (whose crumbles and crumples made her take up exile from homeland itself).

Mathematics and the Diasporic have two important interfaces in the film. One is the moment of human versus machine, female epistemology versus man-made technology, which becomes also West versus the non-western for a brief *cineme*. During a television-show, Shakuntala Rao answers a very complex question by thinking only, and the computer computes it wrongly. Relying on the computer, a metonymy of Western as well as anthropocentric truth, technology and knowledge, the anchor of the television-show dismisses Shakuntala Rao as a fib from the land of magic, not a mathematician. However, phone-calls and messages start coming to the office after some hours, with the proof that the calculations of the computer were wrong and Shakuntala Rao's answer was correct. The second one is the scene of parting between Javier and Shakuntala. After quite a supportive and intimate role in her life amid her initial vulnerabilities and then amid her growing popularities, Javier has to return to his homeland, Spain, and Shakuntala Rao's relationship with him ends.

However, even in London. Shakuntala is shown living by her own standards. As she picks up fluency in English, her vivacious nature also starts radiating. She becomes the toast of the parties, and leads a life of abundance. Her mathematics and her migrancy become symbiotic and co-nourishing. She is named in media and in popular culture as a human computer, a nomenclature that convenes both instead of either/or. Her seamless friendship with mathematics and with her social freedom abroad cannot be read as to distinct acclivities, but as one individual authenticating her-self, negating the being-in-itself her childhood as making her in South India. She is sexually free, vocally amazing, and is at ease with the new land, materially and culturally, as much at ease with her unique playfulness with the numbers.

In another deleted scene of the movie that was not included in the final video, Shakuntala is first asked by Steve how it feels to be a female mathematician, implying it is almost an oxymoron. Shakuntala answers the western man, the interviewer, by asking how it feels to be a female journalist (Deleted Scene 2 — *Shakuntala Devi*, The Interview). The issue soon becomes a gendered-diasporic encounter as the interviewer quips that it must be very difficult to be an outspoken woman hailing from a country like India. Shakuntala answers *tongue-in-cheek* that it is not India but the world that finds it difficult to deal with outspoken omen like her, implying that the diasporic female Subject can scrutinise the phallocentrism of the Western world too, instead of simply being relegated to the social engineering of the non-Western space and culture she comes from. Then she bursts into laughter, re-calling and reciting an Indian maxim in Hindi, which, in translation, means 'dogs do bark at an elephant when she moves undisturbed', and that is how she deals with the world vis-à-vis how the world deals with her. The moment becomes polyglotic, diasporic, and engendered at one go. Effervescence, wit, a combatant attitude dominate the dialogues of this moment, as well as the untranslatable opacity that the diasporic offers to the character Steve while perfectly audible and comprehensible to the Indian audience of the biopic. The Hindi acts as a caesura, a suspension of answerability, a withdrawal of information to Steve and a metis-based code of recognition accessible to the spectators out there in the movie theatre. It is the same inaccessibility that she offers to the western reporter amid communication, that she had offered previously to the transactional nature of relationship with her family back home and then to the boyfriend who had been cheating her. Shakuntala Rao's parole is that of a deserter-communicant.

In Shakuntala Rao's world, men do not stay because they are not given the privilege of being needed. The public accolades that Shakuntala Devi receives as a mathematician and the new land she negotiates with continuously upgraded ease, do not immune her to the familial world. Having met Paritosh Banerjee, she has an accelerated marriage and then becomes a mother. Banerjee is confident that he does not want her to change, yet for a while we find the mathematics and the migration withdrawn as she is a re-patriated wife and mother only. But the mother has to coalesce the three into one, in her own whiz standards and capacities in all three lines of flight: mathematics, migration and motherhood. So she picks up little Anu, the daughter, and goes for international tours. At London before her marriage, she was negotiating a re-territorialised *at-home*-ness, but as the mother seeks mathematics and migration again, this time she becomes truly an itinerant, almost nomadological, an entity of routes and not of the root. Anu has neither a stable address nor a standard school to enrol into. Shakuntala Devi keeps Anu Banerjee away from sedentary institutions, and keeps her into her own cosmopolitan nomadism, with Mathematics as play and Migrancy as playground. But Anu Banerjee breaks free, decides to re-patriate and marry and settle down. It is from this transition that the screen becomes the possibility of a mirror, a retreat [*retrait*] as a re-treat [treating again], a withdrawal as an ipseity drawn with repetition. Seen from a superficial perspective, Shakuntala Devi is doing to Anu the same parental exploitation that her father did to herself: cannibalising her childhood. And Anu is doing exactly the same thing her mother had done — breaking free, going away, finally marrying. One could, here, quote what Mishra has observed:

> "[T]ransgenerational trauma [is depicted in *Shakuntala Devi*]. The movie suggests that Shakuntala Devi was bitter towards her mother because of her mother's submissive nature to her father — who was exploitative. As a result of this, she vowed to be nothing like her mother, and be the independent and confident woman that she is, who is not afraid to voice her mind. Her mother tells her that what goes around comes around, and one day Shakuntala Devi's daughter will come to resent her just like she resents her mother. This is exactly what happens in the movie and it shows the perpetuation of transgenerational trauma in Indian families, but where the movie ended up short, is in its lack of nuance. We hardly get any insight on Shakuntala Devi's troubled relationship with her mother except in the scene where her sister dies because the family did not have enough money to provide her medical care, and Shakuntala blames her sister's death on her mother — for being a silent onlooker all the while, even when her father exploited her for his financial gains" (Mishra).

Seen through the later point of view of Anu (and, according to my interpretation, the fullest anagnorisis comes only after she becomes a mother herself) it is only because of the excessive maternal love for the daughter, and because of Shakuntala Rao's will to keep the daughter away from all that the mother has suffered whenever stuck at a molar, stable, sedentary identity, that she had dissolved motherhood and migrancy earlier, fuelled and sponsored by the global freedom mathematical genius had given her. Not taking the migration-issue into account, Shivani Pegatraju has added another observation—how, in this respect, the film becomes a critique of motherhood within patriarchy:

> "Even if we did take the 'what if' scenario seriously, one would imagine that a man would be okay with travelling the world and not being able to constantly enjoy his child's company at the same time. Neither a man nor woman can 'have it all'; but the crucial difference is that patriarchal society places unreasonable expectations on women to be the 'perfect' mother/wife and prioritize this over their career, while a man is allowed to prioritise his career over family. This social conditioning makes Shakuntala Devi feel undue guilt for being an 'absentee' mother and in her attempt to be a better one, she in fact ends up damaging her relationship with her daughter" (Pegatraju).

We have to remember the aporia that Shakuntala Rao has alleged that her husband is gay but she is also the first author on the-then taboo subject in India, homosexuality, with quite a compassionate view on LGBTQ issues and quite a scholarly grievance that the study of lesbians is further limited (Devi 1977). Such antithetical and paradoxical moments dominate Shakuntala's portrayal in all three dimensions—her mathematics, her diaspora, and her maternity.

One could conclude here by referring to Namrata Joshi's view regarding the combination of the themes of mathematics and maternity of the West-settled Shakuntala Rao:

> "Having covered quite a distance from there, Hindi cinema has of late been offering some freshness, spark and contemporaneity to the mother-daughter dynamic, if not entirely breaking away from the coded formalism, formalities and hierarchies of this zone. The mother might be the confidante, a bestie to her daughter, as in Aditya Chopra's *Dilwale Dulhania Le Jaayenge* (1995). Then there was the rare show of camaraderie

in Advait Chandan's *Secret Superstar* (2017), in which the mother lived her dream vicariously through her daughter even as the daughter worked to liberate her mother from a claustrophobic and abusive marriage. [....] Earlier, Gauri Shinde's *English Vinglish* (2012) underlined a certain callousness towards the mother, who was taken for granted by the family, particularly her daughter. Here was a one-way street—a lot was demanded of the mother but rarely were her own expectations approximated, forget being met. The mother forged an identity away from the family, but without necessarily breaking away from it. Things get a lot more fraught between mothers and daughters in *Shakuntala Devi* though they are still not as thorny as the swing between the adversarial and the friendly in, say, Greta Gerwig's *The Ladybird* (2017). Yet *Shakuntala Devi* does introduce a new narrative—motherhood on the rebound, a reaction against the experiences that women have derived from their mothers. *Shakuntala Devi* makes one look back in appreciation at Rituparno Ghosh's *Unishe April*, which featured an estranged mother (Aparna Sen) and daughter (Debashree Roy), dancer and doctor respectively. On the death anniversary of the father, all their pent-up resentment, pain and anger come storming out. Did the mother's commitment to her art and journey to self-realisation lead her to neglect her daughter? Did the husband nurse a grudge against her popularity and success? Will the misunderstanding, conflict and bitterness between mother and daughter ever clear? Can they forgive and move on? Ghosh's film is what *Shakuntala Devi* is not—an acute, in-depth, intense and well-rounded exploration of two individuals and their relationship—that does not side with one, but is an ally of both. Seen in this light, Bhaskar Hazarika's recent Assamese film, *Kothanodi* ('River of Fables', 2015), is tremendously significant. Refreshingly free of judgment in portraying mothers and as much folksy as edgy, it is based on the Assamese compendium, *Buri Ai'r Sadhu* (Grandma's Tales). It weaves together four stories about four mothers struggling with their inner demons. If one is intent on marrying her daughter with a python, another plots the murder of her stepdaughter. This intriguing film, with its mix of the real and surreal, takes mothers beyond patriarchal frames of reference and gives them liberty to embrace their frailties and dark sides without a care or concern" (Joshi).

Note:

Released by *Sony Pictures* on 31 July 2020, *Shakuntala Devi*—directed by Anupama Menon (b. 1979)—is an Indian (Hindi) biographical-drama-film which focuses on the life of the Bengaluru-born Indian mathematician, Shakuntala Rao (1929-2013). A mathematical genius, politician, astrologer, and culinary artist, Shakuntala Devi—that is, Shakuntala Rao—also published India's first book on homosexuality—*The World of Homosexuals*—in 1977. Her 1964-79-marriage to Paritosh Bandyopadhyay, a homosexual administrative-officer, induced in her an interest in exploring the aspects of homosexuality: as she later said in the documentary *For Straights Only* (2001).

Works cited:

Deleted Scene 1—*Shakuntala Devi* (The Numeral Accident), *Amazon Prime Video—YouTube* 21 August 2020. Accessed on 1 October 2022 <https://youtu.be/AVu7NZpzuiU>

Deleted Scene—2—*Shakuntala Devi* (The Interview), *Amazon Prime Video—YouTube* 14 August 2020. Accessed on 1 October 2022 <https://youtu.be/MMNsKrZWBsM>

Devi, Shakuntala. *The World of Homosexuals*. New Delhi: Vikash Publishing House, 1977.

Joshi, Namrata. "*Burden of Inheritance*: Mothers and Daughters in Shakuntala Devi". *NewsClick* 8 August 2020. Accessed on 2 October 2022 <https://www.newsclick.in/Burden-Inheritance-Mothers-Daughters-Shakuntala-Devi>

Mishra, Soumya. "Film Review: *Shakuntala Devi*—A problematic Portrayal that barely touches upon her Genius". Feminism India 5 August 2020. Accessed on 2 October 2022 <https://feminisminindia.com/2020/08/05/film-review-shakuntala-devi/>

Pegatraju, Shivani. "Shakuntala Devi: A Critique of Motherhood within Patriarchy". *Gaurilankesh News* 10 August 2020. Accessed on 1 October 2022 <https://gaurilankeshnews.com/shakuntala-devi-a-critique-of-motherhood-within-patriarchy/>

Shakuntala Devi (Film). Directed by Anupama Menon. *Sony Pictures*, July 2020.

About the Contributors

Arora, Neha, Ph.D., is an assistant professor of English of the *Central University of Rajasthan* (in the district of Ajmer, Rajasthan). Her areas of interest include diasporic writings, Dalit-literature, comparative literature, Indian writings, and subaltern-studies. She has authored *Dalit Literature Today* (Creative Books, 2015), and has edited/co-edited three critical-anthologies—on New Literature, Mahesh Dattani's plays, and marginalised literature. She has also contributed several research papers in reputed journals and edited volumes.

Bandyopadhyay, Deb Narayan, Ph.D., is the Vice-Chancellor of *Bankura University*, West Bengal, India. In 2001, he gave a course of lectures on 'Nineteenth-century Representations of Shakespeare in India' at the University of Vienna, Shakespeare Society of Vienna, and the University of Salzburg. He also visited the *University of Edinburgh* and lectured at a seminar organised at Mansfield College, Oxford in 2002, with assistance from British Council. He was awarded the *Fulbright Exchange Summer Institute Programme* and worked at Northern Illinois University, University of Chicago, and State University of New York. He was, later, awarded Australian Studies Fellowship in 2005 and 2006. He had held visiting research positions at *Monash University, University of New South Wales, University of Wollongong*, and holds the position of international contributing editor of *Journal of American History* (J.A.H). Bandyopadhyay has worked on Gerontology as the Project Leader in collaboration with University of Swansea under UKIERI-Funding-Programme, and is an awardee of the Andrew Tannahill Fund, University of Glasgow. His most recent publication includes *Transnational Spaces: Australia and India* (Palgrave Macmillan, 2022).

Chattopadhyay, Indrajit, Ph.D., is an associate professor of English of *Kabi Sukanta Mahavidyalaya*, Hooghly, West Bengal, India. Educated at the Universities of Calcutta and

Kalyani, Chattopadhyay has been an academic-counsellor for Post-Graduate course of English Language and Literature of Indira Gandhi National Open University. His most recent publication is *Of Woman Born: Changing Interpretations of Womanhood in Shakespearean Comedies* (Signorina, 2020). His present areas of interest are diasporic literature, cultural studies, and hunting literature.

Chattopadhyay, Sreeparna, Ph.D., is an I.C.S.S.R. Post-doctoral Fellow in Political Science at *Raiganj University*, and is a trained illustrator, painter, and performer. She has worked on documentary-making-teams, and has the experiences of designing book-covers. She has spoken at different international and national-level-conferences and seminars, published research-essays in several international and *U.G.C.-C.A.R.E.*-listed journals and in newspapers, and has the experiences of volunteering as a social-worker.

Dubey, Lata, Ph.D., is professor in the Department of English, *Banaras Hindu University*, Varanasi, India. Her areas of interest include diasporic writings, British fiction, Victoria poetry, linguistics, contemporary fiction, Indian Literatures in English, feminism, contemporary theory, New Literatures in English, narratology. She has published more than two dozen research papers in different international and nationally-circulated journals, and has lectured at several conferences, seminars, and U.G.C.-H.R.D.C. Refresher Courses as resource person.

Dutta, Tanima, Ph.D., works as an assistant professor at the Department of English, *Buniadpur Mahavidyalaya* (Dakshin Dinajpur, West Bengal, India), and edits a reputed multidisciplinary journal, *Exposure*. An activist and a recognised performer, she has spoken at different international and national-level conferences and seminars, and has a number of critically-acclaimed research-publications to her credit. Her doctoral research thesis was highly-appreciated at the *University of Heidelberg*. Dutta is presently co-editing an anthology of critical writings on posthumanism, likely to be published from a reputed eastern U.S.A.-based publishing house.

Fraser, Bashabi, Ph.D., C.B.E., is an eminent litterateur, who is globally respected (principally) as a diasporic poet. A Professor Emerita of English and Creative Writing, *Edinburgh Napier University* (Edinburgh, the United Kingdom), and the Director of the *Scottish Centre of Tagore Studies* (ScoTs), Fraser is also an Associate *Royal Literary Fund* Fellow and an Honorary Fellow at the Centre for South Asian Studies, University of Edinburgh. She has authored and edited 23 books, published several articles and chapters, both academic and creative, and as a poet, has been widely anthologised. She is the Chief Editor of the international e-journal, *Gitanjali and Beyond*. She is the recipient of a *C.B.E.* (2021 Queen's New Year Honours) for Education (academic achievements), Culture (poetry) and Integration (for work connecting Scotland and India) and has been made an Honorary Fellow by the *Association of Scottish Literary Studies* (A.S.L.S.) in 2021. She has been declared *Outstanding Woman of Scotland* by *Saltire Society* in 2015.

Mallick, Saptarshi, Ph.D., works as an assistant professor of English at *Sukanta Mahavidyalaya*, Dhupguri, West Bengal, India (which is a constituent college of the University of North Bengal). In 2016-17 he has been a *Charles Wallace India Trust (Doctoral) Fellow* in the U.K. He was an Associate Staff (Research Fellow) at the *Scottish Centre of Tagore Studies* (ScoTs), *Edinburgh Napier University*, as part of the UKIERI Programme. He is an Ernst Mach Fellow 2019-20 (postdoctoral) at the *Karl-Franzens-Universität Graz*, Austria. He has been visiting faculty in the Summer Semester of 2020 at the *Karl-Franzens-Universität Graz*. He is an Associate Editor of *Gitanjali and Beyond*, an international, open-access e-journal of the *Scottish Centre of Tagore Studies* (ScoTs).

Mukherjee, Rupayan, Ph.D., lectures English at *University B.T. and Evening College*, Cooch Behar (West Bengal, India). He is the co-editor of *Partition Literature and Cinema: A Critical Introduction*

(Routledge, 2020) and *Popular Literature: Texts, Contexts, Contestations* (Ibidem/Columbia University Press, 2022).

Munshi, Auritra, Ph.D., works as an assistant professor at the Department of English, *Raiganj University*, West Bengal, India. He is a co-editor of the book titled *Border and Bordering: Politics, Poetics Precariousness* (Ibidem/Columbia University Press, 2021). He has published many articles in international and national journals such as *Indialogs: Spanish Journal Of India Studies, Postcolonial Interventions: An Interdisciplinary Journal of Postcolonial Studies, Muse India, Journal of the Department of English: Vidyasagar University, Journal of Bodoland University*, and others. His interest includes South Asian diaspora, Coolie diaspora, postcolonialism, and subaltern studies.

Roy, Pinaki, Ph.D., the editor of the present anthology of critical writings, works as a professor of English at Raiganj University (Uttar Dinajpur, West Bengal, India). A resident of Balurghat (Dakshin Dinajpur, West Bengal), and a member of the academic committee of The Vidyasagar Academy (Department of Higher Education, Government of West Bengal), Roy is an anti-plastic-usage-activist, and lectures regularly at different international and national-level conferences. He has also several monographs, edited-volumes, and journal-essays to his credit

Samajdar, Saunak, Ph.D., is an associate professor of the Department of English, *Cooch Behar Panchanan Barma University*, Cooch Behar, West Bengal, India. A *J.N.U.*-alumnus, a movie-buff, and deeply interested in diasporic writings, Samajdar—who resides in Siliguri—is a 'globetrotter' by choice, and has spoken at numerous international and national-level conferences and seminars on areas like visual semiotics and literary and critical theories. His publications have been appreciated globally.

Samanta, Soumyajit, Ph.D., is a former professor of English of the *University of North Bengal* (in the district of Darjeeling, West Bengal, India). Educated at St. Xavier's College, Kolkata, and

Jadavpur University, Samanta's publications include *Lovescape Crucified: A Study of Gerard Manley Hopkins* (Sarup and Sons, 2005) and *James Joyce: A Study of his Novels, Poetry, and Plays* (Atlantic Publishers, 2014). He had been to the *University of Lund*, Sweden, in 2008 and 2010 on fellowships.

Samanta, Subhrajit, M.A.—with degrees in both Mass Communication and English—has pursued adventurous and challenging news stories, covering a range of beats as a full-time general assignment reporter for *The Statesman*, Siliguri. His publications include *Shakuntala and the Natural Sublime: Representations in Literature and Media* (2019), *Psychological Horror in 'Red Dragon' and 'The Silence of the Lambs'* (2022), and *The Mystique of Tibetan Mysticism: An Analysis of Herge's 'Tintin in Tibet'* (2022).

Sarkar, Jaydip, Ph.D., is associate professor of English at *University B.T. and Evening College*, Cooch Behar, a constituent college of University of North Bengal (in the district of Darjeeling, West Bengal, India). Deeply interested in diasporic writings, he has edited and co-edited such books as *Writing Difference: Nationalism, Identity and Literature* (Atlantic, 2013), *A Handbook of Rhetoric and Prosody* (Orient Blackswan, 2018), *Partition Literature and Cinema: A Critical Introduction* (Routledge, 2020), and *Popular Literature: Text, Context, Contestation* (Ibidem/Columbia University Press, 2021). He has attended several national and international conferences in India and abroad.

Sen, Amrit, Ph.D., is a professor at the Department of English, Bhasha Bhavana, *Visva-Bharati* (Santiniketan, West Bengal, India), and is, presently, the Director of *Granthan Vibhaga* (the publishing-section) of *Visva-Bharati* at Kolkata. A recipient of several awards and accolades, including those from the Government of India and the U.G.C., Sen has authored/co-authored 13 books till date, and has published numerous essays and articles in reputed international and national journals. He had been at the University of Edinburgh as Fellow of a UKIERI-programme, and travels all around the world, lecturing at different international conferences, and teaching at numerous universities. Indian diasporic writings, Rabindranath Tagore's literature, and 18th century English literature are on the list of his research-interests.

Sengupta, Ashis, Ph.D., is a professor of English at the University of North Bengal (in the district of Darjeeling, West Bengal, India). A recipient of the Olive I. Reddick Award (1995), Fulbright American Studies Institute Fellowship (2002), Fulbright Visiting Scholarship (2006) and SASNET Guest Lecturer-Grant (2009), he has widely published on American and South Asian theatre in journals of international repute. His edited volumes include *Mapping South Asia through Contemporary Theatre* (Palgrave Macmillan, 2014) and *Islam in Performance* (Bloomsbury Methuen, 2017). His most recent work is *Postdramatic Theatre and India* (Bloomsbury Methuen [Engage], 2022). His areas of interest include literary and cultural theory, and theatre and performance studies.

Singh, Lalan Kishore, Ph.D., is professor of English at *Gauhati University*, Assam, India. He has worked extensively on literary theory and criticism, history and historicism, and ecology and literature. He has also an abiding interest in studying diasporic writings, the historical intersections between historical experience, the Second World War, nationalism, and local cultures of Northeast India.

Swarnakar, Neha, M.Phil, teaches English at *Sripat Singh College* (Jiaganj, Murshidabad, West Bengal, India), and researches at the Department of English, Raiganj University. She has completed her B.A. and M.A from Kalyani University. She has several articles, including those on diasporic writings, to her credit. Her area of interest encompasses resistance literature, new gender studies, and war-literature.

It is a much-needed volume bringing together the varied concepts of diaspora writings through the ages as well as in modern times.

Nibedita Mukherjee, Professor of English,
Sidho-Kanho-Birsa University,
Purulia, West Bengal, India

A comprehensive survey of the important voices of Indian diasporic writers.

Robert Masterson, Poet and Academician,
B.M.C.C., City University of New York,
New York, U.S.A.

A timely tour d' horizon of diasporic cultural practices, encompassing curries and cinema, poetry and drama, fiction and theory.

Peter Paul Schnierer, Professor of English,
University of Heidelberg, Heidelberg, Germany.

ibidem.eu